Easy Everyday
Slow Cooker
Recipes

Easy Everyday
Slow Cooker
Recipes

Donna-Marie Pye

Robert
ROSE

Easy Everyday Slow Cooker Recipes
Text copyright © 2014 Donna-Marie Pye
Cover and text design copyright © 2014 Robert Rose Inc.
Photographs © 2014 Guy Saint-Jean Éditeur

Recipes in this book originated from *Slow Cooker Winners: 300 easy and satisfying recipes*, published by Robert Rose Inc., 2010

A French language version entitled *Les meilleures recettes à la mijoteuse* 2 was published by Guy Saint-Jean Éditeur, 2013

Library and Archives Canada Cataloguing in Publication

Pye, Donna-Marie
    Easy everyday slow cooker recipes / Donna-Marie Pye.

Includes index.
ISBN 978-0-7788-0483-3 (pbk.)

    1. Electric cooking, Slow. 2. Cookbooks. I. Title.

TX827.P93345 2014   641.5'884   C2014-903321-4

Disclaimer
The recipes in this book have been carefully tested by our kitchen and our tasters. To the best of our knowledge, they are safe and nutritious for ordinary use and users. For those people with food or other allergies, or who have special food requirements or health issues, please read the suggested contents of each recipe carefully and determine whether or not they may create a problem for you. All recipes are used at the risk of the consumer. Consumers should always consult their slow cooker manufacturer's manual for recommended procedures and cooking times.

We cannot be responsible for any hazards, loss or damage that may occur as a result of any recipe use.

For those with special needs, allergies, requirements or health problems, in the event of any doubt, please contact your medical adviser prior to the use of any recipe.

Design and Production: Joseph Gisini/PageWave Graphics Inc.
Editors: Sue Sumeraj and Jennifer MacKenzie
Proofreader: Sheila Wawanash
Photographer: Michel Paquet
Food Styling: Éric Régimbald
Prop Styling: Irène Gravelli

Cover image: Zucchini Ratatouille (page 269)

The publisher gratefully acknowledges the financial support of our publishing program by the Government of Canada through the Canada Book Fund.

Published by Robert Rose Inc.
120 Eglinton Avenue East, Suite 800, Toronto, Ontario, Canada M4P 1E2
Tel: (416) 322-6552 Fax: (416) 322-6936
www.robertrose.ca

Printed and bound in USA

1 2 3 4 5 6 7 8 9 CKV 21 20 19 18 17 16 15 14

Contents

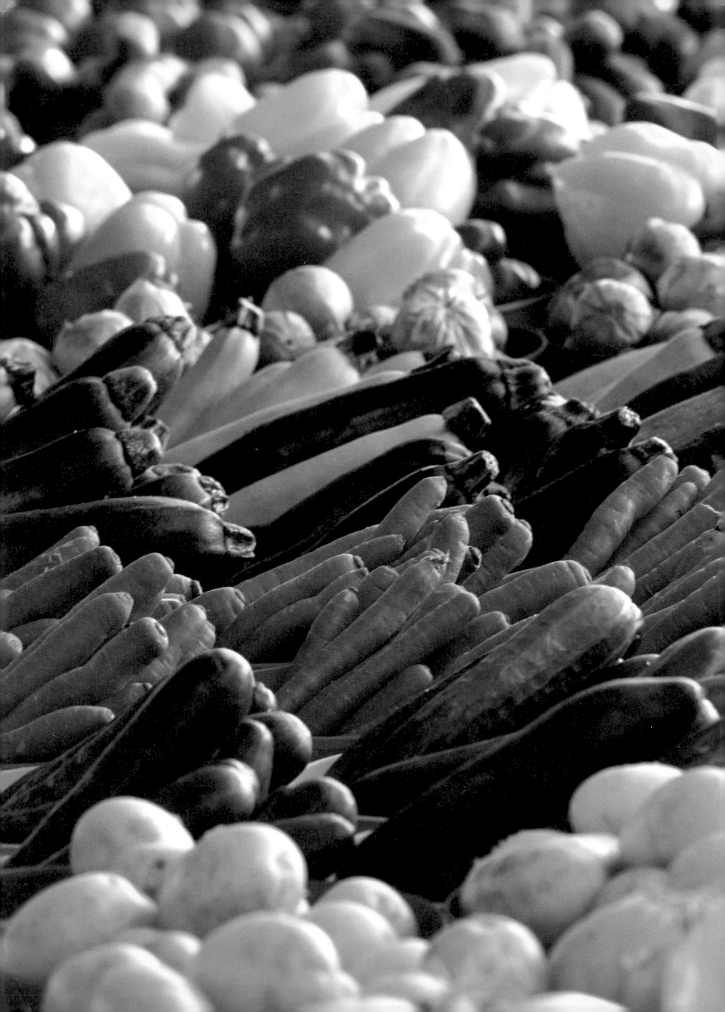

Introduction

Kitchen appliances come and go, but the slow cooker has managed to stand the test of time. It has been almost half a century since the slow cooker arrived in stores, and it now holds a place of prominence on our counters. Most small-appliance manufacturers now include a slow cooker in their product lineup. It's a must-have for any busy, active household.

The reason for this success is that slow cookers are incredibly handy. They come in a variety of sizes, shapes and finishes, and are made to suit any type of household and kitchen decor. All cooks, from busy families to empty nesters to college students to newlyweds, can find a slow cooker to suit their needs. Not only are these appliances useful for cooking a weeknight meal, but they can help streamline preparation for a holiday gathering, when oven space is at a premium. They raise soups, stews and braises to higher levels. They can even help home cooks create delectable preserves and desserts. Who would have imagined that a pot designed to bake beans could prove to be so versatile?

My relationship with the slow cooker began more than 20 years ago, when I first used it to help put dinner on the table after a lengthy commute from my job. Once my children arrived and I began working from home, our lives reached new levels of busyness. Now, with two active, hungry teens, a full schedule of work, a husband with a demanding career and a dog that needs attention too, I still find a need for the slow cooker. It gives us a chance to sit down as a family over a home-cooked meal at least once or twice a week — something we find more difficult to do as time goes on.

Slow cookers are a breeze to use and are time-, cost- and energy-efficient. Stalwart and reliable, they require little or no tending, and very little last-minute cooking is needed. Meats and poultry braise beautifully, resulting in exceptional pot roasts, savory stews and succulent ribs, chilis and curries. Beans, peas and lentils, which are inexpensive, filling and incredibly nutritious, also benefit from long, slow cooking. Slow cookers even offer a heat-free way to cook in the summer. How many other appliances offer so many options?

In this book, you will find 200 recipes to explore and experiment with, featuring the best of North American regional cuisine, as well as globally inspired dishes representing cultures from around the world. I developed these recipes with convenience in mind. While most do require a few extra minutes of preparation, in some you can add all the ingredients at once. I like to use fresh ingredients, but occasionally I use a convenience-food product to make things simpler. I have incorporated many contemporary ingredients — such as balsamic vinegar, chipotle peppers, smoked paprika, roasted red peppers and edamame (soybeans) — to reflect current cooking styles and global influences.

While most of the recipes in this book serve anywhere from four to eight people, I recognized the need for recipes to suit any family and slow cooker size and have included the chapters Meals for Two and Big-Batch Dinners for a Crowd. And who doesn't deserve a break from cooking once in a while? With a bit of advance planning and the inspiring recipes in Double-Duty Dinners, you can turn tonight's dinner into tomorrow's feast, simultaneously banishing the dreaded question "Are we having that again?" The recipes in this chapter are designed to yield extras that come together quickly in a delightful second meal with minimal effort.

Slow cooking has grown up, traveled the world and come home more sophisticated, capable of a broader variety of fresh flavors, cuisines, shapes and textures. Whether you are cooking for two or serving a crowd, this book makes easy work of creating delicious, soul-satisfying meals. Happy slow cooking!

Slow Cooker Know-How

When cooking on Low, a slow cooker uses between 85 and 180 watts of power. The High heat setting uses almost double the power — between 160 and 370 watts.

We all have one thing in common: a busy schedule. But how do you satisfy your eclectic tastes and provide full-flavored dishes made from globally inspired recipes when you are on the go? The answer lies in one of our most trusted kitchen appliances — the slow cooker. Whether you are a family of two, three or more, a first-time cook or an experienced professional, slow cooking both saves you time and creates scrumptious, nutritious food. You can carry on with your day, working, playing or pursuing your passion, while it quietly simmers away on the counter, using its low, moist heat to coax a symphony of flavors from the food. It's like having your own private chef!

Of course, it can't do all the work — you must provide a little input. But with some preplanning and forethought, a little organization and an array of fresh ingredients, you'll have a satisfying meal waiting for you when you're ready for it. Your only job is to pour the wine and make a side dish (and sometimes even that is not necessary).

Simple by Design

Ten years ago, when I wrote my first slow cooker cookbook, I tested all the recipes in the same simple machine that was developed almost 40 years ago. Only two heat settings were available, without an automatic shutoff and with a manual Keep Warm setting. We have come a long way since then. Gone are the bland beige units with cutesy floral patterns on the sides. They have been replaced by sleek black, white and stainless-steel units designed to match our kitchen decor, all with a multitude of electronic settings.

If your slow cooker cooks at specific temperature settings, program it to cook at 200°F (100°C) for Low and 300°F (150°C) for High.

Slow cookers still operate on a high/low principle. The Low setting cooks food at around 200°F (100°C) and the High setting at about 300°F (150°C). The exact cooking temperature varies between models, so when preparing a recipe for the first time, check for doneness at the end of the minimum recommended cooking time. As you become more familiar with your model, you can adjust cooking times accordingly.

The Low setting is used for braises that require longer cooking times (8 hours or more), while the High setting is ideal for cooking and tenderizing food over a shorter time period (4 hours or less). I love the newer machines with programmable timers that allow me to preset the cooking times in half-hour increments; at the end of the set cooking time, the unit drops to a Warm heat setting that keeps the food warm without overcooking it.

Parts of a Slow Cooker

These sleek countertop appliances have some key parts, and different models offer different features. Before buying a slow cooker, you'll want to consider all of the options and decide on the model that best meets your budget and household requirements.

> **If your stoneware insert is removable, the manufacturer's directions will specify whether it is ovenproof, microwaveable and/or able to go under the broiler.**

Casing and Insert

The appliance consists of a metal outer casing and a stoneware insert. Some stoneware is designed so that you can use it to brown meat or sauté vegetables on the stovetop before placing it in the metal casing for slow cooking. But check your manufacturer's instructions to see whether this is possible with your model. If not, it's just as easy to do your browning or sautéing in a skillet, then transfer the food to the stoneware. The recipes in this book assume the use of a skillet.

The metal casing contains thermostatically controlled heating elements, which heat up to warm the air inside the insulated metal walls, thereby cooking the meal. This low-wattage heat never makes direct contact with the stoneware, so there are no hot spots and no need for constant stirring. The slow cooker uses about the same amount of energy as a 100-watt light bulb — substantially less than a conventional oven.

Lid

All slow cookers come with a plastic or glass lid. A good lid seals in moisture and nutrients, so, while a little jiggle is acceptable, you will want to make sure the lid fits snugly. Clear lids are handy, as they allow you to see what is happening inside the slow cooker. Tempting as it might seem, it is important not to lift the lid during cooking — you can lose 20 minutes of cooking time for every lift. Look for lids that are dishwasher-safe. I have

had some heat-resistant plastic ones that started out clear but with time and continued washing became opaque, making it difficult to see what was happening inside.

> **Glass lids get quite hot during the cooking process. When it's time to remove the lid, it's a good idea to use oven mitts or a pot holder.**

Timer and Temperature Probe

Many of today's slow cookers come with a programmable timer. Some of these allow you to use preset times within the High or Low settings; others allow you to set the cooking time, then choose whether to cook on High or Low. Many machines have a Warm setting, which will kick in automatically once the preset cooking time is reached, keeping the contents warm without overcooking them. If the food is forgiving, the Warm setting can also be handy when you're taking cooked food to a potluck. Transport the food in your slow cooker and, once you reach your destination, turn on the Warm setting; the food can safely sit that way for up to 2 hours.

Some slow cookers are also equipped with a temperature probe, which works with the cooker's electronic controls to monitor the internal temperature of meat and automatically shifts to the Warm setting when the desired temperature is reached. Internal temperature is the best way to measure the doneness of some types of meats and poultry, and the probe ensures that these meats are thoroughly cooked according to specified guidelines.

> **The most basic machines do not have features such as a programmable timer or a temperature probe. Before buying one, do make sure it at least has High and Low settings; otherwise, it cannot be considered a true slow cooker.**

Size and Shape

Slow cookers come in an impressive range of sizes and shapes these days. Choose one that is best suited to your needs. You'd be surprised at how many households own two — one for large family meals and another for cooking side dishes, desserts and appetizers.

If you plan to make 4 to 8 servings most of the time, a 4- to 6-quart (4 to 6 L) slow cooker is the best size for you. This capacity will allow you to cook a full meal with leftovers (depending on how hungry everyone is). Most of the recipes in this book were tested in a slow cooker this size. Smaller models, in the 1½- to 3-quart (1.5 to 3 L) range, are ideal for smaller households, and for making warm dips, side dishes and appetizers for which a large pot is simply too big. If you regularly (or even occasionally) feed a crowd, or you simply like to make big batches and freeze your leftovers, you may want to invest in a 6- to 7-quart (6 to 7 L) slow cooker, which is capable of making up to 20 servings.

Slow cookers come in round, oval and rectangular models. While round slow cookers are fine for soups, stews and chilis, oval and rectangular models allow a little more flexibility when it comes to roasts and larger cuts of meat. A rectangular shape also makes more efficient use of cupboard space.

> **The amount of liquid in a recipe can vary considerably, from just a few spoonfuls to enough to submerge the food completely. Ideally, the slow cooker should be no more than two-thirds full of food, with liquid at least 1 inch (2.5 cm) from the rim.**

Handles, Feet and Cord Storage

Slow cookers are popular as tote-along appliances when potluck is the name of the game. Look for easy-to-grip handles that can be grasped with oven mitts on. The stoneware handles heat up when the appliance is cooking, so make sure to protect your hands accordingly.

Because slow cookers can heat up kitchen counters, many people worry about possible heat damage or even fire risk. It is always best to place your slow cooker on a solid, heat-resistant surface. However, to alleviate this problem, some manufacturers have developed slow cookers that have feet, or bases with rubberized bottoms. This feature makes using a slow cooker worry-free.

Finally, some manufacturers have developed retractable electric cords that store conveniently and efficiently inside the base of the slow cooker — a very helpful feature when storage space is at a premium.

> **When cleaning the slow cooker, never immerse the metal housing in water. It only needs a gentle wipe with a damp cloth to remove any dribbles or stickiness. Dry it with a clean kitchen towel so as not to damage the finish.**

8 Essential Tricks of the Trade

Your slow cooker can be used to create any dish — just be adventurous! Here are my top 8 tips to help you use your appliance to its full advantage.

1. Prepare What You Can Ahead of Time

If you plan to start your slow cooker early in the day, here are a few things you can prepare the night before:

- Chop fresh vegetables, place them in airtight containers and refrigerate until the next day. Vegetables that will be used at the same time can be put into the same container to save space.

- Defrost frozen vegetables overnight in the refrigerator.

- Trim fat from meat and poultry and remove skin from poultry. Cut meat and poultry into pieces of the same size. Cubes are the best shape for even cooking, so try to get your pieces as close to cube-shaped as possible. Do *not* brown meat in advance; once it's cut to size, refrigerate it in an airtight container, keeping it separate from any other ingredients. (The exception to this rule is ground meat, which can be browned the night before; however, it still needs to be refrigerated in its own container.)

- Assemble nonperishable ingredients and cooking utensils in a convenient spot for a quick start.

    Recipes in this book that lend themselves to additional advance preparation or cooking are accompanied by make-ahead instructions. Many recipes can also be completely cooked in advance and stored in the refrigerator or freezer for future use.

2. Choose Less Tender Cuts of Meat and Trim Off the Fat

The cuts of meat that benefit from slow cooking are less expensive and often from the tough shoulder area. Slow cooking breaks down the collagen in the muscles' connective tissue, leaving the meat moist and tender. Make sure to trim off all visible fat (and remove skin from poultry) before adding meat to the slow cooker. This will reduce the amount of fat you need to skim from the liquid at the end of the cooking process.

Always read the recipe all the way through first, to make sure you have the necessary ingredients and equipment, and to get a sense of the timing and what needs to happen when.

3. Cut Root Vegetables into Small Pieces

In the slow cooker, root vegetables, such as carrots, parsnips, turnips and potatoes, take longer to cook than meat pieces of the same size, so they should be thinly sliced or cut into cubes no bigger than 1 inch (2.5 cm). It's best to place them as close as possible to the bottom and sides of the stoneware, so that they benefit from proximity to the heat source.

4. Brown Meat and Sauté Vegetables First

Partial cooking or browning may add a few minutes to the preparation process, but in the end, those extra minutes will be worthwhile. Browning meat not only improves its color, but also breaks down the natural sugars, releasing their flavors. Sautéing vegetables with spices and dried herbs before slow cooking produces a richer, more intense sauce.

For browning, the first step is to cut the meat or poultry into pieces of the same size. Next, dredge it in flour, coating evenly. Add it in small batches to a small amount of oil heated over medium-high heat, either in a skillet or in your stoneware if it is designed for stovetop cooking. Stir or turn frequently to brown evenly. If you are using a skillet, transfer each batch to the slow cooker as it is browned. If you're using the stoneware, remove each batch to a plate as it is browned, then return all the meat to the stoneware after deglazing.

Sauté vegetables in a small amount of oil or butter (as called for in the recipe) heated over medium-high heat in a skillet or in stovetop-safe stoneware. For recipes that also contain browned meat, sauté the vegetables after the meat, in the same pan, either with the oil that's left or with added oil or butter. You just need to soften the vegetables — they don't need to be fully cooked or browned. If you overcook them now, they'll acquire a bland flavor during slow cooking.

After browning meat or poultry and sautéing vegetables, deglaze the pan with wine or broth to release the caramelized juices created during browning. Add a small amount of the liquid to the leftover juices and cooked-on food particles in the pan, bring it to a boil, then reduce the heat and simmer for 1 to 2 minutes while scraping up the bits stuck to the bottom of the pan. Pour this aromatic liquid over the browned meat in the slow cooker to maximize the flavor in your finished dish.

5. Don't Overdo the Liquids

Because moisture has no escape from the confines of the slow cooker, the amount of liquid in the stoneware increases as juices and steam are released from the food. Therefore, slow cooker recipes use only about half the liquid called for in conventional recipes. If you're new to slow cooking, keep in mind that the liquid may not cover the solids when you first add the ingredients to the slow cooker.

If you wind up with too much liquid when your meal is done cooking, remove the lid and increase the temperature to High if necessary, then cook, uncovered, for 30 to 45 minutes to allow some liquid to evaporate.

6. Use Whole Herbs and Spices

Whole-leaf dried herbs, such as dried thyme and oregano leaves, and whole or coarsely crushed spices release their flavor slowly throughout the long cooking process, so they are a better choice than ground herbs and spices, which tend to lose their flavor in the slow cooker. Add fresh herbs, such as basil and cilantro, during the last hour of cooking. Always taste your finished dish before serving it and adjust the salt and pepper if needed.

7. Resist the Temptation to Lift the Lid

Always cook with the slow cooker lid on. The lid traps heat as it rises and converts it into steam, which is what cooks the food. Removing the lid will result in major heat loss, which the slow cooker can't quickly recover. You will need to extend the cooking time by at least 20 minutes each time you lift the lid. Do so only when it is time to check for doneness, when adding ingredients or when stirring is recommended.

8. Experiment with Water Baths

Delicate dishes, such as custards, puddings and cheesecakes, are cooked to perfection in a hot-water bath, or bain-marie. In conventional cooking, this technique involves setting the filled baking dish in a larger pan filled with hot water before placing it in the oven. Heat is transferred from the hot water to the dish, cooking the contents gently and slowly, so that it doesn't curdle or form a crust. The technique works wonders in the slow cooker, too:

As a general rule, the slow cooker should be no less than half full and no more than two-thirds to three-quarters full of food once all the ingredients are added.

If you substitute fresh herbs for dried, you will need to use three times as much.

If a recipe in this book instructs you to add or stir ingredients partway through, the resulting heat loss has been accounted for in the overall cooking time.

If the dish fits snugly in the slow cooker, add the water first. Since the water level will rise when you add the filled dish, test it first by pouring about 1 cup (250 mL) water into the stoneware. Add the filled pan and make sure the water rises 1 inch (2.5 cm) up the sides of the dish. If it rises any more than that, remove the pan and ladle some water out.

custards, puddings and cheesecakes stay creamy and smooth, and cheesecakes do not crack. The challenge, however, is finding a dish that will fit properly in the slow cooker. Standard 4-cup (1 L) or 6-cup (1.5 L) ovenproof baking bowls work well in larger slow cookers. If you are making a cheesecake, a 7-inch (18 cm) springform pan should fit nicely.

These water baths add to the heat of your dish. So that you can safely and easily remove the dish from the slow cooker, you'll want to make foil handles to place under the dish when putting it in the stoneware. Cut a 2-foot (60 cm) piece of foil in half lengthwise. Fold each strip in half lengthwise and crisscross the strips in the bottom of the stoneware, bringing the ends up to clear the rim. Place the dish in the slow cooker and pour in enough water to come 1 inch (2.5 cm) up the sides of the dish. Cover the slow cooker with its lid, making sure the ends of the foil are tucked between the rim and the lid. Use the foil handles as lifters to remove the pan from the slow cooker.

Adapting Conventional Recipes

While this book is filled with an array of recipes to suit any palate, it's easy to alter your favorite pot roast, family stew or chili from conventional oven or stovetop directions to a slow-cooking method. You'll just need to follow a few simple guidelines:

- Select a recipe that uses a less tender cut of meat, such as beef brisket or blade roast, short ribs, stew meat, pork shoulder, or chicken or turkey drumsticks or thighs. These will become fork-tender and develop savory flavor during long cooking.

- Start by browning meats as you would for conventional recipes. Then sauté aromatic vegetables, such as onions, garlic, celery and carrots, with dried herbs and spices.

- If you have chosen a recipe with a heavy emphasis on meat, add some vegetables for a convenient way to cook a complete meal all at once. Keep in mind that root vegetables tend to cook more slowly than meat, so cut them into bite-size pieces and place them on the bottom and around the sides of the slow cooker, with the meat on top.

- Soak dried beans, peas and lentils until completely soft before adding them to the slow cooker; otherwise, the sugar and acid in other foods will prevent them from softening (see Basic Beans on page 84 for information on soaking beans).

- Reduce the amount of liquid you use by about half, as moisture is high and evaporation low in the slow cooker.

- If the recipe calls for uncooked rice, add $\frac{1}{4}$ cup (60 mL) extra liquid per $\frac{1}{4}$ cup (60 mL) rice. Long-grain parboiled (converted) white rice will yield the best results in all-day cooking.

- Add pasta and seafood in the last hour of cooking time. Pasta should be cooked to the tender but firm stage before it is added.

- Add tender vegetables, such as peas, broccoli, Brussels sprouts, cauliflower, kale and chard, in the last 15 to 60 minutes of the cooking process. Frozen vegetables, such as peas, corn and green beans, should be thawed first, then added in the last 15 to 30 minutes.

- Stir in cream, milk, sour cream and cheese just before serving. Dairy products can break down during extended cooking.

Organization is the key to successful slow cooking. You can prep many of your ingredients the day before and store them in airtight containers or storage bags in the refrigerator. Cover chopped potatoes with water to keep them from turning brown. Ground meat can be browned the day before, as long as it is fully cooked and refrigerated overnight. Chops, roasts, cubed meat and poultry must all be prepared just before cooking.

When adding ingredients to the slow cooker, leave at least 2 inches (5 cm) between the top of the food and the rim of the slow cooker so the food can come to a simmer.

The chart below will give you an idea of how to adapt cooking times from your favorite conventional oven or stovetop recipes. These times are approximate; you are the best judge of when your food is perfectly cooked.

Conventional Oven or Stovetop Time	Slow Cooker Time
15 to 30 minutes	1½ hours on High
	3 hours on Low
1 hour	3½ hours on High
	6 to 7 hours on Low
2 hours	4½ hours on High
	9 to 10 hours on Low
3 hours	5½ hours on High
	10 to 11 hours on Low

Food Safety Considerations

The U.S. Department of Agriculture assures us that, in a slow cooker that is used properly (the lid is left on and food is cooked at the appropriate heat level for the appropriate length of time), foods will reach their safe internal cooked temperature quickly enough to inhibit bacterial growth.

With that concern off the table, here are a few other kitchen safety details to consider when slow cooking:

Once a dish is completely cooked, you can keep food warm by switching to the Low or Warm setting (many machines will automatically switch to Warm at the end of the preset cooking time). Fully cooked food is safe on these settings for up to 2 hours. Do not use the Warm setting for cooking — it is too low a temperature to cook food safely.

Check for doneness at the minimum time suggested, especially the first time you make a recipe.

- Always start with fresh or thawed meat and poultry. Using frozen or partially frozen meat will increase the time required for the meat's internal temperature to reach the "safe zone" in which bacteria growth is inhibited.

- In general, defrost frozen vegetables, such as peas and corn, before adding them to the slow cooker. This prevents them from slowing down the cooking process. Defrost them in the refrigerator overnight, or place them under cold running water to thaw and separate.

- Cook all ground meat and ground poultry completely before adding it to the slow cooker. (There are some exceptions, and proper cooking directions are given for these in the individual recipes.) If you are cooking ground meat the night before, chill it separately from other ingredients.

- Do not refrigerate uncooked or partially cooked meat or poultry in the slow cooker stoneware, as the insert will become very cold and will slow the cooking process. Partially cook meat or poultry only when transferring it immediately to the slow cooker. Do not refrigerate for later cooking.

- Precut meats and vegetables should be stored separately in the refrigerator. After cutting uncooked meat, never use the same cutting board or knife for other foods without thoroughly washing these utensils with soap and hot water first.

- When cooking whole poultry or meatloaf, use a meat thermometer to accurately test doneness. Insert the thermometer into the thickest part of the thigh or loaf. The U.S. Department of Agriculture recommends cooking poultry and meatloaf to an internal temperature of 165°F (74°C); Health Canada recommends ensuring that the temperature has reached 170°F (77°C).

- Remove leftovers from the stoneware and refrigerate in small portions as quickly as possible.

- Do not reheat cooked food in the slow cooker. Frozen leftovers can be thawed in the refrigerator or microwave, then reheated in a conventional oven or microwave oven, or in a saucepan on the stove.

Know the Limitations

While I am the first to extol the virtues of slow cooking, it's important to remember that, as with any kitchen appliance, slow cookers do have some limitations. If you understand what cooks well in a slow cooker and what doesn't, you won't have any unwanted surprises.

First off, don't even entertain the idea of cooking premium, expensive cuts of meat, such as prime rib or beef filets. As mentioned earlier, slow cooking is designed to tenderize tough, inexpensive cuts of meat by breaking down collagen and fatty tissue. Cuts meant for grilling, broiling and sautéing should be left to those formats for best results.

Nor is it wise to use the slow cooker as a baking tool for items such as cookies and pies, which need dry heat. While we can achieve many wonderful desserts in the slow cooker, traditional baking methods remain the best ways to cook these items.

Finally, take care when working with dairy products and eggs, as it is easy to overcook, separate or toughen these ingredients. To avoid these problems, the recipes that contain dairy products or eggs are very specific about cooking times.

For ease of cleanup, spray the stoneware insert with nonstick cooking spray before adding food. Do not subject the stoneware to sudden changes in temperature. Before cleaning it, let it come to room temperature, then fill it with hot, soapy water and let it soak for an hour or so. Use a nylon scrubber to remove cooked-on pieces. Most stoneware can also be cleaned in the dishwasher.

Ingredient Essentials

When I was developing and testing the recipes in this book, the basic ingredients I used were of standard size and consistency. The recipes make some assumptions about what is standard when it comes to basic ingredients; these distinctions are detailed below. For the best results, always use the recommended ingredient, exactly as called for, unless other options are indicated in a tip.

- Dried herbs are crumbled whole leaves, not ground.

- Table salt is used for cooking unless otherwise indicated. Where a recipe says "season to taste," I used kosher salt.

- All eggs used are large eggs; expect different results if you substitute medium or extra-large eggs.

- I used 2% milk and yogurt unless otherwise specified.

- When sour cream is added to the slow cooker, I used 14%. If using sour cream as a topping or adding it at the end of the cooking process, you can use a lower-fat (5%) version.

- I used salted butter.

- Fresh vegetables and fruits are medium-size unless otherwise indicated. Any inedible peels, skins, seeds and cores are removed unless otherwise indicated.

- "Onions" means regular cooking onions unless otherwise indicated.

- Canned tomatoes are diced, not whole, unless whole is specified.

- Rice is long-grain parboiled (converted), unless otherwise indicated.

- I used fresh, oven-ready lasagna noodles rather than the dried, no-boil type. For all other pasta shapes, I used dried pasta.

- Where recipes call for vegetable oil to brown meats and sauté vegetables, I used a canola/sunflower oil combination.

- When choosing poultry, look for air-chilled products, which have a firmer texture and will hold their shape better and be more tender after the long slow-cooking process.

- Avoid "seasoned" meats and poultry, which have been treated with additional water and sodium phosphate or other ingredients and tend to make slow-cooked foods watery and salty.

For baking recipes, eggs should be brought to room temperature before use; otherwise, they can be used directly from the refrigerator.

When I call for chopped or minced garlic, I used fresh garlic, not the preserved minced garlic available in stores.

When greasing stoneware, I sprayed it with nonstick cooking spray.

Soups

Mexican Minestrone with Cornmeal Dumplings

Makes 6 to 8 servings

There are few things in the world I can eat twice a day for a few consecutive days, but this has proved to be one of them. Super-hearty and delicious, this soup won't disappoint you, I promise, even if you decide you don't want to eat it for six meals in a row.

Tips

Here's a foolproof way to chop an onion: Peel the onion and halve it from top to base. Place each half cut side down on a cutting board. Slice horizontally across each half. Holding the slices together, slice vertically.

Mild green chiles are found in the Mexican foods section of the supermarket. They are sold whole or chopped.

To make sure the dumplings cook through, don't lift the lid of the slow cooker until you are ready to test for doneness.

• Minimum 4-quart slow cooker

1 tbsp	vegetable oil	15 mL
1	onion, finely chopped	1
3	cloves garlic, minced	3
2	potatoes, peeled and coarsely chopped	2
1	can (19 oz/540 mL) chili-style stewed tomatoes, with juice	1
1	can (4½ oz/127 mL) chopped mild green chiles, with liquid	1
2 cups	cooked or canned black beans (see page 84), drained and rinsed	500 mL
2 cups	cooked or canned chickpeas (see page 84), drained and rinsed	500 mL
1 cup	frozen corn kernels, thawed	250 mL
1 cup	chopped green beans	250 mL
1 cup	diced carrots	250 mL
1 tbsp	chopped canned chipotle peppers in adobo sauce	15 mL
1 tsp	ground cumin	5 mL
4 cups	chicken or beef broth	1 L
	Freshly squeezed juice of 1 lime	

Dumplings

⅓ cup	all-purpose flour	75 mL
¼ cup	cornmeal	60 mL
1 tbsp	baking powder	15 mL
⅛ tsp	freshly ground black pepper	0.5 mL
1	egg	1
1 tbsp	milk	15 mL
2 tsp	vegetable oil	10 mL

1. In a large skillet, heat oil over medium-high heat. Sauté onions for 5 minutes or until tender and translucent. Add garlic and sauté for 1 minute. Transfer to slow cooker stoneware.

2. Stir in potatoes, tomatoes with juice, chiles with liquid, black beans, chickpeas, corn, green beans, carrot, chipotle peppers, cumin, broth and lime juice.

continued on page 26…

Substitute 2 cups (500 mL) diced cooked chicken or turkey for the chickpeas.

3. Cover and cook on Low for 6 to 8 hours or on High for 3 to 4 hours, until soup is bubbling and vegetables are tender.

4. *Dumplings:* In a bowl, combine flour, cornmeal, baking powder and pepper. In another bowl, whisk together egg, milk and oil. Add to flour mixture; stir with a fork just until combined.

5. Drop 6 to 8 mounds of dumpling dough onto bubbling soup. Cover and cook on Low for about 30 minutes or until a tester inserted in the center of a dumpling comes out clean.

6. Ladle soup into individual serving bowls, making sure each bowl has at least one dumpling.

Make Ahead

This dish can be assembled up to 12 hours in advance. Prepare through step 2, cover and refrigerate overnight. The next day, place stoneware in slow cooker and proceed with step 3.

Creamy Broccoli Soup with Grilled Cheese Croutons

**Makes
6 servings**

You can serve this flavorful, filling soup at lunch or supper. Be sure to use nice aged Cheddar, as it gives a real lift to this soup.

Tips

You can substitute an equal amount of frozen chopped broccoli.

If you prefer, you can substitute a 12-oz (370 mL) can of evaporated milk for the cream.

● **Minimum 4-quart slow cooker**

2 tbsp	vegetable oil	30 mL
2	onions, finely chopped	2
8 cups	chopped broccoli	2 L
4 cups	vegetable broth	1 L
1 tbsp	Worcestershire sauce	15 mL
1/2 tsp	ground nutmeg	2 mL
1 1/2 cups	light (5%) cream or half-and-half (10%) cream	375 mL
1 cup	shredded sharp (old) Cheddar cheese	250 mL
2 tbsp	dry sherry (optional)	30 mL
	Salt and freshly ground black pepper	
	Grilled Cheese Croutons (see recipe, page 28)	

1. In a large skillet, heat oil over medium-high heat. Sauté onions for 5 minutes or until tender and translucent. Transfer to slow cooker stoneware. Stir in broccoli, broth, Worcestershire sauce and nutmeg.

2. Cover and cook on Low for 4 to 6 hours or on High for 2 to 3 hours, until soup is bubbling and broccoli is tender.

3. Using an immersion blender, or in a food processor or blender, in batches as necessary, purée soup until smooth. (If using food processor or blender, return purée to stoneware.)

4. Stir in cream, cheese and sherry (if using) until cheese has melted. Season to taste with salt and pepper.

5. Ladle into bowls and garnish with croutons.

> **An immersion blender (also called a stick blender, wand blender or hand blender) allows you to blend or purée in almost any container. It is ideal for puréeing soups and emulsifying sauces right in the slow cooker.**

....

These miniature
sandwich-like cubes are
a fun addition to any
creamy soup. Try them
on tomato soup too!

Grilled Cheese Croutons

¼ cup	butter, softened	60 mL
¼ tsp	dried thyme	1 mL
4	slices sandwich bread	4
4 oz	Cheddar cheese, thinly sliced	125 g

1. Heat a large skillet over medium-high heat. In a small bowl, combine butter and thyme. Spread butter mixture over one side of each bread slice. Place 2 slices in the pan, buttered side down. Top each with half the cheese, then with a remaining bread slice, buttered side up.

2. Cook, turning once, for 3 to 5 minutes per side or until toasted on both sides. Let cool slightly, then cut into 1-inch (2.5 cm) squares.

Adobe Sweet Potato and Chile Soup

Makes 4 to 6 servings

Sweet potato soup, Southwest style. It's not too spicy, but has a nice hint of smokiness from the paprika. Serve with a pan of Southwest Cornbread (see recipe, page 30).

Tip

Smoked paprika is made by grinding peppers that have undergone a smoking process. You can find it in various heat levels (from mild to hot). Be careful how much you use, because smoky seasonings can easily overpower the flavor of a dish.

• **Minimum 4-quart slow cooker**

2 tbsp	butter	30 mL
2	onions, finely chopped	2
2	cloves garlic, minced	2
2	sweet potatoes, peeled and chopped	2
1	jalapeño pepper, seeded and finely chopped	1
1 tsp	smoked paprika	5 mL
4 cups	chicken or vegetable broth	1 L
	Freshly squeezed juice of 2 limes (about ¼ cup/60 mL)	
	Salt	
	Sour cream or yogurt	

1. In a large skillet, melt butter over medium-high heat. Sauté onions for 5 minutes or until tender and translucent. Add garlic, sweet potatoes, jalapeño and paprika; sauté for 1 minute. Transfer to slow cooker stoneware. Stir in broth.

2. Cover and cook on Low for 6 to 8 hours or on High for 3 to 4 hours, until soup is bubbling and potatoes are tender.

3. Using an immersion blender, or in a food processor or blender, in batches as necessary, purée soup until smooth. (If using food processor or blender, return purée to stoneware.) Stir in lime juice and season to taste with salt.

4. Ladle into bowls and garnish each with a dollop of sour cream.

This delicious cornbread makes the perfect side dish for any Southern-inspired meal.

Tip

Jalapeño peppers contain volatile oils that can burn your skin and eyes if they come into direct contact. It is best to wear plastic or rubber gloves when chopping jalapeños, and take care not to touch your face or eyes while you work. If your bare hands do touch the peppers, wash your hands and nails well with hot, soapy water.

Southwest Cornbread

- *Preheat oven to 350°F (180°C)*
- *9-inch (23 cm) square or round metal baking pan, greased*

½ cup	all-purpose flour	125 mL
½ cup	cornmeal	125 mL
1 tbsp	baking powder	15 mL
2 tsp	packed brown sugar	10 mL
½ tsp	salt	2 mL
1 tbsp	vegetable oil	15 mL
1	onion, finely chopped	1
1	small jalapeño pepper, seeded and chopped	1
¼ cup	diced red bell pepper	60 mL
¼ cup	diced green bell pepper	60 mL
2	eggs	2
½ cup	vegetable oil	125 mL
1 cup	frozen corn kernels, thawed	250 mL
¼ cup	chopped fresh cilantro	60 mL
½ cup	shredded Cheddar cheese	125 mL

1. In a large bowl, combine flour, cornmeal, baking powder, brown sugar and salt; set aside.

2. In a skillet, heat 1 tbsp (15 mL) oil over medium-high heat. Sauté onion, jalapeño, red pepper and green pepper for 3 to 5 minutes or until softened. Transfer to a large bowl and let cool slightly.

3. In a glass measuring cup, whisk together eggs and ½ cup (125 mL) oil until well combined. Add to the cooled pepper mixture, along with corn and cilantro. Quickly fold vegetable mixture into flour mixture. Fold in cheese. Spoon into prepared baking pan.

4. Bake in preheated oven for 35 to 40 minutes or until golden and firm on top. Cut into squares or wedges.

Jack's Smashed Potato Soup

Makes 6 to 8 servings

This is my son's favorite recipe from the array I developed for this book. Jack even eats it for breakfast! Potatoes blend with Cheddar cheese, cream and roasted garlic in this chunky good-to-the-last-spoonful soup.

Tips

Spread extra roasted garlic on toasted baguette slices, top with a dollop of softened goat cheese, and serve with the soup.

Leftover roasted garlic can be stored in an airtight container in the refrigerator for up to 3 days. It can be mashed and added to soups, stews or pasta sauces.

- **Minimum 4-quart slow cooker**

3½ lbs	thin-skinned potatoes (about 8 medium), cut into ¾-inch (2 cm) cubes	1.75 kg
½ cup	chopped yellow bell pepper	125 mL
4	cloves roasted garlic	4
½ tsp	freshly ground black pepper	2 mL
4½ cups	chicken broth	1.25 L
1 cup	shredded sharp (old) Cheddar cheese	250 mL
½ cup	light (5%) cream	125 mL
½ cup	thinly sliced green onions	125 mL
	Chopped fresh chives (optional)	

1. In slow cooker stoneware, combine potatoes, yellow pepper, garlic, pepper and broth.

2. Cover and cook on Low for 8 to 10 hours or on High for 4 to 5 hours, until soup is bubbling and potatoes are tender.

3. Using an immersion blender or a potato masher, purée or mash potatoes to make a thick soup. Stir in cheese, cream and green onions.

4. Ladle into bowls and garnish with chives (if using).

Make Ahead

This dish can be assembled up to 12 hours in advance. Prepare through step 1, cover and refrigerate overnight. The next day, place stoneware in slow cooker and proceed with step 2.

> ### To Roast Garlic
>
> **Preheat oven to 400°F (200°C). Peel away the outer skins from garlic head, leaving skins of individual cloves intact. With a sharp knife, cut ¼ to ½ inch (0.5 to 1 cm) from the top of the head, exposing individual cloves. Place, base down, on a square of foil or in a garlic baker. Drizzle exposed cloves with oil until well coated; enclose in foil or cover with lid of baker. Bake for 30 to 35 minutes or until cloves feel soft when pressed. Let cool to room temperature, then remove roasted cloves with a cocktail fork or squeeze them out of their skins.**

Curried Split Pea and Sweet Potato Soup

Makes 6 to 8 servings

There are as many variations on split pea soup as there are cooks, and Curried Split Pea and Sweet Potato Soup is one of my favorites.

Tips

For a smoother consistency, you can purée some of the cooked soup after you remove the pork hock. Use an immersion blender right in the slow cooker for ease, and purée until the desired consistency is reached, or transfer 1½ cups (375 mL) to a blender or food processor and process until smooth, then return purée to slow cooker and continue with recipe.

Dried split peas have been mechanically split along the seam so they will cook faster. It's a good idea to sort them before cooking, to remove any tiny stones or discolored pieces. Then place the peas in a colander and rinse under cold running water until the water is no longer foamy.

• **Minimum 5-quart slow cooker**

1 tsp	vegetable oil	5 mL
1 tsp	cumin seeds	5 mL
1 tsp	fennel seeds	5 mL
1 tsp	grated gingerroot	5 mL
1 tsp	finely minced garlic	5 mL
1	large onion, finely chopped	1
1 lb	dried yellow split peas (about 2 cups/500 mL), sorted, rinsed and drained	500 g
1 lb	smoked pork hock	500 g
1½ cups	coarsely chopped celery	375 mL
3	carrots, coarsely chopped	3
2	sweet potatoes, peeled and coarsely chopped	2
1 tbsp	curry powder	15 mL
1 tbsp	dried marjoram, crushed	15 mL
2	bay leaves	2
¼ tsp	freshly ground black pepper	1 mL

1. In a small skillet, heat oil over medium-high heat. Toast cumin and fennel seeds, stirring constantly, for 10 seconds. (Seeds may or may not begin to pop.) Add ginger, garlic and onion; sauté for about 5 minutes or until onions are tender and translucent and spices are fragrant. Transfer to slow cooker stoneware.

2. Stir in peas, pork hock, celery, carrots, sweet potatoes, curry powder, marjoram, bay leaves and pepper. Stir in 6 cups (1.5 L) water.

3. Cover and cook on Low for 9 to 11 hours or on High for 4½ to 5½ hours, until soup is thick and bubbling and peas are tender.

4. Discard bay leaves. Transfer pork hock to a bowl and let cool slightly. When pork hock is cool enough to handle, remove meat from bone. Discard skin and bone. Coarsely chop meat, return to soup and cook on Low for 20 minutes or until heated through.

Make Ahead

This dish can be assembled up to 12 hours in advance. Prepare through step 2, cover and refrigerate overnight. The next day, place stoneware in slow cooker and proceed with step 3.

Kale and Chickpea Soup

Makes
6 servings

I have often thought that the slow cooker and the bread machine should be combined into one appliance. While this hearty and satisfying dinnertime soup simmers away, make a loaf of homemade bread to serve alongside. If you don't have time, pick up a fresh ciabatta loaf from the supermarket.

Tip
You can substitute other greens, such as collard greens, spinach or escarole, for the kale.

* **Minimum 4-quart slow cooker**

2 tbsp	olive oil	30 mL
1	onion, chopped	1
2	cloves garlic, minced	2
1/2 tsp	salt	2 mL
1/2 tsp	freshly ground black pepper	2 mL
1/4 tsp	crumbled dried sage	1 mL
2	sweet potatoes, peeled and cut into 1-inch (2.5 cm) cubes	2
1	red bell pepper, chopped	1
2 cups	cooked or canned chickpeas (see page 84), drained and rinsed	500 mL
1 1/2 cups	cubed cooked ham or smoked turkey breast	375 mL
3 cups	chicken broth	750 mL
3 cups	chopped kale	750 mL
	Parmesan cheese shavings	

1. In a large saucepan, heat oil over medium-high heat. Sauté onion, garlic, salt, pepper and sage for about 5 minutes or until onion is tender and translucent. Transfer to slow cooker stoneware.

2. Stir in sweet potato, red pepper, chickpeas, ham, broth and 1 cup (250 mL) water.

3. Cover and cook on Low for 6 to 8 hours or on High for 3 to 4 hours, until soup is bubbling and potatoes are tender.

4. Stir in kale. Cover and cook on High for 10 to 15 minutes or until kale is tender.

5. Ladle into bowls and top with Parmesan shavings.

> **Kale is a nutrient-packed leafy green. It has been cultivated for over 2,000 years and is a member of the *Brassica* family (which also includes cabbage, Brussels sprouts and collard greens, to name a few). Kale leaves are ruffled and are dark to grayish green in color. It is most flavorful during the cold weather months, although it can be found year-round.**

Creamy Tomato Tortellini Soup

Makes 4 to 6 servings

A package of fresh tortellini or other cheese-filled pasta makes this a satisfying soup the whole family will enjoy. Adding the baby spinach at the end gives it a fresh-from-the-garden flavor.

Tip

To ripen tomatoes, place them in a brown paper bag and store at room temperature. Never store tomatoes in the refrigerator, as it destroys their delicate flavor.

- **Minimum 4-quart slow cooker**

⅓ cup	melted butter	75 mL
⅓ cup	all-purpose flour	75 mL
2 cups	chicken broth	500 mL
3	large tomatoes, coarsely chopped	3
3	cloves garlic, minced	3
1	onion, finely chopped	1
½ tsp	dried basil	2 mL
½ tsp	salt	2 mL
¼ tsp	dried oregano	1 mL
⅛ tsp	cayenne pepper	0.5 mL
1	package (10 oz/300 g) fresh cheese-filled tortellini	1
1	can (12 oz/370 mL) evaporated milk	1
6 cups	baby spinach leaves or chopped trimmed spinach	1.5 L
	Freshly ground black pepper	
	Freshly grated Parmesan cheese	

1. In slow cooker stoneware, whisk together melted butter and flour until a smooth paste forms. Slowly whisk in broth until combined. Stir in tomatoes, garlic, onion, basil, salt, oregano and cayenne.

2. Cover and cook on Low for 6 to 8 hours or on High for 3 to 4 hours, until soup is thick and vegetables are tender.

3. Using an immersion blender, or in a food processor or blender, purée soup until smooth. (If using food processor or blender, return mixture to stoneware.)

4. In a large pot of boiling salted water, cook tortellini according to package directions. Drain and add to stoneware. Stir in evaporated milk and baby spinach.

5. Cover and cook on High for 5 minutes or until spinach is slightly wilted.

6. Ladle into bowls and sprinkle with black pepper and Parmesan.

Make Ahead

This dish can be assembled up to 12 hours in advance. Prepare through step 1, cover and refrigerate overnight. The next day, place stoneware in slow cooker and proceed with step 2.

Lentil Soup with Italian Sausage and Greens

Makes 6 to 8 servings

Nuggets of sausage give a little meatball action to this hearty, no-fuss soup, chock-full of healthy escarole and lentils.

Tips

If you can't find escarole, curly endive is a good substitute, though it is a little more bitter.

Good-quality salad croutons make a quick substitute for homemade.

- **Minimum 4-quart slow cooker**

2 tbsp	olive oil, divided	30 mL
1 lb	mild or hot Italian sausage cut into 1-inch (2.5 cm) pieces	500 g
4	cloves garlic, finely chopped	4
2	carrots, diced	2
2	stalks celery, finely chopped	2
1	onion, finely chopped	1
2 tbsp	tomato paste	30 mL
1½ cups	dried red lentils, rinsed and drained	375 mL
1	bay leaf	1
3 cups	chicken broth	750 mL
8 oz	escarole, chopped (about 4 cups/1 L)	250 g
1 to 2 tbsp	red wine vinegar	15 to 30 mL
	Salt and freshly ground black pepper	
	Cumin Croutons (see recipe, opposite)	

1. In a skillet, heat 1 tbsp (15 mL) of the oil over medium-high heat. Cook sausage, stirring, for 8 to 10 minutes or until browned. Using a slotted spoon, transfer sausage to slow cooker stoneware.

2. Add remaining oil to skillet and reduce heat to medium. Add garlic, carrots, celery and onion; sauté for about 5 minutes or until onion is tender and translucent. Stir in tomato paste. Transfer to stoneware. Stir in lentils, bay leaf, broth and 3 cups (750 mL) water.

3. Cover and cook on Low for 8 to 10 hours or on High for 4 to 5 hours, until soup is bubbling and lentils are tender.

4. Stir in escarole. Cover and cook on High for about 3 minutes or until tender. Stir in vinegar to taste and season to taste with salt and pepper. Discard bay leaf.

5. Ladle into bowls and garnish with croutons.

Make Ahead

This dish can be assembled up to 12 hours in advance. Cook the sausage completely in step 1 and refrigerate it in its own airtight container. Complete step 2, without adding the lentils, cover and refrigerate overnight. The next day, place stoneware in slow cooker, stir in cooked sausage and lentils and proceed with step 3.

Escarole might look like a head of romaine, but it is more flavorful, with thicker, more crumpled-looking leaves and a pale yellow center, or "heart." While it is slightly bitter when raw, it gets milder and sweeter when cooked. Escarole is rich in vitamin A and folate and is a good source of fiber.

Makes 2 cups (500 mL)

Homemade croutons are extremely addictive — I often make a pot of soup just to eat the croutons! The key is to use a good-quality bread, such as ciabatta, whole-grain or hearty specialty bread.

Tip

Croutons can be stored in an airtight container in a cool, dry place for up to 1 day.

Cumin Croutons

2 tbsp	butter	30 mL
2 tsp	ground cumin	10 mL
2 cups	bread cubes	500 mL

1. In a large skillet, melt butter over medium heat. Stir in cumin. Add bread cubes and cook, stirring, for about 5 minutes or until croutons are golden brown and crisp. Remove to a plate lined with paper towels and let cool completely.

Tex-Mex Tomato Rice Soup

Garnish this kid-friendly soup with minced fresh cilantro, shredded chicken and/or sour cream.

Tip

You can also serve this soup garnished with Grilled Cheese Croutons (page 28).

- **Minimum 4-quart slow cooker**

2 tbsp	vegetable oil	30 mL
2	cloves garlic, minced	2
1	onion, chopped	1
1	jalapeño pepper, seeded and minced	1
1/2 tsp	ground cumin	2 mL
1/4 tsp	chili powder	1 mL
2	carrots, chopped	2
1 cup	frozen corn kernels, thawed	250 mL
1/4 cup	long-grain white rice	60 mL
1	can (28 oz/796 mL) diced tomatoes, with juice	1
1/4 cup	minced fresh cilantro (optional)	60 mL
1 tbsp	freshly squeezed lime juice	15 mL
	Salt and freshly ground black pepper	

1. In a large skillet, heat oil over medium-high heat. Sauté garlic, onion, jalapeño, cumin and chili powder for about 5 minutes or until onion is tender and translucent. Transfer to slow cooker stoneware. Stir in carrots, corn, rice, tomatoes with juice and 3 cups (750 mL) water.

2. Cover and cook on Low for 6 to 8 hours or on High for 3 to 4 hours, until soup is bubbling and rice is tender. Stir in cilantro (if using) and lime juice. Season to taste with salt and pepper.

Cathedral Café Red Bean and Barley Soup

Makes 6 to 8 servings

On a car trip home from Florida one year, we stumbled upon the quaint Cathedral Café in Fayetteville, West Virginia. My daughter ordered this soup and enjoyed it so much that I just had to ask for the recipe.

Tip
To avoid tears when chopping onions, put the onions in the freezer for a few minutes first.

• **Minimum 4-quart slow cooker**

4 cups	cooked or canned red kidney beans (see page 84), drained and rinsed	1 L
1	onion, finely chopped	1
1	green bell pepper, finely chopped	1
1 cup	finely chopped carrots	250 mL
1 cup	finely chopped celery	250 mL
1 cup	pearl barley, rinsed	250 mL
1½ tsp	dried basil	7 mL
¼ tsp	freshly ground black pepper	1 mL
4 cups	vegetable broth	1 L
1	can (19 oz/540 mL) diced tomatoes, with juice	1
1 cup	prepared tomato pasta sauce	250 mL
¼ cup	chopped fresh parsley	60 mL

1. In slow cooker stoneware, combine beans, onion, green pepper, carrots, celery, barley, basil, pepper, broth, tomatoes with juice and pasta sauce.

2. Cover and cook on Low for 6 to 8 hours or on High for 3 to 4 hours, until soup is bubbling and barley is tender.

3. Ladle into bowls and garnish with parsley.

Greek Lemon and Rice Soup

**Makes
4 servings**

This classic Greek chicken-egg-lemon soup (known as avgolemono) has been a favorite of children for millennia — it's so cheering on a cold day. A hearty salad and crusty ciabatta bread make this meal complete.

Tip

When cooking rice in the slow cooker, I usually recommend long-grain parboiled (converted) rice; however, for this recipe, short-grain rice, such as Arborio, is recommended. This type of rice softens and absorbs the broth, making the soup thicker. Do not use instant rice.

- **3½- to 5-quart slow cooker**

4 cups	chicken broth	1 L
½ cup	short-grain white rice (see tip, at left)	125 mL
3	egg yolks	3
¼ cup	freshly squeezed lemon juice	60 mL
¼ tsp	salt	1 mL
¼ tsp	freshly ground white pepper	1 mL
4	thin slices lemon (optional)	4
2 tbsp	finely chopped fresh parsley	30 mL

1. In slow cooker stoneware, combine broth and rice.

2. Cover and cook on High for 2 to 3 hours or until rice is tender.

3. Reduce heat to Low. In a bowl, whisk together egg yolks and lemon juice. Whisk a large spoonful of the hot broth mixture into the yolk mixture, adding the hot liquid slowly and whisking constantly. (If hot liquid is added too quickly, the yolk mixture will curdle.) When fully blended, whisk into slow cooker stoneware.

4. Cover and cook on Low for 10 minutes. Season to taste with salt and pepper.

5. Ladle into bowls and garnish each with a lemon slice (if using) and parsley.

Mexican Chicken Tortilla Soup

**Makes
4 servings**

This soup is a snap to prepare because it uses a deli-cooked chicken, frozen vegetables and stewed tomatoes with added chili seasonings.

Tips

Using a deli-cooked chicken not only makes the prep go quickly, it adds immense flavor to the broth. Do not add the skin to the broth; be sure to remove it from the chicken first.

For a little extra heat in this recipe, add 1 to 2 sliced, seeded jalapeño peppers to the soup just before serving.

Serving soup in a warm bowl is an excellent way to help it retain heat. To warm your bowls, place them in a clean sink and run hot water over them. When ready to serve, dry them and use them immediately. If your tap water isn't hot enough, use water from a hot kettle. Alternatively, some ovens are equipped with a warming drawer — if you've never used it, here's your chance!

- **Minimum 4-quart slow cooker**

4 cups	chicken broth	1 L
2	cloves garlic, minced	2
1 tsp	ground cumin	5 mL
1 tsp	ground coriander	5 mL
1	can (19 oz/540 mL) chili-style stewed tomatoes, with juice	1
2 cups	shredded cooked chicken	500 mL
2 cups	frozen bell pepper and onion stir-fry vegetables, thawed	500 mL
½ cup	frozen corn kernels, thawed	125 mL
1 cup	crushed tortilla chips	250 mL
	Sour cream	
2 tbsp	chopped fresh cilantro	30 mL

1. In slow cooker stoneware, combine broth, garlic, cumin, coriander, tomatoes with juice, chicken, stir-fry vegetables and corn.

2. Cover and cook on Low for 6 to 7 hours or on High for 3 to 3½ hours, until soup is bubbling and vegetables are tender.

3. Ladle soup into warmed bowls and top each with tortilla chips, a dollop of sour cream and a sprinkling of cilantro.

Make Ahead

This dish can be assembled up to 12 hours in advance. Prepare through step 1, cover and refrigerate overnight. The next day, place stoneware in slow cooker and proceed with step 2.

Edamame and Chicken Corn Chowder

Makes 4 to 6 servings

This hearty and nutritious "stoup" is chock-full of goodness.

Tip

Look for edamame in the freezer section of your grocery store. Lima beans are a good alternative if you can't find edamame.

- **4- to 5-quart slow cooker**

3	slices bacon (4 oz/125 g)	3
1 lb	boneless skinless chicken breasts, cut into 1-inch (2.5 cm) pieces	500 g
1	onion, chopped	1
3 cups	chicken broth	750 mL
2	red potatoes, cut into 1/2-inch (1 cm) cubes	2
1	can (14 oz or 341 mL) cream-style corn	1
2 cups	frozen shelled edamame, thawed	500 mL
1	large red bell pepper, diced	1
1	jalapeño pepper, minced	1
1/2 tsp	dried oregano	2 mL
2 tbsp	all-purpose flour	30 mL
1/2 cup	heavy or whipping (35%) cream	125 mL
	Salt and freshly ground black pepper	
	Shredded Monterey Jack cheese	

1. In a large saucepan, cook bacon for 5 to 6 minutes or until browned and crisp. Transfer to paper towels to drain. Pour off all but 1 tbsp (15 mL) fat from pan. Crumble bacon, transfer to an airtight container and refrigerate until ready to use.

2. Add chicken and onion to pan and sauté for 4 to 5 minutes or until onions are tender and translucent. Using a slotted spoon, transfer to slow cooker stoneware. Stir in broth, potatoes, corn, edamame, red pepper, jalapeño and oregano.

3. Cover and cook on Low for 6 to 8 hours or on High for 3 to 4 hours, until chicken is no longer pink inside and vegetables are tender.

4. In a bowl, whisk together flour and cream until smooth. Gently stir into soup. Cover and cook on High for 15 to 20 minutes or until slightly thickened. Season to taste with salt and pepper. Ladle chowder into individual serving bowls and garnish with reserved bacon and cheese.

Vietnamese Chicken Pho

Makes 6 to 8 servings

This classic Asian soup, prepared with leftover shredded chicken, packs tons of flavor.

Tip

Hoisin sauce is a thick, reddish brown sauce made from soybeans and used primarily in Thai and Chinese dishes. It can be found in the Asian aisle of the supermarket.

• **Minimum 4-quart slow cooker**

8 cups	chicken broth	2 L
2 cups	shredded cooked chicken (see tip, page 42)	500 mL
8 oz	bean sprouts (about 4 cups/1 L)	250 g
4 oz	dried rice vermicelli noodles	125 g
2 tbsp	chopped fresh Thai basil	30 mL
	Hoisin sauce	
	Lime wedges	

1. In slow cooker stoneware, combine broth and chicken.

2. Cover and cook on Low for 6 to 7 hours or on High for 3 hours, until soup is bubbling.

3. Stir in bean sprouts, noodles and basil. Cover and cook for 10 to 12 minutes or until noodles are soft.

4. Ladle soup into bowls and drizzle with hoisin sauce. Garnish each bowl with a lime wedge.

> **Thai basil is used as a condiment in Thai and Vietnamese dishes. It can be found in Asian supermarkets. It has purplish stems and flowers, shiny green leaves and a slight anise, almost citrusy, flavor. If you can't find it, you can substitute Italian basil.**

Smoky Turkey and Black Bean Soup

Makes 6 to 8 servings

....

This is one of my mother's favorite soups. She likes to put it on to cook before she heads out to the golf course, so it is waiting for her when she gets home. Look for smoked turkey legs in the deli section of your grocery store.

Tips

If you have a small, round slow cooker, use a smoked turkey thigh or chopped smoked turkey sausage (such as turkey kielbasa) instead.

Supermarkets are full of many varieties of canned beans. For this recipe, you can try using kidney or pinto beans.

● **Minimum 5-quart slow cooker**

1 tbsp	vegetable oil	15 mL
1	onion, diced	1
2	cloves garlic, minced	2
1	jalapeño pepper, minced	1
6 cups	chicken broth	1.5 mL
4 cups	cooked or canned black beans (see page 84), drained and rinsed	1 L
1/4 cup	tomato paste	60 mL
1	smoked turkey leg (about 1 1/4 lbs/625 g)	1
2	green bell peppers, diced	2
1	tomato, diced	1
1/4 cup	sour cream	60 mL
1/3 cup	chopped fresh cilantro	75 mL

1. In a nonstick skillet, heat oil over medium-high heat. Sauté onion for 2 to 3 minutes or until tender and translucent. Add garlic and jalapeño; sauté for 1 minute. Transfer to slow cooker stoneware. Stir in broth, black beans and tomato paste. Add turkey leg.

2. Cover and cook on Low for 6 to 8 hours or on High for 3 to 4 hours, until turkey meat is falling off the bone.

3. Using a slotted spoon, transfer turkey leg to a bowl; remove meat from the bone, chop and set aside. (Discard bone.)

4. Using an immersion blender, or in a food processor or blender, in batches as necessary, purée soup until smooth. (If using food processor or blender, return purée to stoneware.)

5. Add green peppers, tomato and chopped turkey to soup; stir to combine. Cover and cook on High for 10 minutes or until vegetables are warmed through.

6. Ladle into bowls and top each with a dollop of sour cream and a sprinkling of cilantro.

Make Ahead

This dish can be assembled up to 12 hours in advance. Prepare through step 1, without adding the smoked turkey leg, cover and refrigerate overnight. The next day, place stoneware in slow cooker, add the turkey leg and proceed with step 2.

Asian Turkey and Rice Soup

Slices of mushroom, slivers of bok choy and chunks of turkey mingle in a soy- and ginger-flavored broth, giving this savory soup all the essence of a stir-fry.

Tip

Grating gingerroot is easiest if you keep a nub of it in the freezer. (Ginger tends to get moldy and soft too quickly when it's stored in the refrigerator.) Use a Microplane-style grater for best results. Microplanes have tiny razor-like edges that make quick and easy tasks of both grating and cleaning. You will find Microplanes in good kitchenware and department stores.

- **Minimum 4-quart slow cooker**

1 lb	turkey thighs, skin removed	500 g
4	cloves garlic, minced	4
2	carrots, cut into thin strips, about 2 inches (5 cm) long	2
2 cups	sliced assorted mushrooms, such as cremini, button and shiitake	500 mL
1/2 cup	chopped onion	125 mL
2 tsp	grated gingerroot	10 mL
3 cups	chicken broth	750 mL
2 tbsp	soy sauce	30 mL
2 cups	cooked brown rice	500 mL
1 1/2 cups	sliced bok choy	375 mL

1. In slow cooker stoneware, combine turkey thighs, garlic, carrots, mushrooms, onion, ginger, broth, soy sauce and 1 1/2 cups (375 mL) water.

2. Cover and cook on Low for 6 to 8 hours or on High for 3 to 4 hours, until turkey is no longer pink inside.

3. Using a slotted spoon, transfer turkey thighs to a cutting board and let cool slightly; remove meat from bones. (Discard bones.) Using two forks, shred meat into bite-size pieces. Return to slow cooker stoneware.

4. Stir in rice and bok choy. Cover and cook on High for 10 to 15 minutes or until rice is warmed through and bok choy is tender.

Variation

Substitute boneless skinless chicken thighs for the turkey thighs.

> Bok choy, also known as Chinese cabbage, is one of the most popular Asian greens. It has a large, loose head with crisp white stalks and dark green, flat leaves. The greens have a very mild cabbage flavor when cooked, and the stalks become creamy and tender. The miniature version, called baby bok choy, is equally delicious and is perfect in soup.

Nonna's Mini-Meatball Soup

Makes 6 to 8 servings

This soup reminds of the one I'm served when I visit my friend Maria's house. Her mother always has a pot of soup on the stove, or if she doesn't, she will quickly make one for you with whatever ingredients she has on hand.

Tip

If you don't have homemade chicken stock, use ready-to-use chicken broth. I like to keep 32-oz (1 L) Tetra Paks of broth on hand, especially the sodium-reduced variety. They come in handy when you're making soups and stews. Another option is to use three 10-oz (284 mL) cans of broth and add enough water to make 6 cups (1.5 L). Avoid broth cubes and powders, which tend to be salty.

- **Minimum 5-quart slow cooker**

1 lb	lean ground beef	500 g
1 lb	lean ground pork	500 g
1 cup	finely grated Parmesan cheese	250 mL
1 cup	fine dry Italian bread crumbs	250 mL
2	eggs, lightly beaten	2
1	bunch flat-leaf (Italian) parsley, finely chopped (about 1 cup/250 mL)	1
½ tsp	salt	2 mL
½ tsp	freshly ground black pepper	2 mL
6 cups	chicken broth	1.5 L
2 cups	packed baby spinach, coarsely chopped, or chopped escarole	500 mL
2 cups	cooked small pasta, such as elbows, tubetti, shells or stars	500 mL
	Freshly grated Parmesan cheese (optional)	

1. In a large bowl, combine beef, pork, Parmesan, bread crumbs, eggs, parsley, salt and pepper. Using your hands, roll into ¾-inch (2 cm) meatballs. Place meatballs in slow cooker stoneware. Gently pour in broth.

2. Cover and cook on Low for 8 to 9 hours or on High for 4½ to 5 hours, until soup is bubbling and meatballs are cooked through.

3. Stir in spinach. Cover and cook on High for 10 to 15 minutes or until greens are wilted, bright green and tender. Stir in cooked pasta.

4. Ladle into bowls and sprinkle with additional Parmesan, if desired.

Steak and Potato Cowboy Soup

**Makes
6 servings**

Salsa is the key to the sensational flavors in this soup. Kick up the heat a little by using a hot salsa.

Tip

Broth (or stock) is one of the most indispensable pantry staples. Commercial broth cubes and powders are loaded with salt and just don't deliver the flavor of homemade stock or prepared broth. I like to keep 32-oz (1 L) Tetra Paks on hand, especially the sodium-reduced variety. They come in handy when you're making soups and stews.

- **Minimum 4-quart slow cooker**

1½ lbs	boneless beef shoulder or blade steak, trimmed and cut into 1-inch (2.5 cm) cubes	750 g
2	potatoes, peeled and cut into 1-inch (2.5 cm) cubes	2
1	onion, sliced crosswise and separated into rings	1
2 cups	frozen corn kernels	500 mL
2	cloves garlic, minced	2
1	jar (23 oz/650 mL) mild or hot thick and chunky salsa	1
2 cups	beef broth	500 mL
1 tsp	dried basil	5 mL
	Shredded Monterey Jack cheese or Tex-Mex cheese blend (optional)	

1. In slow cooker stoneware, combine beef, potatoes, onion and corn.

2. In a bowl, stir together garlic, salsa, broth and basil, then pour over beef and vegetables.

3. Cover and cook on Low for 8 to 10 hours or on High for 4 to 5 hours, until soup is bubbling and beef is tender.

4. Ladle into bowls and top with cheese (if using).

Make Ahead

This dish can be assembled up to 12 hours in advance. Prepare through step 2, cover and refrigerate overnight. The next day, place stoneware in slow cooker and proceed with step 3.

Red Curry Beef Noodle Soup

Makes 4 to 6 servings

This beef noodle soup is very popular in Laos and Thailand. In our northern climate, it brings much comfort on a cold winter day. You can pick up most of the ingredients in the Asian section of the supermarket.

Tips

To soak rice noodles, place them in a large heatproof bowl, add enough boiling water to cover and let soak for 10 minutes. Drain; rinse under cold running water, drain again and set aside.

Look for a cut of beef labeled "simmering steak" for this recipe. To yield the best results, it needs to be a cut that can take a long, moist-heat method of cooking.

Thai basil can be found in Asian supermarkets. If you can't find it, you can substitute Italian basil.

- **Minimum 4-quart slow cooker**

2 tbsp	vegetable oil	30 mL
1 lb	boneless beef shoulder or blade steak, cut into 1-inch (2.5 cm) strips	500 g
2 tsp	Thai red curry paste	10 mL
8 oz	green beans, trimmed and cut into 1-inch (2.5 cm) pieces	250 g
4 cups	chicken broth	1 L
1 tbsp	fish sauce (approx.)	15 mL
1 tsp	granulated sugar	5 mL
4	green onions, sliced	4
1/4 cup	slivered fresh Thai basil or basil	60 mL
2 tbsp	rice wine vinegar	30 mL
2 tbsp	soy sauce	30 mL
8 oz	rice stick noodles, soaked (see tip, at left)	250 g
1 cup	bean sprouts	250 mL
1/2 cup	fresh cilantro leaves	125 mL
1/2 cup	unsalted roasted peanuts, coarsely chopped (optional)	125 mL

1. In a skillet, heat 1 tbsp (15 mL) of the oil over medium-high heat. Add beef and cook for 2 to 3 minutes or until browned. Using a slotted spoon, transfer to slow cooker stoneware.

2. Add the remaining oil to the skillet. Add curry paste and cook, stirring, for 1 minute or until fragrant. Add green beans and stir-fry for 1 minute; transfer to stoneware. Stir in broth, fish sauce and sugar.

3. Cover and cook on Low for 7 to 9 hours or on High for 3½ to 4½ hours, until soup is bubbling and beef is tender. Stir in green onions and basil. Taste soup and add more fish sauce, if desired.

4. Meanwhile, in a small bowl, combine vinegar and soy sauce. Divide noodles evenly between individual soup bowls. Ladle soup evenly over noodles. Top with bean sprouts, cilantro and peanuts (if using), then drizzle with vinegar mixture. Serve immediately.

> **Fish sauce is the salt of Asia, and one of the most important ingredients in Thai cooking. It is made of fermented, salted anchovies and is used both in cooking and as a condiment on the table.**

Sweet-and-Sour Moroccan Lamb Soup

Makes 4 to 6 servings

There are some nights — particularly cold nights — when soup is what everyone is craving. Be sure to serve plenty of pita bread to go along with this hearty soup. The ingredients are so simple to assemble, it can be put together in a snap before you head out the door in the morning.

Tip

Despite its shape, orzo is not rice, but is pasta made of hard wheat semolina. It was originally made from barley.

• **Minimum 4-quart slow cooker**

2 tbsp	olive oil (approx.)	30 mL
1 lb	boneless lamb shoulder, trimmed and cut into thin strips	500 g
1 tsp	salt	5 mL
1 tsp	ground ginger	5 mL
1 tsp	ground turmeric	5 mL
½ tsp	freshly ground black pepper	2 mL
2 cups	cooked or canned chickpeas (see page 84), drained and rinsed	500 mL
1	can (28 oz/796 mL) plum tomatoes, drained	1
1	large onion, chopped	1
1	3-inch (7.5 cm) cinnamon stick	1
2 tbsp	chopped fresh cilantro	30 mL
1 cup	orzo	250 mL
1 cup	dates, finely chopped	250 mL
	Freshly squeezed juice of 1 lemon, divided	
	Chopped fresh cilantro (optional)	

1. In a large nonstick skillet, heat half the oil over medium-high heat. In batches, cook lamb for 3 to 5 minutes or until browned all over, adding oil as necessary between batches. Using a slotted spoon, transfer to slow cooker stoneware.

2. Add salt, ginger, turmeric and pepper; stir to coat lamb evenly. Stir in chickpeas, tomatoes, onion, cinnamon stick, cilantro and 7 cups (1.75 L) water.

3. Cover and cook on Low for 10 to 12 hours or on High for 5 to 6 hours, until soup is bubbling and lamb is tender. Remove cinnamon stick.

4. In a pot of boiling salted water, cook orzo for 6 to 8 minutes or until al dente. Drain.

5. Add orzo, dates and 2 tbsp (30 mL) of the lemon juice to the slow cooker and stir to combine. Taste and adjust the seasoning with more lemon juice, if desired.

6. Ladle into bowls and garnish with additional cilantro, if desired.

Variation

This soup is also very good made with lentils instead of chickpeas.

Stews

Golden Lentil Stew

Makes 6 to 8 servings

· ·

This slightly sweet Moroccan lentil and chickpea stew is brightened by mixing a combination of sweet and savory spices in the stew and adding a twist of lemon at the end.

Tips

Broth (or stock) is one of the most indispensable pantry staples. Commercial broth cubes and powders are loaded with salt and just don't deliver the flavor of homemade stock or prepared broth. I like to keep 32-oz (1 L) Tetra Paks on hand, especially the sodium-reduced variety. They come in handy when you're making soups and stews.

Tomato paste is now available in tubes in many supermarkets and delis. It keeps for months in the refrigerator.

Orzo is a small, rice-shaped pasta. You can substitute any small pasta for the orzo or break spaghetti noodles into short pieces.

• **Minimum 4-quart slow cooker**

1 tbsp	olive oil	15 mL
1	onion, finely chopped	1
3	cloves garlic, minced	3
½ tsp	sweet paprika	2 mL
½ tsp	ground turmeric	2 mL
½ tsp	ground ginger	2 mL
½ tsp	ground coriander	2 mL
¼ tsp	ground nutmeg	1 mL
4	stalks celery, finely chopped	4
1	can (19 oz/540 mL) diced tomatoes, with juice	1
2 cups	vegetable broth	500 mL
2 cups	cooked or canned chickpeas (see page 84), drained and rinsed	500 mL
1 cup	dried red lentils, rinsed	250 mL
1 tbsp	tomato paste	15 mL
3	whole cloves	3
1	3-inch (7.5 cm) cinnamon stick	1
¼ tsp	freshly ground black pepper	1 mL
½ cup	cooked orzo or other small pasta	125 mL
½ cup	chopped pitted dates	125 mL
2 tbsp	coarsely chopped fresh parsley	30 mL
2 tbsp	finely chopped fresh cilantro	30 mL
1 tbsp	freshly squeezed lemon juice	15 mL
1	lemon, cut into wedges	1

1. In a large nonstick skillet, heat oil over medium-high heat. Sauté onion for 3 to 5 minutes or until tender and translucent. Add garlic, paprika, turmeric, ginger, coriander and nutmeg; sauté for 1 minute or until fragrant. Transfer to slow cooker stoneware.

2. Stir in celery, tomatoes with juice, broth, chickpeas, lentils, tomato paste, cloves, cinnamon stick and pepper.

continued on page 58…

If you have any
leftovers, this stew
stores very well in the
refrigerator for up to
5 days. Store in an
airtight container and
reheat as necessary,
adding a little water
if the stew is too
thick.

3. Cover and cook on Low for 8 to 10 hours or on High for 4 to 5 hours, until stew is bubbling.

4. Stir in orzo and dates. Cover and cook on High for 10 to 15 minutes or until heated through. Discard cinnamon stick. Stir in parsley, cilantro and lemon juice. Serve garnished with lemon wedges.

Make Ahead

This dish can be assembled up to 12 hours in advance. Prepare through step 2, but don't add the lentils. Cover and refrigerate overnight. The next day, stir in lentils, place stoneware in slow cooker and proceed with step 3.

Keep the Lid On!

When something is cooking in the slow cooker, resist the temptation to lift the lid. The domed lid allows condensation to run into the stoneware, forming a water seal. This seal keeps in the heat; if you remove the lid, the seal is broken and the heat escapes. It takes the cooker a long time to restore the heat level. Slow cooker recipes shouldn't need stirring, but if you need to add ingredients, do so and replace the lid quickly. If you lift the lid without being instructed to do so, add about 20 more minutes to the cooking time.

Spanish Chicken with Chickpeas

Makes 4 to 6 servings

On a trip to Spain with our Swiss friends Patrizia and Thomas, my husband and I whiled away the afternoon in a cozy restaurant in the small mountain village of Ronda. The owner made a version of this fragrant dish, and we soaked up the remnants of it with slices of warm, crusty bread while sipping glasses of local red wine. I thought I was in heaven.

Tip

Chorizo, a flavorful pork sausage, gets its distinctive smokiness and deep color from the smoked paprika used to make it. It can be found fresh or cured, but I prefer the cured, smoked European variety for this recipe. You can find it in the deli section of well-stocked supermarkets or in specialty stores that sell Spanish sausage.

- **4- to 6-quart slow cooker**

¼ cup	all-purpose flour	60 mL
1 tsp	salt	5 mL
½ tsp	freshly ground black pepper	2 mL
2 lbs	boneless skinless chicken thighs (8 to 10)	1 kg
8 oz	cured chorizo sausage, cut into ½-inch (1 cm) pieces	250 g
2 cups	cooked or canned chickpeas (see page 84), drained and rinsed	500 mL
3	large cloves garlic, smashed	3
1 tsp	dried oregano	5 mL
1	can (14 oz/398 mL) diced tomatoes, with juice	1
2 tsp	sherry vinegar	10 mL
Pinch	saffron threads	Pinch

1. In a bowl, combine flour, salt and pepper. Dredge chicken in flour mixture to coat and shake off any excess. Arrange chicken in slow cooker stoneware. Sprinkle with sausage, chickpeas, garlic and oregano. Discard any excess flour mixture.

2. In a blender or food processor, purée tomatoes with juice, ½ cup (125 mL) water, vinegar and saffron. Pour over chicken mixture.

3. Cover and cook on Low for 8 to 10 hours or on High for 4 to 6 hours, until juices run clear when chicken is pierced. Remove garlic cloves, if desired. Season to taste with salt and pepper.

North African Chicken Stew

Makes 4 servings

With this stew, you can enjoy the flavors of North African cuisine without having to go to an exotic grocery store to buy the ingredients. Ladle it over couscous and serve it with some warm flatbread to soak up the savory sauce.

Tips

You can add a little more heat to this recipe by increasing the amount of cayenne pepper. Or you can add some hot sauce at the end of the cooking time, if you prefer to taste the level of heat before adding extra spice.

Look for precut fresh squash in the produce department of your supermarket. It will save a lot of preparation time, since the peel and seeds have already been removed. Simply cut it into 1-inch (2.5 cm) cubes.

- **Minimum 4-quart slow cooker**

1½ lbs	boneless skinless chicken thighs, cut into 2-inch (5 cm) pieces	750 g
1½ tbsp	freshly squeezed lemon juice	22 mL
1 tsp	ground cumin	5 mL
½ tsp	ground allspice	2 mL
½ tsp	cayenne pepper	2 mL
2	cloves garlic, minced	2
1	red onion, chopped	1
1	butternut or other winter squash, peeled and cubed (about 6 cups/1.5 L)	1
2 cups	cooked or canned chickpeas (see page 84), drained and rinsed	500 mL
½ cup	chicken broth	125 mL
	Salt and freshly ground black pepper	
4	green onions, chopped	4
	Hot cooked couscous	
	Chopped fresh cilantro or parsley	
4	lemon slices	4

1. Place chicken in slow cooker stoneware. Drizzle with lemon juice and toss chicken to coat.

2. In a small bowl, combine cumin, allspice and cayenne. Sprinkle over chicken. Arrange garlic, red onion, squash and chickpeas on top. Pour in broth.

3. Cover and cook on Low for 5 to 7 hours or on High for 2½ to 4 hours, until chicken is no longer pink inside. Season to taste with salt and black pepper.

4. Add green onions. Cover and cook on High for 10 minutes.

5. Ladle over couscous and garnish each serving with cilantro and lemon slices.

Italian Chicken Stew with Crisp Polenta

Makes 4 to 6 servings

This rustic, country-style Italian stew cooks in a rich tomato-mushroom sauce. You can serve it over mashed potatoes, but picking up a package of ready-made polenta is much faster and easier.

Tips

Bone-in thighs cook a little more slowly than boneless, so they are ideal for this dish. If you can't find skinless bone-in chicken thighs, purchase them with the skin on. It is easy to remove and discard the skin yourself.

To prepare mushrooms, wipe them with a damp paper towel. Don't rinse or soak them, or they'll absorb water and turn mushy when cooked.

- **Minimum 4-quart slow cooker**
- *Rimmed baking sheet*

Italian Chicken Stew

2 tbsp	all-purpose flour	30 mL
1 tsp	salt	5 mL
½ tsp	freshly ground black pepper	2 mL
8 to 12	skinless bone-in chicken thighs (about 3 lbs/1.5 kg)	8 to 12
2 tbsp	olive oil (approx.)	30 mL
1 lb	mushrooms, quartered	500 g
2	onions, sliced	2
4	cloves garlic, sliced	4
½ cup	dry white wine	125 mL
1	can (19 oz/540 mL) tomatoes, with juice	1
1 tsp	dried Italian seasoning	5 mL
⅓ cup	pitted green olives, halved	75 mL
	Chopped fresh parsley	

Crisp Polenta

1	tube (1 lb/500 g) plain prepared polenta, cut into 12 slices	1
1 tbsp	olive oil	15 mL
	Salt and freshly ground black pepper	

1. *Stew:* In a bowl, combine flour, salt and pepper. Dredge chicken in flour mixture to coat. (Reserve remaining flour.)

2. In a large nonstick skillet, heat half the oil over medium-high heat. Cook chicken in batches, adding more oil as needed, for 2 to 3 minutes per side or until browned all over. Using a slotted spoon, transfer to slow cooker stoneware. Add mushrooms.

3. Return skillet to medium-high heat. Add onions to remaining drippings in pan, adding more oil if pan is dry, and sauté for 3 to 5 minutes or until tender and translucent. Add garlic and sauté for 1 minute. Sprinkle with reserved flour mixture and stir until onion mixture is coated. Pour in wine, stirring until blended.

continued on page 62…

Tip

Cooking times can vary a great deal between slow cooker manufacturers. Always let your food cook for the minimum amount of time before testing for doneness.

4. Pour onion mixture over chicken and mushrooms. Stir in tomatoes with juice and Italian seasoning, using a wooden spoon to break up tomatoes slightly.

5. Cover and cook on Low for 8 to 10 hours or on High for 4 to 6 hours, until juices run clear when chicken is pierced. Sprinkle with olives, cover and cook for about 5 minutes.

6. *Crisp Polenta:* Meanwhile, preheat broiler, with rack positioned 6 to 8 inches (15 to 20 cm) from the heat. Brush both sides of each polenta slice with oil and place on baking sheet. Season to taste with salt and pepper. Broil, without turning, for 10 to 15 minutes or until deep golden brown.

7. Arrange polenta on individual plates or bowls, spoon stew over top and garnish with parsley.

Italian Chicken Stew with Crisp Polenta ▶

Tex-Mex Beef Stew

The blend of spices gives this stew the most wonderful flavor. At the end of the long cooking time, and before adding the dumpling batter, add an extra pinch of chili powder and cinnamon to brighten the flavors.

Tips

Here's a foolproof way to chop an onion: Peel the onion and halve it from top to base. Place each half cut side down on a cutting board. Slice horizontally across each half. Holding the slices together, slice vertically.

Jalapeño peppers contain volatile oils that can burn your skin and eyes if they come into direct contact. It is best to wear plastic or rubber gloves when chopping jalapeños, and take care not to touch your face or eyes while you work. If your bare hands do touch the peppers, wash your hands and nails well with hot, soapy water.

- **4- to 6-quart slow cooker**

Stew

4	slices smoked bacon, diced	4
3 lbs	boneless stewing beef, cut into 1-inch (2.5 cm) cubes	1.5 kg
	Vegetable oil	
½ cup	dark beer	125 mL
1	can (28 oz/796 mL) tomatoes, with juice	1
4	cloves garlic, minced	4
2	onions, diced	2
1	red onion, diced	1
1	yellow bell pepper, diced	1
1	jalapeño pepper, seeded and chopped	1
1 tbsp	ancho chile powder	15 mL
2 tsp	dried oregano	10 mL
½ tsp	ground cinnamon	2 mL

Cornmeal Dumplings

½ cup	all-purpose flour	125 mL
2 tbsp	cornmeal	30 mL
½ tsp	salt	2 mL
1	egg, lightly beaten	1
⅓ cup	milk	75 mL
1 tbsp	butter, melted	15 mL
	Lime wedges	

1. *Stew:* In a large nonstick skillet, cook bacon over medium-high heat, stirring, for 5 to 7 minutes or until crisp. Using a slotted spoon, transfer to a plate lined with paper towels to drain, reserving drippings in pan.

2. Return skillet to medium-high heat. Cook beef in batches, adding more oil as needed, for 5 minutes or until browned all over. Using a slotted spoon, transfer to slow cooker stoneware.

Tips

Most recipes use large eggs. If a recipe doesn't specify a size, assume you need large.

When browning meat in hot oil, avoid overfilling the skillet. If the pan is too full, the meat will steam rather than brown. Turn the meat frequently and cook it as quickly as possible, then use a slotted spoon to remove it.

Resist the urge to lift the lid and taste or smell whatever is inside the slow cooker as it's cooking. Every peek will increase the cooking time by 20 minutes.

3. Add beer to pan and bring to a boil, scraping up any brown bits from pan. Transfer to stoneware. Stir in bacon, tomatoes with juice, garlic, onions, red onion, yellow pepper, jalapeño, chile powder, oregano and cinnamon.

4. Cover and cook on Low for 8 to 10 hours or on High for 4 to 6 hours, until beef and vegetables are tender and stew is bubbling.

5. *Cornmeal Dumplings:* In a bowl, combine flour, cornmeal and salt. In a separate bowl, whisk together egg, milk and butter. Stir into flour mixture just until combined.

6. Drop spoonfuls of dumpling batter onto bubbling stew. Cover and cook on High for 20 to 25 minutes or until tester inserted into center of dumplings comes out clean. Serve garnished with lime wedges.

Make Ahead

This dish can be assembled up to 12 hours in advance, as long as the beef is left out. Cook the bacon in step 1 and refrigerate it in its own airtight container. Skip over step 2 and complete step 3. Cover and refrigerate overnight. The next day, brown the beef in 2 tbsp (30 mL) vegetable oil. Place stoneware in slow cooker, add beef and bacon and proceed with step 4.

Ancho chile powder, also called ground ancho chile pepper, is the most commonly used chile powder in Mexican cooking. It is ground from dried ancho (poblano) peppers and has a smoky flavor and mild to medium heat. If you can't find ancho chile powder, you can substitute regular chili powder.

Country Italian Beef Stew

Makes 6 to 8 servings

This stew features the wonderful flavors of the Mediterranean — fennel, basil and rosemary. Fennel has a distinctive mild licorice flavor, but even if you are not a licorice fan, you will enjoy the bold flavors of this beef stew.

Tip

Crush dried rosemary between your thumb and fingers before adding it to a dish. This helps release the full aromatic flavor of the herb.

- **Minimum 4-quart slow cooker**

3 tbsp	all-purpose flour	45 mL
1 tsp	salt	5 mL
1 tsp	freshly ground black pepper, divided	5 mL
2 lbs	stewing beef, cut into 1-inch (2.5 cm) cubes	1 kg
2 tbsp	vegetable oil (approx.)	30 mL
6	tiny new potatoes, halved or quartered	6
2	parsnips, cut into 1- to 2-inch (2.5 to 5 cm) pieces	2
1	fennel bulb, trimmed and cut into $\frac{1}{2}$-inch (1 cm) wedges	1
1 cup	chopped onion	250 mL
1 cup	beef broth	250 mL
$\frac{1}{2}$ cup	dry red wine	125 mL
1	can (7$\frac{1}{2}$ oz/213 mL) pizza sauce	1
4	cloves garlic, minced	4
1 tsp	dried rosemary, crumbled	5 mL
1 cup	fresh baby spinach leaves	250 mL

1. In a heavy plastic bag, combine flour, salt and $\frac{1}{2}$ tsp (2 mL) of the pepper. In batches, add beef to bag and toss to coat with flour mixture. Discard excess flour mixture.

2. In a large nonstick skillet, heat half the oil over medium-high heat. Cook beef in batches, adding more oil as needed, for 5 minutes or until browned all over. Using a slotted spoon, transfer to slow cooker stoneware. Stir in potatoes, parsnips, fennel and onion.

3. In a 2-cup (500 mL) measuring cup, combine broth, wine, pizza sauce, garlic, rosemary and the remaining pepper. Pour over beef mixture.

4. Cover and cook on Low for 8 to 10 hours or on High for 4 to 5 hours, until bubbling. Just before serving, stir in spinach until wilted.

Lemony Veal Milanese

Makes 6 to 8 servings

....

This hearty dish is as much of a hit with young children as it is with sophisticated adults. Serve the stew atop egg noodles, to sop up the rich sauce. The noodles take no time to cook after a long day at work.

Tips

To get the most juice from a lemon, let it warm to room temperature, then roll it on the counter, pressing down with the palm of your hand, before squeezing it.

When browning meat in hot oil, avoid overfilling the skillet. If the pan is too full, the meat will steam rather than brown. Turn the meat frequently and cook it as quickly as possible, then use a slotted spoon to remove it.

- **Minimum 4-quart slow cooker**

½ cup	all-purpose flour	125 mL
¾ tsp	freshly ground black pepper	3 mL
2½ lbs	boneless stewing veal, cut into 1-inch (2.5 cm) cubes	1.25 kg
¼ cup	olive oil	60 mL
½ cup	dry white wine	125 mL
1½ cups	chicken broth	375 mL
6	stalks celery, chopped	6
4	carrots, chopped	4
4	cloves garlic, minced	4
2	leeks (white and light green parts only), sliced	2
2	small onions, chopped	2
1	can (19 oz/540 mL) diced tomatoes, with juice	1
2 tsp	dried basil	10 mL
2 tsp	dried rosemary	10 mL
2 tsp	dried Italian seasoning	10 mL
¼ cup	chopped fresh parsley	60 mL
1 tsp	grated lemon zest	5 mL
2 tbsp	freshly squeezed lemon juice	30 mL
1 tsp	salt	5 mL

1. In a heavy plastic bag, combine flour and pepper. In batches, add veal to bag and toss to coat with flour mixture. Discard excess flour mixture.

2. In a large nonstick skillet, heat 2 tbsp (30 mL) of the oil over medium-high heat. Cook veal in batches, adding more oil as needed, for 5 minutes or until browned all over. Using a slotted spoon, transfer to slow cooker stoneware.

3. Add wine to skillet and boil, scraping up any brown bits from pan, for 2 to 3 minutes or until reduced by half. Add broth and simmer for 1 minute. Pour over veal. Stir in celery, carrots, garlic, leeks, onions, tomatoes with juice, basil, rosemary and Italian seasoning.

4. Cover and cook on Low for 6 to 7 hours or on High for 3 to 3½ hours, until stew is bubbling. Stir in parsley, lemon zest, lemon juice and salt.

Pork Paprikash

Makes 4 to 6 servings

While old-school Hungarian cooks would use lard instead of oil, and probably double the amount of sour cream, this lighter version of traditional paprikash is equally delicious. My taste testers gave this recipe a Triple-A rating, and recommended serving it over hot, buttered egg noodles.

Tip

Broth (or stock) is one of the most indispensable pantry staples. Commercial broth cubes and powders are loaded with salt and just don't deliver the flavor of homemade stock or prepared broth. I like to keep 32-oz (1 L) Tetra Paks on hand, especially the sodium-reduced variety.

- **4- to 5-quart slow cooker**

2 lbs	boneless pork shoulder blade (butt), trimmed and cut into 1-inch (2.5 cm) cubes	1 kg
2 tbsp	sweet paprika	30 mL
½ tsp	dried marjoram	2 mL
1	onion, chopped	1
1	can (19 oz/540 mL) tomatoes, drained	1
½ cup	chicken broth	125 mL
1	green bell pepper, coarsely chopped (optional)	1
8 oz	egg noodles	250 g
1 tbsp	butter, cut into pieces	15 mL
	Chopped fresh parsley	
½ cup	sour cream	2 mL
	Salt and freshly ground black pepper	

1. In slow cooker stoneware, toss together pork, paprika and marjoram. Stir in onion, tomatoes and broth.

2. Cover and cook on Low for 7 to 8 hours or on High for 3½ to 4 hours, until pork is tender.

3. Stir in green pepper (if using). Cover and cook on High for 15 to 20 minutes or until pepper is bright green and tender-crisp.

4. Meanwhile, in a pot of boiling salted water, cook noodles according to package directions. Drain and toss with butter and parsley.

5. Stir sour cream into paprikash. Season to taste with salt and pepper. Divide noodles among individual serving bowls and ladle paprikash over top. Garnish with additional parsley.

> Although paprika is made from ground chiles and looks pretty, it doesn't taste like much. But when it's heated, this spice comes to life, exuding a sweet flavor with rich, earthy undertones and varying heat levels. Try to purchase Hungarian or Spanish paprika (found in colorful tins) rather than the generic paprika found in the spice aisle of the supermarket.

Pesto Meatball Stew

Makes 4 to 6 servings

Sometimes we just want a quick, throw-it-together meal the whole family will enjoy. My friend Christopher taste-tested this one with his family, and it has since become a staple meal in their busy household.

Tip

Keeping a box of premade cooked meatballs in the freezer makes for really quick dinner prep. You can use beef, pork, turkey or chicken meatballs for this recipe — they will all taste great in the stew.

• **Minimum 4-quart slow cooker**

2	carrots, finely chopped	2
2	stalks celery, finely chopped	2
1	red bell pepper, finely chopped	1
1	box (2 lbs/1 kg) frozen cooked Italian-style meatballs, thawed	1
1	can (28 oz/796 mL) Italian-style stewed tomatoes, with juice	1
2 cups	cooked or canned white kidney beans (see page 84), drained and rinsed	500 mL
$\frac{1}{4}$ cup	basil pesto	60 mL
2 cups	cooked short pasta, such as rotini or penne	500 mL
$\frac{1}{2}$ cup	finely shredded Parmesan cheese	125 mL

1. In slow cooker stoneware, combine carrots, celery, red pepper, meatballs, tomatoes with juice, beans, pesto and $\frac{1}{2}$ cup (125 mL) water.

2. Cover and cook on Low for 5 to 7 hours or on High for $2\frac{1}{2}$ to $3\frac{1}{2}$ hours, until vegetables are tender and stew is bubbling.

3. Stir in pasta. Cover and cook for 15 to 20 minutes or until heated through. Serve sprinkled with cheese.

> Pesto is a dark green, fragrant spread that originated in Italy. In Italian, *pesto* means "pounded," and the spread got its name because the herb and garlic were originally pounded together (likely using a pestle, a tool whose name comes from the same root).

Cinderella Stew

Makes 4 to 6 servings

I came across a recipe with this name and couldn't resist it, since *Cinderella* is my daughter Darcy's all-time favorite princess movie! In fact, we nicknamed her "Darc-arella" when she was little, because it was the only movie she would watch. If you have time, you can carve out a pumpkin and fill it with this stew for a unique presentation. All the princes and princesses in your family will love it!

Tips

To avoid tears when chopping onions, put the onions in the freezer for a few minutes first.

You can make your own pumpkin pie spice using 1 tbsp (15 mL) ground cinnamon and ¼ tsp (1 mL) each ground ginger, nutmeg and cloves.

- **Minimum 4-quart slow cooker**

2	large sweet onions, chopped	2
2	cloves garlic, minced	2
¼ cup	all-purpose flour	60 mL
1 tsp	salt	5 mL
¼ tsp	freshly ground black pepper	1 mL
3 lbs	boneless pork shoulder blade (butt), trimmed and cut into 1-inch (2.5 cm) cubes	1.5 kg
2 tbsp	vegetable oil (approx.)	30 mL
1 tbsp	butter	15 mL
1	can (19 oz/540 mL) tomatoes, with juice	1
1	sweet potato, chopped	1
1	Granny Smith or other tart apple, chopped	1
3 tbsp	dried currants	45 mL
½ tsp	pumpkin pie spice	2 mL
¼ tsp	ground cumin	1 mL
1	bay leaf	1

Topping

1½ cups	plain yogurt	375 mL
½ cup	chopped green onions	125 mL

1. Layer onions and garlic in slow cooker stoneware.

2. In a heavy plastic bag, combine flour, salt and pepper. In batches, add pork to bag and toss to coat with flour mixture. Discard excess flour mixture.

3. In a large nonstick skillet, heat half the oil and the butter over medium-high heat. Cook pork in batches, adding oil as needed, for about 4 minutes or until browned all over. Using a slotted spoon, transfer to stoneware.

continued on page 74…

4. Stir in tomatoes with juice, sweet potato, apple, currants, pumpkin pie spice, cumin and bay leaf.

5. Cover and cook on Low for 8 to 10 hours or on High for 4 to 5 hours, until pork is tender. Discard bay leaf.

6. *Topping:* In a bowl, combine yogurt and green onions. Ladle stew into individual serving bowls and top each with a dollop of yogurt mixture.

Make Ahead

This dish can be assembled up to 12 hours in advance, as long as the pork is left out. Complete step 1, skip over steps 2 and 3, then complete step 4. Cover and refrigerate overnight. The next day, dredge and brown the pork as directed in steps 2 and 3. Place stoneware in slow cooker, add pork and proceed with step 4.

> There are several varieties of sweet onions, including Vidalia, Walla Walla, Maui and Sweetie Sweet. Although all onions have natural sugars, sweet onions have a lower sulfur content and higher water content, which emphasizes their sweetness and makes them less pungent.

Sausage, Spinach and White Bean Stew

Makes 4 servings

....

This wonderful stew is a variation on a classic Italian bean soup. My family loved the flavor, and the spinach gives the stew an authentic rustic quality. Don't forget to add the croutons at the end, for some added crunch.

Tips

You can use chopped Swiss chard, escarole or arugula in place of the spinach.

Use a hearty bread, such as ciabatta, to make the bread cubes.

- **Minimum 4-quart slow cooker**

Stew

1 tbsp	olive oil	15 mL
1	onion, chopped	1
1 lb	hot Italian sausage, bulk or casings removed	500 g
2	cloves garlic, minced	2
4 cups	cooked or canned white kidney beans (see page 84), drained and rinsed	1 L
1 cup	chicken broth	250 mL
2 cups	packed baby spinach leaves	500 mL
1½ tsp	red wine vinegar (approx.)	7 mL
	Salt	
¼ cup	freshly grated Parmesan cheese	60 mL

Rustic Croutons

2 tbsp	olive oil	30 mL
2 cups	lightly packed bread cubes	500 mL
	Salt	

1. *Stew:* In a heavy skillet, heat oil over medium heat. Sauté onion for 5 to 6 minutes or until tender and translucent. Add sausage, increase heat to medium-high and cook, stirring and breaking up sausage with a spoon, for 8 to 10 minutes or until lightly browned and no longer pink inside. Using a slotted spoon, transfer to slow cooker stoneware. Stir in garlic, beans and broth.

2. Cover and cook on Low for 6 to 7 hours or on High for 3 to 4 hours, until stew is bubbling.

3. Stir in spinach and vinegar. Cover and cook on High for 8 to 10 minutes or just until spinach is wilted. Season to taste with salt.

4. *Rustic Croutons:* Meanwhile, in a nonstick skillet, heat oil over medium-high heat. Add bread cubes, stirring to coat and seasoning to taste with salt. Cook, stirring, for 2 to 4 minutes or until crisp and browned all over.

5. Ladle stew into bowls, sprinkle with Parmesan and garnish with croutons.

Chili Verde

**Makes
4 servings**

This warm, hearty stew is based on an authentic Mexican recipe in which chunks of pork are slow-cooked in a green chili sauce made with tomatillos, garlic and jalapeños. It is wonderful on its own, served over rice with some tortilla chips for scooping up extra sauce, or as a filling for a burrito or taco, with toppings such as shredded lettuce and avocado.

Tips

You can use cubed trimmed boneless pork shoulder blade (butt) instead of the tenderloin, but increase the cooking time to 8 to 10 hours on Low or 4 to 5 hours on High.

Browning the pork before it is placed in the slow cooker gives the dish an extra-rich flavor and eliminates some of the fat. If you are pressed for time, however, you can place the pork directly into the slow cooker stoneware without browning it first.

• **Minimum 4-quart slow cooker**

1 tbsp	vegetable oil	15 mL
1	pork tenderloin (about 12 oz/375 g), trimmed and cut into 1-inch (2.5 cm) cubes	1
1	large onion, thinly sliced	1
6	cloves garlic, sliced	6
1	can (14 oz/400 mL) tomatillos, drained, rinsed and coarsely chopped (or 1 lb/500 g fresh tomatillos, husked, rinsed and coarsely chopped)	1
1	can ($4\frac{1}{2}$ oz/127 mL) diced mild green chiles	1
2 cups	cooked or canned great Northern or white kidney beans (see page 84), drained and rinsed	500 mL
$1\frac{1}{2}$ cups	chicken broth	375 mL
1 tsp	ground cumin	5 mL
	Salt and freshly ground black pepper	
$\frac{1}{2}$ cup	lightly packed fresh cilantro, chopped	125 mL
1	jalapeño pepper, sliced (optional)	1

1. In a large nonstick skillet, heat oil over medium-high heat. Cook pork for about 4 minutes or until browned all over. Using a slotted spoon, transfer to slow cooker stoneware. Stir in onion, garlic, tomatillos, green chiles, beans, broth and cumin.

2. Cover and cook on Low for 5 to 7 hours or on High for $2\frac{1}{2}$ to 3 hours, until pork is tender.

3. Season to taste with salt and pepper. Stir in cilantro. Cover and cook on Low for 10 minutes. Serve garnished with jalapeño (if using).

> The tomatillo, a staple in Mexican cooking, is a relative of the tomato. It is about the size of a table tennis ball and has a light brown, papery husk around the outside. Although tomatillos are available year-round, they aren't always available fresh. But you can substitute canned tomatillos in any recipe that calls for fresh.

Indonesian Pork Satay Stew

Makes 4 to 6 servings

Satay is an Indonesian specialty of spicy marinated meat that is skewered, then broiled or grilled. Here I've taken all the great flavors of a pork satay and created a lively stew.

Tips

Grating gingerroot is easiest if you keep a nub of it in the freezer. (Ginger tends to get moldy and soft too quickly when it's stored in the refrigerator.) Use a Microplane-style grater for best results. Microplanes have tiny razor-like edges that make quick and easy tasks of both grating and cleaning. You will find Microplanes in good kitchenware and department stores.

To store gingerroot, peel it and place it in a jar with a tight-fitting lid. Add enough sherry to cover. The sherry will saturate and preserve the ginger. Refrigerate for up to 1 month. Use the infused wine to flavor other chicken dishes.

- **4- to 6-quart slow cooker**

2 tbsp	all-purpose flour	30 mL
½ tsp	salt	2 mL
½ tsp	freshly ground black pepper	2 mL
2 lbs	boneless pork shoulder blade (butt), cut into 1-inch (2.5 cm) cubes	1 kg
2 tbsp	vegetable oil (approx.)	30 mL
2	red or green bell peppers, cut into 1-inch (2.5 cm) pieces	2
1	large red onion, cut into wedges	1
1 cup	thick and chunky salsa (mild or hot)	250 mL
½ cup	creamy peanut butter	125 mL
1 tbsp	soy sauce	15 mL
1 tbsp	freshly squeezed lime juice	15 mL
1½ tsp	grated gingerroot	7 mL
½ tsp	ground turmeric	2 mL
½ tsp	ground coriander	2 mL
½ cup	light (5%) cream or evaporated milk	125 mL
1 tbsp	cornstarch	15 mL
3 cups	hot cooked white or brown rice	750 mL
⅓ cup	chopped dry-roasted peanuts	75 mL
2	green onions, sliced	2

1. In a heavy plastic bag, combine flour, salt and pepper. In batches, add pork to bag and toss to coat with flour mixture. Discard excess flour mixture.

2. In a large nonstick skillet, heat half the oil over medium-high heat. Cook pork in batches, adding more oil as needed, for about 4 minutes or until browned all over. Using a slotted spoon, transfer to slow cooker stoneware.

3. Stir in bell peppers, red onion, salsa, peanut butter, soy sauce, lime juice, ginger, turmeric and coriander.

4. Cover and cook on Low for 8 to 10 hours or on High for 4 to 6 hours, until pork is tender.

5. In a jar with a tight-fitting lid, combine cream and cornstarch; shake until blended. Stir into stew. Cover and cook on High for 10 to 15 minutes or until sauce has thickened.

6. Divide rice among bowls and ladle stew over top. Garnish with peanuts and green onions.

Make Ahead

Combine the ingredients in step 3 in the stone cooker stoneware. Cover and refrigerate overnight. The next day, dredge and brown the pork as directed in steps 1 and 2. Place stoneware in slow cooker, add pork and proceed with step 4.

Provençal Lamb Stew

This stew is full of flavors from the south of France, and is one of those dishes that tastes even better the day after it is made. Serve it over a heaping mound of garlic mashed potatoes, with a simple steamed green vegetable, such as fresh green beans.

Tip

The best cuts for lamb stew come from the shoulder or shank. Avoid using lamb loin — it can be very expensive and will overcook quickly.

Make Ahead

In slow cooker stoneware, combine onions, garlic, carrot, celery, wine, tomatoes, beans, broth, rosemary and bay leaf. Cover and refrigerate overnight. The next day, dredge and brown the lamb as directed in steps 1 and 2. Place stoneware in slow cooker, add lamb and proceed with step 4.

• **Minimum 4-quart slow cooker**

2 tbsp	all-purpose flour	30 mL
1/2 tsp	salt	2 mL
1/4 tsp	freshly ground black pepper	1 mL
1 1/2 lbs	boneless lamb shoulder, trimmed and cut into 1-inch (2.5 cm) cubes	750 g
2 tbsp	olive oil (approx.)	30 mL
2	onions, chopped	2
2	cloves garlic, minced	2
1	carrot, chopped	1
1	stalk celery, chopped	1
1/2 cup	dry white wine	125 mL
1	can (19 oz/540 mL) tomatoes, drained and chopped	1
2 cups	cooked or canned white kidney beans (see page 84), drained and rinsed	500 mL
1/2 cup	chicken broth	125 mL
1 tbsp	chopped fresh rosemary	15 mL
1	bay leaf	1
	Chopped fresh parsley	

1. In a heavy plastic bag, combine flour, salt and pepper. In batches, add lamb to bag and toss to coat with flour mixture. Discard excess flour mixture.

2. In a large nonstick skillet, heat half the oil over medium-high heat. Cook lamb in batches, adding more oil as needed, for 5 minutes or until browned all over. Using a slotted spoon, transfer to slow cooker stoneware. Sprinkle with onions, garlic, carrot and celery.

3. Add wine to the skillet and bring to a boil, scraping up any brown bits from pan. Pour over lamb mixture. Stir in tomatoes, beans, broth, rosemary and bay leaf.

4. Cover and cook on Low for 8 to 10 hours or on High for 4 to 5 hours, until lamb and vegetables are tender and stew is bubbling. Discard bay leaf. Season to taste with salt and pepper. Serve garnished with parsley.

Variation

If you are not a lamb fan, you can substitute cubes of lean pork shoulder blade (butt) or stewing beef.

Chilis and Beans

Basic Beans

The slow cooker is very useful for cooking dried beans, peas and lentils, which can be tiresome to prepare using other methods. This is great news for anyone who wants to avoid the salt and preservatives added to precooked canned beans — and you'll save money if you buy dried beans in bulk.

Many of the legume recipes in this book call for cooked beans by volume, so that you can use your own cooked beans instead of relying on canned beans — but whether to use cooked or canned is entirely up to you. (Some recipes call for dried beans; in those recipes, the beans are cooked right in the method, and canned beans cannot be substituted.) It is important to remember that dried beans will more than double in size after cooking. One pound (500 g), or about 2 cups (500 mL), of dried beans yields 4 to 5 cups (1 to 1.25 L) of cooked beans.

Transforming dried legumes into tender, edible beans, peas and lentils requires a three-step process: sorting, soaking and cooking. The cooking time depends on the type of slow cooker used, the variety, age and quality of the bean, your altitude and whether you use hard or soft water for cooking. The best way to test for doneness is to taste them. Cooked beans are free of any raw, starchy taste, and are tender.

Step 1: Sorting

To prepare dried beans for cooking, start by sorting and discarding any damaged, broken or cracked beans and foreign material. Then place in a colander and give them a thorough rinse under cold water.

Step 2: Soaking

Soaking the beans is an important step in the preparation process, helping to replace the water that was removed in the drying process, shortening the cooking time and improving the flavor, texture, appearance and digestibility of the beans. Most dried beans (the exception is lentils) must be soaked for several hours before they are cooked. The most time-efficient strategy is to soak your beans overnight, then start the cooking process in the morning. Never let beans sit in water for more than 18 hours.

I have provided instructions for both a long soak (the best option for making beans more digestible) and a quick soak (which may be more convenient if you're short on time). Once the soak is finished, drain the beans, discarding the soaking liquid, and rinse well.

1 *Long Soak:* Place the beans in your slow cooker or a large bowl and add 10 cups (2.5 L) boiling water. Cover and let soak for 12 hours or overnight. Drain and rinse thoroughly under cold running water. The beans are now ready to cook.

Quick Soak: Place the beans in a large saucepan or stockpot (be sure pot is large enough to allow beans to expand to two and a half times the size). Add 10 cups (2.5 L) water and bring to a boil over high heat. Reduce heat and simmer for 3 minutes. Remove from heat, cover and let soak for 1 hour. Drain and rinse thoroughly under cold running water. The beans are now ready to cook.

Step 3: Cooking

Place drained presoaked beans in the slow cooker stoneware. Add enough fresh cold water to completely cover beans with three times their volume of water. For additional flavor, you can add seasonings, such as a bay leaf, garlic or a bouquet garni (made from your favorite herbs tied together in a cheesecloth bag), to the cooking liquid. Beans must be completely cooked before they are combined with salt, sugar or acidic foods such as molasses or tomatoes (all of which prevent beans from softening).

Cover and cook on Low for 4 to 6 hours. Don't worry if the beans have not absorbed all of the water. They should be tender, but not mushy. Drain and rinse thoroughly under cold running water. The beans are now fully cooked and ready for use in your favorite recipe.

Storing Cooked Beans

Once beans are completely cool, divide them into 1- or 2-cup (250 or 500 mL) portions and pack into storage containers or freezer bags and label the portion size. This makes it convenient for recipe preparation, since this is the amount usually called for in recipes. The beans will store nicely in the refrigerator for up to 1 week or in the freezer for up to 1 month, so while you're going to the trouble of preparing cooked beans, you might as well make enough for several meals. Thaw beans first before adding to any recipe. This is to ensure the cooking process is not slowed down.

Canned Beans

Canned beans are a quick and easy substitute for cooked dried beans. Although can sizes vary, the difference won't affect the results of most cooked recipes. A standard 19-oz (540 mL) can of beans yields about 2 cups (500 mL) drained and rinsed beans. If you have smaller or larger cans, you can use the volume called for or just add the amount from your can (unless otherwise specified in the recipe). Drain canned beans in a colander and rinse thoroughly under cold running water before adding them to your recipe.

Holy Mole Chili

Makes 4 to 6 servings

With its notes of cumin, cinnamon and chocolate playing off the gentle spices, this meatless chili combines the best of a mole sauce and a Cincinnati-style chili. Its rich body makes it a seriously satisfying dinner any night of the week.

Tip

If you can't find mole paste, substitute 1 tbsp (15 mL) unsweetened cocoa powder and ½ tsp (2 mL) ground cinnamon.

- **Minimum 4-quart slow cooker**

4	cloves garlic, minced	4
1	large green bell pepper, diced	1
1	onion, finely chopped	1
1	can (19 oz/540 mL) diced tomatoes, with juice	1
1	can (14 oz/398 mL) baked beans in tomato sauce	1
2 cups	cooked or canned romano or pinto beans (see page 84), drained and rinsed	500 mL
2 cups	cooked or canned black beans (see page 84), drained and rinsed	500 mL
1 tbsp	chili powder	15 mL
2 tsp	ground cumin	10 mL
2 tsp	ground coriander	10 mL
¼ cup	mole paste (see tip, at left)	60 mL
½ cup	vegetable or chicken broth	125 mL
	Crushed tortilla chips, chopped fresh cilantro, shredded Cheddar cheese (optional)	

1. In slow cooker stoneware, combine garlic, green pepper, onion, tomatoes with juice, beans in tomato sauce, romano beans, black beans, chili powder, cumin and coriander.

2. In a bowl, combine mole paste and broth. Using a fork, gently stir together into a thin sauce. Stir into bean mixture.

3. Cover and cook on Low for 5 to 6 hours or on High for 2½ to 3 hours, until vegetables are tender and chili is bubbling. Serve topped with tortilla chips, cilantro and cheese (if using).

Make Ahead

This dish can be assembled up to 12 hours in advance. Prepare through step 2, cover and refrigerate overnight. The next day, place stoneware in slow cooker and proceed with step 3.

> Mole paste is a rich, dark, reddish brown sauce used in many Mexican poultry dishes. It is a smooth cooked blend of onions, garlic, several varieties of chiles, ground seeds (such as pumpkin or sesame) and a small amount of Mexican chocolate, which adds richness without being overly sweet. You can find mole paste in the Mexican foods section of the supermarket or in specialty stores.

White Bean and Toasted Cumin Chili with Lime Cream

Makes 4 to 6 servings

Toasting the cumin seeds intensifies their flavor, giving this chili a rich, nutty taste.

Tips

To toast cumin seeds, place in a dry nonstick skillet over low heat. Cook, stirring often, for about 8 minutes or until fragrant. Remove from heat and let cool.

Once opened, transfer canned chipotle peppers and their sauce to a glass jar with a tight-fitting lid and store in the refrigerator for up to 10 days. For longer storage, transfer the peppers and sauce to a freezer bag and gently press out the air, then seal the bag. Manipulate the bag to separate the peppers, so it will be easy to break off a frozen section of pepper and sauce without thawing the whole package.

- **Minimum 4-quart slow cooker**

3	cloves garlic, minced	3
1	onion, finely chopped	1
1	canned chipotle pepper in adobo sauce, chopped	1
1	can (28 oz/796 mL) tomatoes, with juice, chopped	1
1	bottle (12 oz/341 mL) dark beer	1
4 cups	cooked or canned white kidney beans (see page 84), drained and rinsed	1 L
1½ cups	diced winter squash	375 mL
1 tbsp	cumin seeds, toasted (see tip, at left)	15 mL
1 tsp	granulated sugar	5 mL
½ cup	sour cream	125 mL
2 tbsp	freshly squeezed lime juice	30 mL
1 tbsp	snipped fresh chives	15 mL

1. In slow cooker stoneware, combine garlic, onion, chipotle, tomatoes with juice, beer, beans, squash, cumin seeds and sugar.

2. Cover and cook on Low for 8 to 10 hours or on High for 4 to 5 hours, until bubbling.

3. In a small bowl, combine sour cream, lime juice and chives. Spoon chili into bowls and top with sour cream mixture.

Make Ahead

This dish can be assembled up to 12 hours in advance. Prepare through step 1, cover and refrigerate overnight. The next day, place stoneware in slow cooker and proceed with step 2.

Greek Chicken Chili

**Makes 6 to
8 servings**

Greek chili? My
assistant, Leslie, came
up with this recipe
to please her teenage
daughter, who only eats
poultry. It's certainly not
something you would
be served in Greece,
but this chili uses
some of the flavors and
seasonings found in
Greek dishes.

Tip

For this recipe,
I used the bottled
sun-dried tomatoes
packed in olive oil,
but you can also use
the packaged dried
ones found in the
produce section of
the supermarket.
To rehydrate the
packaged tomatoes,
simply cover them
with boiling water
and let soak for
30 minutes or until
soft and pliable.

• **4- to 6-quart slow cooker**

2 tsp	olive oil	10 mL
8	boneless skinless chicken thighs (about 1½ lbs/750 g), cut into 1-inch (2.5 cm) pieces	8
3	cloves garlic, minced	3
1	zucchini, diced	1
1	red bell pepper, diced	1
1 cup	chopped red onion	250 mL
2 tbsp	chili powder	30 mL
1 tbsp	packed brown sugar	15 mL
1 tsp	freshly ground black pepper	5 mL
1 tsp	ground cumin	5 mL
1 tsp	dried oregano	5 mL
1	can (19 oz/540 mL) diced tomatoes, with juice	1
2 cups	cooked or canned chickpeas (see page 84), drained and rinsed	500 mL
1½ cups	tomato pasta sauce	375 mL
¼ cup	diced drained oil-packed sun-dried tomatoes (see tip, at left)	60 mL
2 tbsp	chopped fresh cilantro	30 mL
⅓ cup	crumbed feta cheese	75 mL

1. In a large nonstick skillet, heat oil over medium-high heat. Add chicken and cook for 3 to 5 minutes or until browned all over. Using a slotted spoon, transfer to slow cooker stoneware.

2. Stir in garlic, zucchini, red pepper, onion, chili powder, brown sugar, pepper, cumin, oregano, tomatoes with juice, chickpeas, pasta sauce and sun-dried tomatoes.

3. Cover and cook on Low for 5 to 7 hours or on High for 2½ to 3½ hours, until juices run clear when chicken is pierced. Stir in cilantro. Serve sprinkled with cheese.

Make Ahead

The ingredients in step 2 can be assembled in the stoneware up to 12 hours in advance. Cover and refrigerate overnight. The next day, brown the chicken as directed in step 1. Place stoneware in slow cooker, stir in chicken and proceed with step 3.

Red and White Chili

This robust chili is a satisfying change from the traditional, heavier beef chilis. Leftovers can be served in a warmed pita the next day, or reheated as a nacho dip.

Tips

Mild green chiles are found in the Mexican foods section of the supermarket. They are sold whole or chopped.

Whole turkey thighs are a perfect addition to this chili. There is a lot of meat on thighs, so 2 are plenty.

Variation

If you have difficulty finding turkey thighs, you can substitute approximately 4 turkey drumsticks or 9 bone-in chicken thighs.

- **4- to 6-quart slow cooker**

2	cloves garlic, finely chopped	2
1	onion, chopped	1
2	cans (each 4½ oz/127 mL) chopped mild green chiles	2
3½ cups	chicken broth	875 mL
2 cups	cooked or canned white kidney beans (see page 84), drained and rinsed	500 mL
2 cups	cooked or canned red kidney beans (see page 84), drained and rinsed	500 mL
2 tsp	ground cumin	10 mL
⅛ tsp	cayenne pepper	0.5 mL
2 lbs	turkey thighs (about 2), skin removed	1 kg
1 cup	frozen corn kernels, thawed	250 mL
2 tbsp	all-purpose flour	30 mL
1	lime, cut into wedges (optional)	1

1. In slow cooker stoneware, combine garlic, onion, chiles, broth, white beans, red beans, cumin and cayenne. Place turkey thighs on top.

2. Cover and cook on Low for 8 to 10 hours or on High for 4 to 5 hours, until bubbling.

3. Transfer turkey to a cutting board. Remove meat from bones and cut into bite-size pieces. (Discard bones.) Return turkey to slow cooker, along with corn; stir to combine.

4. In a small bowl, combine flour and ¼ cup (60 mL) water. Stir into turkey mixture. Cover and cook on High for 20 to 30 minutes or until heated through and slightly thickened. If desired, serve garnished with lime wedges to squeeze over chili.

Make Ahead

This dish can be partially assembled up to 12 hours in advance. Prepare through step 1, without adding the turkey thighs. Cover and refrigerate vegetable mixture overnight. The next day, place stoneware in slow cooker, add turkey thighs and proceed with step 2.

East-West Fruit and Nut Chili

Makes 6 to 8 servings

This chili melds curry from the East with chili and chocolate from the West, for an interesting version that is surprisingly good. Make sure you serve it with some crusty rolls or naan bread and, of course, a beer or two for the adults!

Tip

A good chili is dependent on the quality of the chili powder used. Most chili powders are a blend of ground chiles and cumin, oregano, garlic and salt. Don't confuse chili powder with cayenne pepper or hot pepper flakes, which are much hotter.

- **Minimum 4-quart slow cooker**

1½ lbs	lean ground beef	750 g
3	cloves garlic, minced	3
2	large onions, finely chopped	2
3 tbsp	chili powder	45 mL
2 tbsp	unsweetened cocoa powder	30 mL
1 tbsp	curry powder	15 mL
1	red bell pepper, chopped	1
1	tart apple, such as Granny Smith, chopped	1
2	cans (each 4½ oz/127 mL) diced mild green chiles, drained	2
1	can (28 oz/796 mL) diced tomatoes, with juice	1
1	can (14 oz/398 mL) tomato sauce	1
2 cups	cooked or canned red kidney beans (see page 84), drained and rinsed	500 mL
1 cup	chicken broth	250 mL
1 tsp	ground cinnamon	5 mL
⅔ cup	toasted slivered almonds	150 mL
⅔ cup	raisins	150 mL
	Plain yogurt (optional)	

1. In a large nonstick skillet, cook beef, garlic and onions over medium-high heat, breaking up beef with the back of a spoon, until vegetables are tender and beef is no longer pink. Add chili powder, cocoa powder and curry powder and cook for 1 minute. Using a slotted spoon, transfer beef mixture to slow cooker stoneware, draining off any excess fat and liquid.

2. Stir in red pepper, apple, chiles, tomatoes with juice, tomato sauce, beans, broth and cinnamon.

3. Cover and cook on Low for 8 to 10 hours or on High for 4 to 5 hours, until bubbling.

4. Just before serving, stir in almonds and raisins. Ladle into bowls and top each with a dollop of yogurt (if using).

Make Ahead

This chili can be assembled up to 12 hours in advance. Prepare through step 2, keeping beef mixture and bean mixture separate. Cover each and refrigerate overnight. The next day, combine beef and bean mixtures in slow cooker stoneware, place in slow cooker and proceed with step 3.

Canadian Maple Turkey Chili

**Makes 6 to
8 servings**

This chili is slightly sweet, but has lots of meat. It's sure to become a family favorite.

Tips

Ground turkey is a good substitute for other ground meats in many dishes, but it has a milder flavor than beef or pork. Don't be afraid to increase the seasoning, adding at least twice what you would when using other ground meats.

It's important to fully cook ground meat before adding it to the slow cooker. Cook ground meat until no longer pink inside. Use the back of a wooden spoon to break up the meat as it cooks; otherwise, you will end up with large chunks of meat.

Make Ahead

This dish can be assembled up to 24 hours in advance. Prepare through step 2, keeping turkey mixture and bean mixture separate. Cover each and refrigerate overnight. The next day, combine turkey and bean mixtures in stoneware, place in slow cooker and proceed with step 3.

- **Minimum 4-quart slow cooker**

1 tsp	vegetable oil	5 mL
6	slices bacon, chopped	6
1	onion, finely chopped	1
1 lb	lean ground turkey (see tips, at left)	500 g
10	mushrooms, sliced	10
2	stalks celery, finely chopped	2
1	large tomato, chopped	1
1/2	green bell pepper, finely chopped	1/2
1/2	red bell pepper, finely chopped	1/2
1	can (10 oz/284 mL) sodium-reduced condensed tomato soup	1
1	can (14 oz/398 mL) baked beans in tomato sauce	1
2 cups	cooked or canned mixed beans (see page 84), drained and rinsed	500 mL
1 cup	chopped carrots	250 mL
2 tbsp	pure maple syrup	30 mL
1 tbsp	chili powder	15 mL
1 tbsp	ground cumin	15 mL
1/2 tsp	salt	2 mL
1/2 tsp	freshly ground black pepper	2 mL
1/8 tsp	cayenne pepper	0.5 mL
1 cup	frozen corn kernels, thawed	250 mL

1. In a large skillet, heat oil over medium-high heat. Add bacon and cook, stirring, for 3 to 5 minutes or until slightly crisp. Drain all but 1 tbsp (15 mL) fat from pan. (Discard drained fat.)

2. Add onion and sauté for 3 to 5 minutes or until tender and translucent. Add turkey and cook, breaking up with the back of a wooden spoon, for 5 to 7 minutes or until no longer pink inside. Transfer to slow cooker stoneware.

3. Stir in mushrooms, celery, tomato, green pepper, red pepper, soup, baked beans in tomato sauce, mixed beans, carrots, maple syrup, chili powder, cumin, salt, pepper and cayenne.

4. Cover and cook on Low for 8 to 10 hours or on High for 4 to 5 hours, until bubbling. Stir in corn and cook for 20 minutes.

Touchdown Beer Chili and Nachos

Makes 6 to 8 servings

Watching football makes people hungry. All the rooting and cheering really stirs up an appetite. Game day is a good time to take advantage of the ease a slow cooker delivers. This simple, hearty chili with nacho chips will keep everyone satisfied, charged up and focused on the game.

Tip

It is always best to brown ground meat thoroughly before adding it to the slow cooker. This ensures that the meat reaches the recommended cooked temperature of 160°F (71°C), or 165°F (74°C) for ground poultry. If you have a good nonstick skillet, you will not need to add cooking oil unless you are browning ground turkey or chicken, which is generally very lean.

- **Minimum 4-quart slow cooker**
- *Preheat oven to 350°F (180°C)*
- *Rimmed baking sheet*

1½ lbs	lean ground beef	750 g
4	cloves garlic, finely chopped	4
1	large sweet onion, finely chopped	1
1	can (19 oz/540 mL) diced tomatoes, with juice	1
1	can (4½ oz/127 mL) diced mild green chiles	1
1	bottle (12 oz/341 mL) dark beer	1
2 cups	cooked or canned red kidney beans (see page 84), drained and rinsed	500 mL
1 cup	frozen corn kernels, thawed	250 mL
3 tbsp	chili powder	45 mL
2 tbsp	liquid honey	30 mL
1 tbsp	hot pepper sauce	15 mL
1 tsp	curry powder	5 mL
1	bag (8 oz/225 g) multigrain or blue corn tortilla chips	1
2 cups	shredded Cheddar cheese or Monterey Jack cheese	500 mL
1	can (8 oz/220 mL) sliced jalapeño peppers, drained	1
	Sour cream (optional)	

1. In a large nonstick skillet, cook beef, garlic and onion over medium-high heat, breaking up beef with the back of a wooden spoon, until vegetables are tender and beef is no longer pink. Using a slotted spoon, transfer beef to slow cooker stoneware, draining excess fat and liquid from the pan.

2. Stir in tomatoes with juice, chiles, beer, beans, corn, chili powder, honey, hot pepper sauce and curry powder.

3. Cover and cook on Low for 6 to 8 hours or on High for 3 to 4 hours, until bubbling.

4. Meanwhile, spread tortilla chips over baking sheet. Top with cheese and jalapeños. Bake in preheated oven for 10 to 15 minutes or until Cheddar has melted but is not browned. Transfer to a serving bowl.

5. Ladle chili into bowls and top each with a dollop of sour cream (if using). Serve tortilla chips alongside.

Make Ahead

This chili can be assembled up to 12 hours in advance. Prepare through step 2, keeping beef mixture and bean mixture separate. Cover each and refrigerate overnight. The next day, combine beef and bean mixtures in slow cooker stoneware, place in slow cooker and proceed with step 3.

White Bean Salad with Sun-Dried Tomatoes

Makes 4 to 6 servings

This bean salad can be eaten as a side dish with grilled chicken or pork. It is also a light, tasty salad on its own.

Tips

To zest a lemon, use the fine side of a box cheese grater, making sure not to grate the white pith underneath. Or use a zester to remove the zest, then finely chop it. Zesters are inexpensive and widely available at specialty kitchenware shops.

To extract the most juice from a lemon, let it warm to room temperature, then roll it on the counter, pressing down with the palm of your hand, before squeezing it. Or microwave a whole lemon on High for 30 seconds, then roll it. The juice can be frozen in ice cube trays, then the frozen cubes stored in sealable plastic bags for later use. Lemon zest can also be wrapped and frozen for later use.

- **4- to 5-quart slow cooker**

1 lb	dried great Northern beans or white kidney beans (about 2 cups/500 mL), sorted, rinsed and soaked (see page 84)	500 g
3	cloves garlic, finely chopped	3
1½ tsp	dried basil	7 mL
¼ tsp	freshly ground black pepper	1 mL
¾ cup	finely chopped drained oil-packed sun-dried tomatoes	175 mL
2 tbsp	oil from sun-dried tomatoes	30 mL
	Grated zest and freshly squeezed juice of 2 lemons	
3	green onions, finely chopped	3
2	stalks celery, finely chopped	2
1½ cups	sliced black olives	375 mL
¼ cup	chopped fresh flat-leaf (Italian) parsley	60 mL
½ cup	crumbled feta cheese	125 mL
	Salt	

1. In a large saucepan, combine beans and enough water to cover beans by three times their volume. Bring mixture to a boil; reduce heat and simmer for 3 minutes. Remove from heat, cover and stand for 1 hour. Drain and rinse beans.

2. In slow cooker stoneware, combine soaked beans, garlic, basil, pepper and 6 cups (1.5 L) water.

3. Cover and cook on Low for 4 to 6 hours or until beans are tender.

4. Drain beans and transfer to a bowl. Stir in sun-dried tomatoes, oil, lemon zest and lemon juice. Add green onions, celery, olives, parsley and cheese to beans; toss to combine. Season to taste with salt and pepper. Serve warm or at room temperature.

Make Ahead

The salad can be prepared through step 3, covered and refrigerated for up to 1 day. To serve, let beans warm to room temperature and proceed with step 4.

Italian Baked Beans

**Makes
6 servings**

These beans bear no resemblance to their traditional cousins from Boston. This dish is packed with the robust flavors of good spaghetti. All you need is a crusty loaf of bread and a salad of lettuce, tomatoes and cucumbers to make this a hearty meal for a cold winter night.

Tips

To make fresh bread crumbs, lightly pulse a few slices of bread in your food processor until processed to a light, fluffy crumb mixture.

Tomato paste is now available in tubes in many supermarkets and delis. It keeps for months in the refrigerator.

- **4- to 6-quart slow cooker**

2	carrots, coarsely chopped	2
2	stalks celery, coarsely chopped	2
2	cloves garlic, minced	2
1	onion, finely chopped	1
1	green bell pepper, finely chopped	1
1	can (28 oz/796 mL) diced tomatoes with Italian seasonings, with juice	1
2 cups	cooked or canned white kidney beans (see page 84), drained and rinsed	500 mL
2 cups	cooked or canned chickpeas (see page 84), drained and rinsed	500 mL
2 cups	cubed mozzarella cheese	500 mL
2 tbsp	tomato paste	30 mL
2 tsp	dried Italian seasoning	10 mL
Pinch	hot pepper flakes	Pinch
Pinch	granulated sugar	Pinch
1 cup	fresh bread crumbs (see tip, at left)	250 mL
2 tbsp	freshly grated Parmesan cheese	30 mL
2 tbsp	finely chopped fresh flat-leaf (Italian) parsley	30 mL
2 tbsp	butter, melted	30 mL

1. In slow cooker stoneware, combine carrots, celery, garlic, onion, green pepper, tomatoes, kidney beans, chickpeas, mozzarella, tomato paste, Italian seasoning, hot pepper flakes and sugar.

2. Cover and cook on Low for 7 to 9 hours or on High for 3 to 4 hours, until bubbling and vegetables are tender.

3. In a bowl, combine bread crumbs, Parmesan and parsley. Stir in butter. Sprinkle evenly over beans and cook for 1 hour.

Christmas Cake Beans and Couscous

**Makes
6 servings**

Don't worry: there aren't actually any bits of Christmas cake in this recipe. But the golden raisins and dried fruit, which add sweetness to this delicious combination of beans and couscous, remind me of the flavors of my favorite holiday treat. Loaded with fiber and protein, this dish is wonderful with a salad at the end of a long day at any time of year.

Tip

Dried candied fruit are the type used to make old-fashioned Christmas fruit cake. Do not use larger dried fruit, such as apricots, apples and prunes.

- **4- to 6-quart slow cooker**

2 cups	cooked or canned pinto beans (see page 84), drained and rinsed	500 mL
2 cups	frozen shelled edamame, thawed	500 mL
1 cup	golden raisins	250 mL
1 cup	chopped candied fruit	250 mL
2 tsp	grated gingerroot	10 mL
1/2 tsp	salt	2 mL
1/4 tsp	hot pepper flakes	1 mL
1 cup	vegetable broth	250 mL
1 3/4 cups	unsweetened orange or pineapple juice	425 mL
1/2 cup	couscous	125 mL
1 tbsp	olive oil	15 mL
1/2 cup	sliced toasted almonds (see tip, page 101)	125 mL
	Sliced green onion	

1. In slow cooker stoneware, combine beans, edamame, raisins, dried fruit, ginger, salt, hot pepper flakes, broth and orange juice.

2. Cover and cook on Low for 6 to 7 hours or on High for 3 to 3 1/2 hours, until bubbling.

3. Turn off heat and stir in couscous and oil. Cover and let stand for 5 to 10 minutes or until couscous is tender. Fluff mixture with a fork. Serve garnished with almonds and green onion.

> **Edamame are sweet, green soybeans commonly used in Japanese cooking. They are rich in proteins and vitamins A, B and C, making them a nutrition powerhouse. In the supermarket, they are generally found frozen in the health food section or with the frozen vegetables.**

Maple Mochaccino Beans

Makes 4 to 6 servings

This may look like an odd combination of ingredients, but trust me, it is fantastic! The recipe was passed along to me by a good friend, who takes these beans to family parties all the time and earns rave reviews. The ground coffee gives the beans a dark, rich brown color, and the maple syrup lends a touch of sweetness.

Tip

By baked beans in tomato sauce, I mean the canned "pork and beans" style. They are available with additional flavorings, such as maple syrup or chipotle seasonings. Be adventurous and give these a try.

- **4- to 6-quart slow cooker**

6	slices bacon, chopped	6
1	large red onion, very thinly sliced	1
3	cans (each 14 oz/398 mL) baked beans in tomato sauce	3
2 tbsp	finely ground coffee or espresso	30 mL
1 tsp	dry mustard	5 mL
½ cup	pure maple syrup	125 mL

1. In a large nonstick skillet, cook bacon over medium-high heat, stirring, for 4 to 5 minutes or until lightly browned but not crisp. Using a slotted spoon, transfer to a plate lined with paper towels, leaving drippings in pan.

2. Return pan to medium-high heat. Sauté onion for 4 to 6 minutes or until tender and translucent. Remove from heat.

3. Sprinkle half the bacon over bottom of slow cooker stoneware. Cover with half the onions, then with 1 can of beans. Repeat layers. Sprinkle ground coffee evenly over top.

4. In a bowl, combine mustard and maple syrup; pour over bean mixture.

5. Cover and cook on Low for 7 to 9 hours or on High for 3 to 4 hours, until bubbling and sauce has thickened.

Make Ahead

This dish can be assembled up to 12 hours in advance. Prepare through step 3, cover and refrigerate overnight. The next day, place stoneware in slow cooker and proceed with step 4.

Hot Curried Beans

This bean dish — perfect as a side dish or on its own for a potluck — is a real hit with my vegetarian daughter, Darcy, who loves the combination of beans, crunchy apples and sweet raisins. She is not a cilantro fan, but my husband and I enjoy a sprinkling of cilantro on top. The chutney lends some sweetness, with a little heat, while the nuts add a nice crunch.

Tip

To toast almonds, spread nuts in a single layer in a shallow baking pan or rimmed baking sheet. Bake in a 350°F (180°C) oven, stirring or shaking once or twice, for 5 to 10 minutes or until golden brown and fragrant.

- **4- to 6-quart slow cooker**

1 lb	dried red kidney beans (about 2 cups/500 mL), sorted, rinsed and soaked (see page 84)	500 g
1	onion, sliced	1
8 oz	button mushrooms, sliced	250 g
½ cup	golden raisins	125 mL
1 tbsp	curry powder	15 mL
½ tsp	freshly ground black pepper	2 mL
1½ cups	vegetable or chicken broth	375 mL
1	large red or green apple, chopped	1
	Hot cooked couscous	
	Mango chutney	
	Chopped toasted almonds (see tip, at left)	

1. In slow cooker stoneware, combine soaked beans, onion, mushrooms, raisins, curry powder, pepper, broth and ¾ cup (175 mL) water.

2. Cover and cook on Low for 4 to 6 hours or until beans are tender. Stir in apples and cook for 15 minutes.

3. Spoon beans over couscous, top each serving with a dollop of chutney and sprinkle with almonds.

Carolyn's Boozy Baked Beans

Makes 8 to 10 servings

This recipe was passed along to me by my friend Carolyn Culp. She is always the hit of the family reunion when she turns up with this. You can omit the rum, if you want, but it really adds spirit to this dish.

Tip

If using fresh pineapple, substitute 1½ cups (375 mL) fresh pineapple chunks and ½ cup (125 mL) unsweetened apple juice for the pineapple juice.

- **4- to 5-quart slow cooker**

1 lb	dried white pea beans (about 2 cups/500 mL), rinsed and sorted	500 g
1	can (14 oz/398 mL) pineapple chunks, with juice	1
4 oz	salt pork	125 g
½ cup	amber or dark rum	125 mL
¼ cup	light (fancy) molasses	60 mL
¼ cup	packed dark brown sugar	60 mL
2 tsp	dry mustard	10 mL
1 tsp	salt	5 mL

1. In a large saucepan, combine beans and 10 cups (2.5 L) water; bring to a boil over high heat. Reduce heat and simmer for 3 minutes. Remove from heat, cover and let soak for 1 hour. Drain and rinse, reserving 1 cup (250 mL) of the soaking liquid.

2. In slow cooker stoneware, combine reserved soaking liquid, pineapple with juice, salt pork, rum, molasses, brown sugar and mustard. Stir in beans.

3. Cover and cook on Low for 8 hours or until bubbling. Season with salt.

> White pea beans, also known as navy beans or *alubias chicas*, are the type of cooked bean you will find in canned baked beans in tomato sauce (aka pork and beans). The term "navy bean" was adopted during the Second World War, when pork and beans was regularly fed to the troops.

Poultry

Creamy Chicken Artichoke Casserole

Makes 6 servings

I love recipes that let me use some ready-made ingredients to make a simple, tasty dish. The crushed salad croutons on the casserole give it a crunchy topping. Serve with rice and a crisp green salad to finish this dish nicely.

Tip

You can substitute light Alfredo sauce and mayonnaise for the regular versions called for in this recipe.

- **4- to 6-quart slow cooker, stoneware greased**

1	red bell pepper, chopped	1
3 cups	chopped cooked chicken	750 mL
1 cup	shredded Asiago cheese	250 mL
¼ cup	chopped green onions	60 mL
1	can (14 oz/398 mL) artichoke hearts, drained and chopped	1
1	container (10 oz/300 mL) Alfredo sauce	1
½ cup	mayonnaise	125 mL
1½ cups	croutons, coarsely crushed	375 mL
	Sliced green onions (optional)	

1. In a large bowl, combine red pepper, chicken, Asiago, green onions, artichokes, Alfredo sauce and mayonnaise. Transfer to prepared slow cooker stoneware. Sprinkle with croutons.

2. Cover and cook on Low for 5 to 6 hours or on High for 2½ to 3 hours, until bubbling. If desired, sprinkle with sliced green onions.

Braised Chicken in Riesling

....

Traditionally, this dish is made with red wine, but when you use white wine, such as Riesling, it is lighter and equally delicious. You can also substitute an equal amount of chicken broth or apple juice, if you prefer not to use wine. Serve over cooked brown rice.

Tip

Tomato paste is now available in tubes in many supermarkets and delis. It keeps for months in the refrigerator.

- **Minimum 4-quart slow cooker**

6	skinless bone-in chicken thighs, trimmed	6
½ tsp	salt	2 mL
¼ tsp	freshly ground black pepper	1 mL
1 tbsp	olive oil	15 mL
1	onion, thinly sliced	1
1½ cups	finely shredded green cabbage	375 mL
1 cup	chopped baby carrots	250 mL
3	cloves garlic, minced	3
¾ cup	Riesling or other dry white wine	175 mL
¾ cup	chicken broth	175 mL
2 tbsp	tomato paste	30 mL
2 tbsp	all-purpose flour	30 mL

1. Sprinkle chicken with salt and pepper. In a large nonstick skillet, heat oil over medium-high heat. Cook chicken for 2 to 3 minutes per side or until browned all over. Using a slotted spoon, transfer to slow cooker stoneware.

2. Add onion and cabbage to skillet. Reduce heat to medium and sauté for about 5 minutes or until onion is tender and translucent and cabbage is softened. Stir into chicken and top with carrots and garlic.

3. In a glass measuring cup, whisk together wine, broth and tomato paste. Pour over chicken mixture.

4. Cover and cook on Low for 5 to 6 hours or on High for 3 to 4 hours, until juices run clear when chicken is pierced. Using a slotted spoon, transfer chicken and vegetables to a platter and keep warm.

5. In a bowl, whisk together flour and ⅓ cup (75 mL) water until smooth. Whisk in about ¼ cup (60 mL) hot liquid from stoneware until blended. Stir flour mixture into stoneware. Cover and cook on High for about 15 minutes or until liquid has thickened. Season to taste with salt and pepper. Spoon over chicken and vegetables.

Chicken with Sourdough Mushroom Stuffing

Makes 4 to 6 servings

Since I first made Thanksgiving stuffing in the slow cooker more than 10 years ago, I have maintained that this is the best way to ensure that this side dish is moist and delicious. Now I have combined the stuffing with chicken and vegetables to make a complete one-dish meal.

Tips

To zest a lemon, use the fine side of a box cheese grater, making sure not to grate the white pith underneath. Or use a zester to remove the zest, then finely chop it. Zesters are inexpensive and widely available at specialty kitchenware shops.

Sourdough bread is a little heavier than regular French bread, making it a great choice for the slow cooker, but if you wish to use a French loaf, you can.

● **Minimum 4-quart slow cooker, stoneware greased**

2 tbsp	grated lemon zest, divided	30 mL
1 tbsp	dried sage	15 mL
1 tsp	salt	5 mL
1 tsp	freshly ground black pepper	5 mL
8	skinless bone-in chicken drumsticks or thighs (about 2 lbs/1 kg)	8
1/4 cup	butter	60 mL
2	cloves garlic, minced	2
1	onion, finely chopped	1
4 cups	quartered assorted mushrooms, such as cremini, portobello, shiitake or button	1 L
8 cups	cubed sourdough bread (1 inch/2.5 cm cubes)	2 L
1 cup	coarsely shredded carrots	250 mL
1/2 cup	dried cranberries (optional)	125 mL
1 cup	chicken broth	250 mL
1/4 cup	finely chopped fresh parsley	60 mL

1. Set aside 1 tsp (5 mL) of the lemon zest. In a small bowl, combine the remaining zest, sage, salt and pepper. Sprinkle over chicken and rub all over. Place chicken in prepared slow cooker stoneware.

2. Meanwhile, in a skillet, melt butter over medium-high heat. Sauté garlic, onion and mushrooms for 3 to 5 minutes or until mushrooms are tender.

3. In a large bowl, combine bread cubes, carrots and cranberries (if using). Add mushroom mixture. Drizzle with broth and toss gently to combine. Lightly pack over chicken in stoneware.

4. Cover and cook on High for 4 to 5 hours or on Low for 8 to 10 hours, until juices run clear when chicken is pierced. Using a slotted spoon, transfer stuffing and chicken to a warmed platter. (Discard juices in stoneware.)

5. In a small bowl, combine parsley and the reserved lemon zest. Sprinkle over chicken and stuffing.

Fennel and Pear Chicken Thighs

Makes 6 servings

If you can't find dried pears, this dish is equally delicious with dried apples. And fennel? Well, I just can't say enough wonderful things about it. I love the flavor it gives this or any other recipe.

Tips

Store mushrooms in a paper bag, with the top loosely folded over once or twice, or place them in a glass container and cover it with a tea towel or moist paper towel. Be sure to allow air circulation. Store in the refrigerator (but not in the crisper) and use within a few days — or a week, if they are packaged and unopened.

To prepare mushrooms, first trim off the bottoms of the stems, then wipe off the mushrooms. Don't rinse or soak the mushrooms, or they'll absorb water and turn mushy when you cook them.

- **4- to 6-quart slow cooker**

1	fennel bulb with fronds	1
8 oz	mushrooms, sliced	250 g
1/2 cup	chopped dried pears or apples	125 mL
2 1/2 lbs	boneless skinless chicken thighs (about 12)	1.25 kg
3/4 tsp	salt	3 mL
1/2 tsp	freshly ground black pepper	2 mL
1/2 tsp	dried thyme	2 mL
1 cup	unsweetened pear nectar or apple juice	250 mL
	Hot cooked couscous	
2 tbsp	cornstarch	30 mL
2 tbsp	cold water	30 mL

1. Remove and reserve green fronds from fennel bulb and cut bulb and the remaining stalks into 1/2-inch (1 cm) slices.

2. In slow cooker stoneware, combine fennel slices, mushrooms and pears. Arrange chicken on top and sprinkle with salt, pepper and thyme. Pour pear nectar over chicken.

3. Cover and cook on Low for 7 to 8 hours or on High for 3 1/2 to 4 hours, until juices run clear when chicken is pierced.

4. Spoon hot couscous onto a warmed platter. Using a slotted spoon, arrange chicken and vegetables on top and keep warm.

5. In a small bowl, whisk together cornstarch and water. Whisk into liquid in stoneware. Cover and cook on High for 10 to 15 minutes or until sauce is thickened. Spoon over chicken and vegetables. Garnish with reserved fennel fronds.

> **Look for dried pears and apples in the produce, baking or bulk departments of the supermarket.**

Salsa Cinnamon Chicken

**Makes
6 servings**

You might think the combination of peanut sauce (Asian) and salsa (Mexican) is an unlikely fusion. However, these two ingredients, along with the fresh basil, are a wonderful complement to the chicken.

Tips

Feel free to substitute red kidney beans for the black beans in this dish.

If using a combination of chicken breasts, drumsticks and thighs, place the breasts on top to prevent them from getting overcooked.

● **4- to 6-quart slow cooker, stoneware greased**

2 cups	cooked or canned black beans (see page 84), drained and rinsed	500 mL
1 cup	corn kernels, thawed if frozen	250 mL
1 cup	medium or hot salsa, divided	250 mL
3 lbs	bone-in chicken pieces (skin-on breasts, skinless drumsticks and/or thighs)	1.5 kg
¼ cup	chopped fresh basil, divided	60 mL
1 tsp	ground cinnamon	5 mL
¾ cup	peanut sauce	175 mL

1. In prepared slow cooker stoneware, combine beans and corn. Pour half the salsa over bean mixture. Layer chicken on top (see tip, at left).

2. In a bowl, combine 2 tbsp (30 mL) of the basil, cinnamon, peanut sauce and the remaining salsa. Pour over chicken.

3. Cover and cook on Low for 5 to 6 hours or on High for 2½ to 3 hours, until breasts are no longer pink inside and/or juices run clear when drumsticks and thighs are pierced. Serve sprinkled with the remaining basil.

Make Ahead

This dish can be assembled up to 12 hours in advance. Prepare through step 2, cover and refrigerate overnight. The next day, place stoneware in slow cooker and proceed with step 3.

> **Peanut sauce is commonly used in Thai cuisine, where it is served with satays, spring rolls and raw vegetables. It is generally a mixture of ground peanuts, chile peppers and oil, with seasonings such as ginger, garlic and lemongrass. I used a store-bought version for this recipe, but if you have a recipe for homemade, so much the better!**

Italian Lemon Chicken with Gremolata

Makes 6 to 8 servings

Everyone loves chicken, and this is an easy dish you can serve to company. Serve it with steamed rice and a salad of Italian greens tossed in a light vinaigrette.

Tips

The gremolata can be prepared in advance and refrigerated for up to 4 hours.

Pearl onions are easy to prepare. Simply cut an X into the base of each onion. Bring a pot of water to a boil over medium-high heat. Drop onions into pot and boil for 1 minute. Drain and immediately immerse in ice-cold water. Let cool, then squeeze the onions out of their skins.

- **4- to 6-quart slow cooker**

2 lbs	skinless bone-in chicken thighs and drumsticks	1 kg
1 tsp	salt	5 mL
1/2 tsp	freshly ground black pepper	2 mL
2	cans (each 14 oz/398 mL) artichoke hearts, drained and quartered	2
2 cups	pearl onions, skins removed (see tip, at left)	500 mL
2 cups	baby carrots	500 mL
1 tsp	crumbled dried rosemary	5 mL
1/2 cup	chicken broth	125 mL
1/4 cup	dry vermouth or white wine	60 mL
1 tbsp	freshly squeezed lemon juice	15 mL
Gremolata		
2	cloves garlic, minced	2
3 tbsp	chopped fresh parsley	45 mL
1 tbsp	coarsely chopped lemon zest	15 mL

1. Arrange chicken in slow cooker stoneware. Sprinkle with salt and pepper. Arrange artichokes, onions and carrots around chicken. Sprinkle chicken and vegetables with rosemary.

2. In a bowl, combine broth, vermouth and lemon juice. Pour over chicken and vegetables.

3. Cover and cook on Low for 6 to 8 hours or on High for 3 to 4 hours, until juices run clear when chicken is pierced.

4. *Gremolata:* In a bowl, combine garlic, parsley and lemon zest. Sprinkle over chicken and vegetables before serving.

Jamaican Chicken Casserole

Makes 4 servings

Create an easy one-dish dinner by baking chicken in a Caribbean-inspired rub. The flavors give the dish a delightful warmth that makes it a perfect meal for a cold night.

Tip

If your liquid honey has crystallized (or if you are using solid creamed honey instead), place the jar (or as much as you need in a small heatproof bowl) in a saucepan of hot water and let warm until the crystals dissolve and the honey is melted. Or heat in the microwave on Medium-High (70%) for about 1 minute, stirring after 30 seconds, until melted.

• **Minimum 4-quart slow cooker, stoneware greased**

1 tsp	salt	5 mL
¾ tsp	ground allspice	3 mL
¾ tsp	dried thyme	3 mL
½ tsp	pumpkin pie spice	2 mL
¼ tsp	cayenne pepper	1 mL
8	boneless skinless chicken thighs	8
2 tbsp	vegetable oil (approx.)	30 mL
1	large sweet potato, peeled and cubed (about 3 cups/750 mL)	1
2 cups	cooked or canned black beans (see page 84), drained and rinsed	500 mL
¼ cup	liquid honey	60 mL
¼ cup	freshly squeezed lime juice	60 mL
2 tbsp	cornstarch	30 mL
1 tbsp	cold water	15 mL
2	green onions, chopped	2

1. In a bowl, combine salt, allspice, thyme, pumpkin pie spice and cayenne. Add chicken and rub all over with spices.

2. In a large nonstick skillet, heat half the oil over medium-high heat. Cook chicken in batches, adding more oil as needed, for 2 to 3 minutes per side or until browned all over. Set aside.

3. In prepared slow cooker stoneware, combine sweet potato and beans. Top with chicken.

4. In a small saucepan, combine honey and lime juice. Bring to a boil and cook, stirring, for 1 minute. Pour over chicken.

5. Cover and cook on Low for 4 to 6 hours or on High for 2½ to 3 hours, until juices run clear when chicken is pierced. Using a slotted spoon, transfer chicken and vegetables to a platter and keep warm.

6. In a small bowl, whisk together cornstarch and water. Whisk into liquid in stoneware. Cover and cook on High for 10 to 15 minutes or until sauce has thickened. Spoon over chicken and vegetables. Garnish with green onions.

Easy Chicken Rarebit

Makes 4 to 6 servings

....

This dish is reminiscent of Welsh rarebit, also known as "rabbit" in Great Britain, where it originated. Rarebit is toasted bread topped with savory sauce made from melted cheese and seasonings. The addition of chicken makes it a satisfying meal on its own, but serve it with a crisp kosher dill pickle on the side.

Tips

This recipe uses boneless skinless chicken breasts, which require a very short cooking time. If you want to cook this recipe for longer, use boneless skinless chicken thighs, cut into strips, instead, to ensure that you don't overcook the chicken. Increase the cooking time to 6 to 8 hours on Low or 3 to 4 hours on High, until juices run clear when chicken is pierced.

If you can, purchase single cans of specialty beer at the liquor store. This recipe uses dark beer, but a good ale is also acceptable.

- **4- to 6-quart slow cooker**

1	large onion, halved crosswise and thinly sliced	1
2 lbs	boneless skinless chicken breasts, cut diagonally into ½-inch (1 cm) thick slices	1 kg
2 tbsp	butter	30 mL
2 tbsp	all-purpose flour	30 mL
1 tsp	Dijon mustard	5 mL
1 tsp	Worcestershire sauce	5 mL
½ tsp	salt	2 mL
½ tsp	freshly ground black pepper	2 mL
½ cup	dark beer, such as porter or stout	125 mL
¾ cup	heavy or whipping (35%) cream	175 mL
1½ cups	shredded Cheddar cheese	375 mL
Dash	hot pepper sauce	Dash
6	pumpernickel or rye buns, split and toasted	6
4	slices bacon, cooked crisp and crumbled (optional)	4
1	tomato, chopped (optional)	1

1. Arrange onion on bottom of slow cooker stoneware and lay chicken on top.

2. In a saucepan, melt butter over medium-high heat. Cook flour, whisking constantly and being careful not to let it brown, for 2 minutes. Whisk in mustard, Worcestershire sauce, salt and pepper until smooth. Whisk in beer until combined. Add cream and cook, stirring, until smooth. Pour over chicken.

3. Cover and cook on Low for 4 to 5 hours or on High for 2 to 2½ hours, until chicken is no longer pink inside. Using a slotted spoon, transfer chicken to a plate and keep warm.

4. Stir Cheddar and hot pepper sauce into liquid in stoneware. Cover and cook on High for 10 minutes or until cheese has melted.

5. Arrange chicken evenly on bottom halves of buns and ladle cheese mixture on top. Sprinkle with bacon and tomato (if using). Cover with top halves of buns.

Spanish Paella with Chicken and Garden Vegetables

Makes 6 to 8 servings

· ·

This dish is traditionally made with a variety of meats, seafood and vegetables. This simple slow cooker version uses chicken, sausage and vegetables, and it's absolutely delicious.

Tip

For an easier version, substitute 2 cups (500 mL) thawed frozen mixed vegetables for the red pepper, zucchini and peas. Stir in about 20 minutes before the end of cooking.

- **Minimum 4-quart slow cooker**

1 tbsp	olive oil	15 mL
6	boneless skinless chicken thighs	6
1	onion, chopped	1
1	clove garlic, minced	1
1	can (19 oz/540 mL) tomatoes, with juice	1
1 lb	smoked hot sausage, sliced into rounds	500 g
3 cups	chicken broth	750 mL
1 cup	long-grain parboiled (converted) white rice	250 mL
1 tsp	dried thyme	5 mL
Pinch	saffron threads	Pinch
1	red or yellow bell pepper, chopped	1
1	zucchini, chopped	1
½ cup	frozen peas, thawed	125 mL

1. In a large nonstick skillet, heat oil over medium-high heat. Cook chicken for 2 to 3 minutes per side or until browned all over. Using a slotted spoon, transfer to slow cooker stoneware.

2. Add onion to skillet and sauté for 3 to 4 minutes or until tender and translucent. Stir in garlic, tomatoes with juice, sausage, broth, rice, thyme and saffron; cook for 5 minutes. Spoon over chicken.

3. Cover and cook on Low for 6 to 8 hours or on High for 3 to 4 hours, until juices run clear when chicken is pierced and rice is tender. About 20 minutes before the end of cooking, stir in red pepper, zucchini and peas.

Chicken and Pepperoni Bake

**Makes
4 servings**

If you love the flavors of pizza, this recipe will be a favorite. The pepperoni slices add a great dimension to the sauce. I've even used small pepperettes in this recipe, as I seem to always have some in the refrigerator for my son, Jack. Serve this with noodles and a cooked green vegetable, for a complete meal.

Tip

To extract the most juice from a lemon, let it warm to room temperature, then roll it on the counter, pressing down with the palm of your hand, before squeezing it. Or microwave a whole lemon on High for 30 seconds, then roll it. The juice can be frozen in ice cube trays, then the frozen cubes stored in sealable plastic bags for later use. Lemon zest can also be wrapped and frozen for later use.

- **4- to 6-quart slow cooker**

½ cup	all-purpose flour	125 mL
1 tbsp	dried thyme	15 mL
½ tsp	salt	2 mL
3 lbs	skinless bone-in chicken thighs and drumsticks	1.5 kg
4	cloves garlic, minced	4
2	onions, finely chopped	2
1	can (28 oz/796 mL) tomatoes, drained	1
1 cup	thinly sliced pepperoni	250 mL
¼ tsp	hot pepper flakes	1 mL
½ cup	dry red wine	125 mL
2 tbsp	tomato paste	30 mL
¾ cup	sliced kalamata olives	175 mL
2 tbsp	chopped fresh oregano	30 mL
2 tsp	freshly squeezed lemon juice	10 mL

1. In a heavy plastic bag, combine flour, thyme and salt. In batches, add chicken to bag and toss to coat with flour mixture. Transfer chicken to slow cooker stoneware. Reserve the remaining flour mixture.

2. Add garlic, onions, tomatoes, pepperoni and hot pepper flakes to stoneware.

3. In a bowl, combine wine and tomato paste. Pour over chicken and vegetables.

4. Cover and cook on Low for 5 to 6 hours or on High for 2½ to 3 hours, until juices run clear when chicken is pierced. Using a slotted spoon, transfer chicken to a platter and keep warm.

5. In a bowl, combine the reserved flour mixture and 2 tbsp (30 mL) water. Whisk into liquid in stoneware. Cover and cook on High for 10 to 15 minutes or until sauce is thickened. Stir in olives, oregano and lemon juice. Season to taste with salt. Spoon sauce over chicken.

Braised Chicken Marbella-Style

Makes 6 to 8 servings

This recipe is inspired by one of my favorites from *The Silver Palate Cookbook*. The chicken is marinated overnight for moistness and flavor, then braised with dried fruit. All you need alongside is a crisp green salad and some rice to soak up the juices.

Tips

If using a combination of chicken breasts, drumsticks and thighs, place the breasts on top to prevent them from getting overcooked.

Cooking times for poultry may be longer for larger slow cookers and/or where there is a relatively high proportion of dark to white meat. For predominantly white meat dishes, be sure to avoid overcooking. It is best to check doneness at the earliest time suggested in the recipe.

• **4- to 6-quart slow cooker**

3	cloves garlic, minced	3
1	bay leaf	1
2 tbsp	packed brown sugar	30 mL
1 tsp	dried oregano	5 mL
1 tsp	salt	5 mL
½ tsp	freshly ground black pepper	2 mL
½ cup	dry white wine	125 mL
2 tbsp	red wine vinegar	30 mL
3 lbs	bone-in chicken pieces (skin-on breasts, skinless drumsticks and/or thighs)	1.5 kg
½ cup	pitted prunes, chopped	125 mL
½ cup	dried figs, chopped	125 mL
¼ cup	whole pitted Spanish green olives	60 mL
2 tbsp	capers, drained	30 mL
2 tbsp	chopped fresh parsley	30 mL

1. In a glass measuring cup, combine garlic, bay leaf, brown sugar, oregano, salt, pepper, wine and vinegar. Place chicken in a sealable plastic bag and pour in garlic mixture. Seal bag and massage marinade around the meat. Refrigerate overnight.

2. Transfer chicken and marinade to slow cooker stoneware (see tip, at left). Add prunes and figs.

3. Cover and cook on Low for 5 to 6 hours or on High for 2½ to 3 hours, until breasts are no longer pink inside and/or juices run clear when drumsticks and thighs are pierced. About 10 minutes before the end of cooking, stir in olives and capers. Discard bay leaf. Serve sprinkled with parsley.

> **Capers are the flower buds of a bush native to the Mediterranean. Once picked, the buds are sun-dried, then pickled in a vinegar brine. They can be found in various sizes, from petite to small (about the size of your little fingertip). If desired, rinse capers before using to remove excess salt.**

Moroccan Chicken

Makes 4 to 6 servings

I have acquired a taste for Middle Eastern cuisine in the past few years. While you're cooking this exotic dish, the pungent aromas of curry and lemon will emanate throughout the house.

Tips

Preserved lemons are a key ingredient in many Moroccan dishes. Their flavor is mildly tart and intensely lemony. You can find them in gourmet food shops. If you can't find one, simply omit it.

If using a combination of chicken breasts, drumsticks and thighs, place the breasts on top to prevent them from getting overcooked.

Cooking times for poultry may be longer for larger slow cookers and/or where there is a relatively high proportion of dark to white meat. For predominantly white meat dishes, be sure to avoid overcooking. It is best to check doneness at the earliest time suggested in the recipe.

- **4- to 6-quart slow cooker**

½ cup	all-purpose flour	125 mL
1 tbsp	garam masala or curry powder	15 mL
1 tsp	salt	5 mL
½ tsp	freshly ground black pepper	2 mL
3 lbs	bone-in chicken pieces (skin-on breasts, skinless drumsticks and/or thighs)	1.5 kg
2 tbsp	olive oil (approx.)	30 mL
2	onions, chopped	2
2	cloves garlic, minced	2
½ cup	dry white wine	125 mL
½ cup	chicken broth	125 mL
	Finely grated zest and freshly squeezed juice of 1 lemon	
1	preserved lemon (see tip, at left), finely chopped	1
½ cup	pitted ripe kalamata olives	125 mL
¼ cup	chopped fresh cilantro	60 mL

1. In a heavy plastic bag, combine flour, garam masala, salt and pepper. In batches, add chicken to bag and toss to coat with flour mixture. (Once all the chicken is coated, reserve the remaining flour mixture.)

2. In a large skillet, heat half the oil over medium-high heat. Cook chicken in batches, adding more oil as needed, for 2 to 3 minutes per side or until browned all over. Using a slotted spoon, transfer to slow cooker stoneware (see tip, at left).

3. Add onions to skillet, reduce heat to medium and sauté for about 2 minutes or until tender and translucent. Add garlic and reserved flour mixture; cook, stirring, for about 3 minutes or until flour is toasted. Add wine and broth; cook, stirring, until thickened. Remove from heat and stir in ½ tsp (2 mL) of the lemon zest. Pour over chicken. Scatter preserved lemon on top.

4. Cover and cook on Low for 5 to 6 hours or on High for 2½ to 3 hours, until breasts are no longer pink inside and/or juices run clear when drumsticks and thighs are pierced.

5. Using a slotted spoon, transfer chicken to a platter. Stir remaining lemon zest, lemon juice, olives and cilantro into sauce. Spoon over chicken.

Slow Roast Chicken with Peas and Prosciutto

**Makes
6 servings**

Don't be daunted by
the fusion of French
and Italian flavors in
this recipe; it works well
with the mild flavor of
the chicken.

Tips

If a whole chicken is
too large to fit into
your slow cooker, cut
it into pieces with a
sharp knife, placing
the breast portion on
top in the stoneware.

Herbes de Provence
is a blend of dried
basil, fennel seed,
lavender, marjoram,
rosemary, sage,
summer savory and
thyme. Look for it
in the spice aisle of
the supermarket.

- **Minimum 5-quart slow cooker**

1	whole roasting chicken (about 2½ lbs/1.25 kg)	1
1 tbsp	herbes de Provence	15 mL
1 tsp	lemon pepper	5 mL
½ tsp	salt	2 mL
1 tsp	olive oil	5 mL
1	onion, finely chopped	1
5 oz	prosciutto, chopped	150 g
½ cup	dry white wine	125 mL
1 cup	frozen green peas, thawed	250 mL
½ cup	evaporated milk or heavy or whipping (35%) cream	125 mL
3 tbsp	cornstarch	45 mL
2 tbsp	cold water	30 mL
	Hot cooked linguine pasta	

1. Rinse chicken, inside and out, under cold running water and pat dry with paper towels. (Discard any giblets, but reserve chicken neck for another use, if desired).

2. In a bowl, combine herbes de Provence, lemon pepper and salt. Rub oil over skin of chicken and sprinkle with herb mixture. Place chicken, breast side up, in slow cooker stoneware. Arrange onion and prosciutto evenly around chicken. Pour wine over top.

3. Cover and cook on Low for 8 to 10 hours or until a meat thermometer inserted in the thickest part of a thigh registers 170°F (77°C). About 30 minutes before the end of cooking, add peas and evaporated milk to cooking liquid.

4. With two large spoons or pancake flippers, carefully transfer chicken to a plate and let stand for 15 minutes before carving.

5. Meanwhile, in a small bowl, whisk together cornstarch and cold water. Whisk into liquid in stoneware. Cover and cook on High for 10 to 15 minutes or until sauce is thickened.

6. Carve chicken. Divide cooked pasta evenly among individual serving plates. Arrange chicken on pasta and ladle sauce over top.

Bollywood Chicken Loaf with Chutney Glaze

Makes 4 to 6 servings

In this dish, ground chicken is spiced with tandoori curry paste for a zesty change from the usual meatloaf. Serve with roasted potatoes, and cauliflower seasoned with curry powder. A little yogurt sauce on the side cools down the taste buds (although this is not a particularly spicy dish).

Tip

You can also line the stoneware with cheesecloth, using a large enough piece to drape over the rim, and use it to lift out the cooked meatloaf.

Variation

Substitute 2 lbs (1 kg) lean ground beef or turkey for the ground chicken, or combine 1 lb (500 g) ground beef with 1 lb (500 g) ground turkey or chicken.

- **Minimum 4-quart slow cooker**

2 lbs	lean ground chicken	1 kg
2	cloves garlic, minced	2
1	egg, lightly beaten	1
1/3 cup	crushed pappadams or fine dry bread crumbs	75 mL
2 tbsp	tandoori curry paste	30 mL
2 tsp	garam masala or curry powder	10 mL
Pinch	salt	Pinch
1/4 tsp	freshly ground black pepper	1 mL
1/4 cup	mango chutney	60 mL

Spiced Yogurt Sauce

1/2 cup	plain nonfat yogurt	125 mL
1/2 tsp	minced fresh garlic	2 mL
1/2 tsp	ground coriander	2 mL
1/4 tsp	ground cumin	1 mL

1. Cut a 2-foot (60 cm) length of foil in half lengthwise to make 2 strips. Fold each strip in half lengthwise. Crisscross the strips on the bottom of the slow cooker stoneware, bringing the ends up the sides and over the rim.

2. In a large bowl, combine chicken, garlic, egg, pappadams, curry paste, garam masala, salt and pepper. Using your hands, blend well. Mound into a loaf shape and place in prepared stoneware. Spread chutney over top.

3. Tucking strip ends under lid, cover and cook on Low for 4 to 6 hours or on High for 2½ to 3 hours, until a meat thermometer inserted in the center of the loaf registers 170°F (77°C). Remove lid and grasp strip ends to lift out meatloaf. Transfer to a platter.

4. *Sauce:* Meanwhile, in a bowl, combine yogurt, garlic, coriander and cumin. Refrigerate until ready to serve. Serve on the side.

> **Garam masala is a blend of spices used in Indian cooking. *Garam* means "warm" or "hot" in Hindi and *masala* means "mixture," so as you might expect, this blend adds a pleasant heat to dishes. If you can't find garam masala, an equal amount of curry powder will work almost as well.**

Sweet Butter Chicken

Makes 4 to 6 servings

Here's one of my favorite menu offerings at an Indian restaurant. The smooth sauce and tender chicken melt in your mouth — like butter! It's perfect served over cooked basmati rice, with a crisp cucumber salad and savory pappadams (crisp Indian flatbreads) on the side.

Tips

The most flavorful paprika comes from Hungary. Types range from mild to hot. Use the type that suits your taste.

Evaporated milk holds up extremely well in the slow cooker and will not curdle when it is cooked over a long period of time. Don't confuse evaporated milk with the sweetened condensed milk used in desserts and candies.

Toasting cashews brings out their sweet, buttery flavor. Spread nuts in a single layer on a rimmed baking sheet and toast in a 350°F (180°C) oven for about 10 minutes or until golden and fragrant.

- **4- to 6-quart slow cooker**

2 tbsp	melted butter, divided	30 mL
2 tbsp	tandoori curry paste or tikka curry paste, divided	30 mL
1 tbsp	minced gingerroot	15 mL
1 tsp	ground cumin	5 mL
1 tsp	paprika	5 mL
1	can (12 oz/370 mL) evaporated milk	1
1	can (5½ oz/156 mL) tomato paste	1
1 tbsp	packed brown sugar	15 mL
8	boneless skinless chicken thighs	8
½ cup	plain yogurt	125 mL
2 tbsp	freshly squeezed lime juice	30 mL
	Hot cooked basmati rice	
2 tbsp	chopped fresh cilantro	30 mL
2 tbsp	chopped toasted cashews	30 mL

1. In a saucepan, cook 1 tbsp (15 mL) of the butter until just beginning to brown. Add 1 tbsp (15 mL) of the curry paste, ginger, cumin and paprika; cook, stirring, for about 2 minutes or until fragrant. Stir in evaporated milk, tomato paste and brown sugar; bring to a boil. Reduce heat and simmer, stirring often, for about 10 minutes or until thickened.

2. Add the remaining butter to slow cooker stoneware and swirl to coat bottom and sides.

3. In a bowl, combine chicken, yogurt and the remaining curry paste. Arrange in stoneware and pour sauce evenly over top.

4. Cover and cook on Low for 5 to 6 hours or on High for 3 hours, until juices run clear when chicken is pierced. Stir in lime juice.

5. Serve over rice, sprinkled with cilantro and cashews.

> **Tandoori and tikka curry pastes are complex blends of freshly ground spices and herbs, preserved in vegetable oil to seal in freshness. Both are mild blends and can be mixed with broth, yogurt or canned tomatoes to create a delicious sauce for meat, poultry, seafood or vegetables. Once opened, curry paste can be stored in the refrigerator for up to 6 months.**

Sweet Thai Chili Chicken

Makes 5 to 6 servings

This Thai chicken dish is so good that everyone will want seconds. It blends all of the great flavor profiles found in Thai cooking — sweet, salty, spicy and sour. Serve over hot cooked rice noodles, with Ginger Snow Peas and Peppers (see recipe, below) on the side.

- **4- to 6-quart slow cooker**

10 to 12	boneless skinless chicken thighs	10 to 12
2	cloves garlic, minced	2
2 tsp	paprika	10 mL
¼ tsp	Chinese five-spice powder	1 mL
½ cup	sweet Thai chili sauce	125 mL
¼ cup	ketchup	60 mL
2 tbsp	fish sauce	30 mL

1. Place chicken thighs in slow cooker stoneware. In a bowl, combine garlic, paprika, five-spice powder, chili sauce, ketchup, fish sauce and 2 tbsp (30 mL) water. Pour evenly over chicken.

2. Cover and cook on Low for 5 to 6 hours or on High for 2½ to 3 hours, until juices run clear when chicken is pierced.

> **If you want to make your own Chinese five-spice powder, you'll need equal amounts of ground cinnamon, cloves, star anise, fennel seeds and Szechuan peppercorns. (You can substitute freshly ground black pepper for the Szechuan peppercorns.) Use a clean coffee grinder or a mortar and pestle to finely grind the spices together.**

Ginger Snow Peas and Peppers

Makes 6 servings

This quick, easy side dish is an excellent accompaniment to an Asian entrée.

8 oz	snow peas, trimmed	250 mL
2	bell peppers (any color), cut into ¾-inch (2 cm) strips	2
2 tbsp	rice vinegar	30 mL
1 tbsp	vegetable oil	15 mL
1 tsp	grated gingerroot	5 mL
	Salt and freshly ground black pepper	

1. Place a steamer basket in a saucepan filled with 1 inch (2.5 cm) water. Bring to a gentle boil. Add snow peas and bell peppers. Cover and cook for 2 to 4 minutes or until tender-crisp.

2. In a serving bowl, whisk together vinegar, oil and ginger. Add snow peas and peppers and toss to coat. Season to taste with salt and pepper. Serve immediately.

Chicken Sausage and Bean Casserole

Makes 6 to 8 servings

....

Warm up a cold winter night with this rustic, sage-infused sausage and bean casserole. It's especially good served with a crisp green salad, a crusty baguette and white wine.

Tips

Any white bean can be used in this recipe. If you're not a fan of chickpeas, try white kidney beans. For some added color, use red kidney beans.

For the wine, try a Sauvignon Blanc or Chardonnay.

- **4- to 6-quart slow cooker, stoneware greased**
- *Food processor*

½	crusty baguette, torn into pieces	½
¼ cup	olive oil, divided	60 mL
	Kosher salt and freshly ground black pepper	
⅓ cup	fresh sage leaves (about 25)	75 mL
4	cloves garlic, minced	4
1	large onion, finely chopped	1
1 lb	chicken or turkey sausage, casings removed	500 g
4 cups	canned or cooked chickpeas (see page 84), drained and rinsed	1 L
½ cup	dry white wine	125 mL

1. In food processor, pulse baguette pieces to very coarse crumbs. Add 2 tbsp (30 mL) of the oil and pulse briefly to moisten crumbs. Season with salt and pepper; set aside.

2. In a skillet, heat the remaining oil over medium-high heat. Sauté sage for 2 to 3 minutes or until crisp. Using a slotted spoon, transfer sage to a plate lined with paper towels and set aside.

3. Add garlic and onion to skillet; sauté for 5 to 7 minutes or until onion is tender and translucent. Add sausage and cook, breaking up sausage with the back of a wooden spoon, for 3 to 5 minutes or until no longer pink inside. Stir in chickpeas and wine. Transfer to prepared slow cooker stoneware. Sprinkle with reserved bread crumbs.

4. Cover and cook on Low for 6 to 8 hours or on High for 3 to 5 hours, until bubbling. Season to taste with salt and pepper. Before serving, crumble reserved sage leaves over top.

Buffalo Chicken and Potatoes

**Makes
6 servings**

This fun dish reminds me of my favorite bar food: chicken wings. Team it up with a plate of celery and carrot sticks and lots of cold beer, and you have a guaranteed party!

Tips

Look for precut raw chicken tenders in your local supermarket, so you can save chopping time when making this recipe.

Traditional Buffalo-style chicken wing sauce is composed of two ingredients: butter and a vinegar-based cayenne pepper hot sauce. It is readily available in the sauce and condiment aisle of the supermarket.

- • **4- to 5-quart slow cooker, stoneware greased**

1¼ lbs	boneless skinless chicken breasts (about 2 large), cut into 1-inch (2.5 cm) strips	625 g
⅓ cup	Buffalo wing sauce	75 mL
1	can (10 oz/284 mL) condensed cream of celery soup	1
6 cups	frozen hash brown potatoes, thawed	1.5 L
1 cup	ranch or blue cheese salad dressing	250 mL
½ cup	shredded Cheddar cheese	125 mL
½ cup	fine dry bread crumbs or crushed corn flakes cereal	125 mL
2 tbsp	butter, melted	30 mL
3	green onions, chopped	3

1. In a bowl, combine chicken and Buffalo wing sauce, stirring to coat chicken. Place on bottom of prepared slow cooker stoneware.

2. In a large bowl, combine soup, potatoes, dressing and cheese. Spoon over chicken.

3. In a small bowl, stir together bread crumbs and butter. Sprinkle evenly over chicken mixture.

4. Cover and cook on Low for 6 to 8 hours or on High for 3 to 4 hours, until potatoes are tender and chicken is no longer pink inside. Serve sprinkled with green onions.

Chicken in Orange Sesame Sauce

**Makes
4 servings**

This recipe is a fusion of two classic dishes, orange chicken and sesame chicken. Serve it with a crisp green vegetable, such as broccoli, on the side.

Tips

Broth (or stock) is one of the most indispensable pantry staples. Commercial broth cubes and powders are loaded with salt and just don't deliver the flavor of homemade stock or prepared broth. I like to keep 32-oz (1 L) Tetra Paks on hand, especially the sodium-reduced variety. They come in handy when you're making soups and stews.

The simplest way to toast sesame seeds is in a small dry skillet over medium heat. Cook, shaking the pan constantly, until the seeds are fragrant, about 3 minutes.

- **4- to 6-quart slow cooker**

2	oranges	2
1 tbsp	ground coriander	15 mL
½ tsp	cayenne pepper	2 mL
	Salt and freshly ground black pepper	
3 lbs	skinless bone-in chicken thighs or drumsticks	1.5 kg
2 tbsp	vegetable oil (approx.)	30 mL
1 tsp	sesame oil	5 mL
3	cloves garlic, minced	3
1 tbsp	minced gingerroot	15 mL
¼ tsp	hot pepper flakes	1 mL
½ cup	chicken broth	125 mL
3 tbsp	tamari or dark soy sauce	45 mL
2 tbsp	cornstarch	30 mL
2 tbsp	cold water	30 mL
3	green onions, thinly sliced	3
½	red bell pepper, thinly sliced	½
1 cup	snow peas, trimmed	250 mL
	Hot cooked rice noodles or steamed rice	
2 tbsp	toasted sesame seeds	30 mL

1. Grate zest from oranges and set aside. Using a paring knife, remove peel and all of the pith from each orange, discarding peel and pith. Cut each orange into ¼-inch (0.5 cm) slices and set aside.

2. In a bowl, combine coriander, cayenne, ½ tsp (2 mL) salt and ¼ tsp (1 mL) black pepper. Rub all over chicken.

3. In a large nonstick skillet, heat half the vegetable oil and the sesame oil over medium-high heat. Cook chicken in batches, adding more oil as needed, for 2 to 3 minutes per side or until browned all over. Using a slotted spoon, transfer to slow cooker stoneware.

4. Add garlic, ginger and hot pepper flakes to skillet; sauté for 1 to 2 minutes. Stir in broth and tamari; increase heat to high and cook for 1 minute. Pour over chicken. Sprinkle with 1 tsp (5 mL) of the reserved orange zest and arrange orange slices on top.

5. Cover and cook on Low for 5 to 6 hours or on High for 2½ to 3 hours, until juices run clear when chicken is pierced.

6. In a small bowl, whisk together cornstarch and cold water. Stir into stoneware, along with green onions, red pepper and snow peas. Cover and cook on High for 10 to 15 minutes or until sauce is thickened. Season to taste with salt and pepper.

7. Arrange noodles on a platter. Place chicken on noodles and spoon vegetables and sauce over top. Sprinkle with the remaining orange zest and sesame seeds.

> **Tamari is similar to soy sauce, but is thicker in consistency and darker in color. It has a distinctly mellow flavor and is often used as a condiment or dipping sauce. It can be found in the Asian foods aisle of the supermarket or in an Asian market.**

Santa Fe Turkey Breast

**Makes
8 servings**

This simple turkey roast evokes the flavors of the American Southwest. The chipotle pepper gives the salsa a nice smoky taste. It is best to use a chunky salsa, to thicken the sauce. For an authentic flair, serve with Mexican Corn (see recipe, below) on the side.

- **Minimum 4-quart slow cooker**

1	bone-in skin-on turkey breast (about 4 lbs/2 kg)	1
1 cup	thick and chunky salsa	250 mL
2 tbsp	liquid honey	30 mL
1 tbsp	chopped chipotle pepper in adobo sauce	15 mL
2 tbsp	cornstarch	30 mL
2 tbsp	cold water	30 mL

1. Place turkey, bone side down, in prepared slow cooker stoneware. In a small bowl, combine salsa, honey and chipotle pepper. Pour over turkey.

2. Cover and cook on Low for 6 to 8 hours or until a meat thermometer inserted in the thickest part of the breast registers 170°F (77°C). Using tongs, remove turkey from stoneware and let stand for 10 minutes before carving.

3. Meanwhile, in a small bowl, whisk together cornstarch and cold water. Stir into liquid in stoneware. Cover and cook on High for 10 to 15 minutes or until liquid is thickened.

4. Remove skin from turkey and discard. Slice turkey and arrange on a heated platter. Drizzle some of the gravy over turkey and serve the rest in a warmed gravy boat.

Mexican Corn

**Makes 4 to
6 servings**

This colorful side dish exhibits bold Southwestern flavors. It is delicious served hot, but makes a great picnic or barbecue side dish served at room temperature.

2 tbsp	butter	30 mL
1	onion, finely chopped	1
1	red bell pepper, finely chopped	1
1	jalapeño pepper, seeded and finely chopped	1
2 cups	frozen corn kernels, thawed	500 mL
	Salt and freshly ground black pepper	
1 tbsp	chopped fresh cilantro (optional)	15 mL

1. In a skillet, melt butter over medium-low heat. Sauté onion, red pepper, jalapeño and corn for 6 to 8 minutes or until vegetables are tender. Season to taste with salt and pepper. Serve garnished with cilantro (if using).

Turkey Osso Buco

**Makes
6 servings**

. . . .

Although classic Italian osso buco is made with veal shanks, this slow cooker version is tasty proof that turkey thighs can be a first-rate substitute.

Tips

This comforting meal could also be served over mashed potatoes instead of pasta.

Look for turkey parts after holidays, such as Thanksgiving and Christmas, when they can be purchased more economically. Freeze them to have on hand for dishes like this one.

● **Minimum 5-quart slow cooker**

2 tbsp	all-purpose flour	30 mL
1/2 tsp	salt	2 mL
1/4 tsp	freshly ground black pepper	1 mL
3 lbs	turkey thighs, skin removed	1.5 kg
2 tbsp	olive oil (approx.)	30 mL
6	cloves garlic, minced	6
3	carrots, chopped	3
3	stalks celery, chopped	3
1	onion, finely chopped	1
1	can (7 1/2 oz/213 mL) tomato sauce	1
1/2 cup	dry white wine	125 mL
1/4 cup	chicken broth	60 mL
1 tsp	grated lemon zest	5 mL
1 tsp	dried thyme	5 mL
3 cups	hot cooked pasta, such as penne or farfalle	750 mL

1. In a bowl, combine flour, salt and pepper. Sprinkle over turkey, coating evenly.

2. In a large skillet, heat half the oil over medium-high heat. Cook turkey in batches, adding more oil as needed, for 3 to 4 minutes per side or until browned all over. Remove from heat.

3. In slow cooker stoneware, combine garlic, carrots, celery and onion. Arrange turkey on top.

4. In a bowl, combine tomato sauce, wine, broth, lemon zest and thyme. Pour over turkey.

5. Cover and cook on Low for 6 to 8 hours or on High for 3 to 4 hours, until meat is falling off the bones. Using a slotted spoon, transfer turkey to a cutting board. Remove meat from bones and cut into large chunks. (Discard bones.)

6. Stir pasta into liquid in stoneware. Using a slotted spoon, spoon pasta onto individual serving plates and top with turkey. Ladle sauce over top.

Turkey Bolognese with Spaghetti Squash

Makes 6 to 8 servings

Now here's a twist: a mildly flavored Bolognese sauce served over spaghetti squash instead of pasta.

Tips

Choose a squash that is heavy for its size and has a hard, firm, deep-colored rind free of any blemishes or moldy spots.

To cook squash, halve it lengthwise and scoop out the seeds. Place cut side down on a rimmed baking sheet and bake in a 350°F (180°C) oven for 55 to 60 minutes or until strands of flesh separate easily when raked with a fork. Let cool slightly, then use a fork to rake the flesh into spaghetti-like strands.

To save time getting this meal on the table, cook the squash the day before and refrigerate the whole halves until ready to use. Reheat it gently in the microwave on Medium (50%) power for 2 minutes or in a 350°F (180°C) oven for 10 to 12 minutes or until warmed through. Rake into strands before serving.

- **4- to 5-quart slow cooker**

2 tbsp	butter	30 mL
2 tbsp	olive oil	30 mL
1	onion, finely chopped	1
1	small carrot, finely chopped	1
1	stalk celery, finely chopped	1
1½ lbs	lean ground turkey	750 g
4 oz	thickly sliced pancetta, finely chopped	125 g
	Salt and freshly ground black pepper	
½ cup	dry white wine	125 mL
1	can (28 oz/796 mL) crushed tomatoes	1
½ cup	chicken broth	125 mL
¼ cup	hot evaporated milk or heavy or whipping (35%) cream	60 mL
	Salt and freshly ground black pepper	
1	spaghetti squash (2 to 3 lbs/1 to 1.5 kg), cooked (see tips, at left)	1

1. In a large skillet, heat butter and oil over medium-high heat. Sauté onion, carrot and celery for 5 to 7 minutes or until onion is tender and translucent. Add turkey and pancetta; cook, breaking up turkey with the back of a wooden spoon, for 3 to 5 minutes or until turkey is no longer pink. Add wine and cook, stirring, for 3 to 5 minutes or until wine has almost evaporated. Transfer to slow cooker stoneware. Stir in tomatoes and broth.

2. Cover and cook on Low for 6 to 8 hours or on High for 3 to 4 hours, until bubbling. Just before serving, stir in evaporated milk. Season to taste with salt and pepper. Serve over spaghetti squash.

> **Pancetta is an Italian bacon that is cured with salt and spices but is not smoked. It is sold in a sausage-like roll in the deli department of the supermarket. Tightly wrapped, it can be stored in the refrigerator for up to 3 weeks or frozen for up to 6 months.**

Turkey and Couscous Stuffed Peppers

**Makes
4 servings**

Do you like stuffed peppers? Get a head start on dinner with this fresh take on a slow-simmered meal. Make a batch when peppers are in season. If there are just two of you, cook all 4 peppers, and you'll have a second meal ready to go — these peppers reheat surprisingly well.

Tip

Use an apple corer to cut a small hole in the bottom of each pepper. This will allow moisture and steam to penetrate, promoting even cooking.

- **4- to 5-quart slow cooker**

4	large red or green bell peppers	4
8 oz	lean ground turkey	250 g
½ cup	chopped onion	125 mL
1	clove garlic, finely chopped	1
1	can (14 oz/398 mL) tomato sauce	1
½ tsp	ground cumin	2 mL
¼ tsp	ground cinnamon	1 mL
¼ tsp	salt	1 mL
⅛ tsp	cayenne pepper	0.5 mL
⅔ cup	couscous	150 mL
	Crumbled feta or goat cheese (optional)	
	Pine nuts (optional)	
	Chopped fresh cilantro (optional)	

1. Cut around stem on each bell pepper to remove stem. Scoop out seeds and membranes. Rinse peppers.

2. In a nonstick skillet, cook turkey, onion and garlic over medium-high heat, breaking up turkey with the back of a wooden spoon, for about 5 minutes or until turkey is no longer pink. Drain off any liquid. Stir in tomato sauce, cumin, cinnamon, salt and cayenne. Stir in couscous.

3. Spoon turkey mixture into peppers, dividing evenly. Pour ½ cup (125 mL) water into slow cooker stoneware. Set peppers upright in water.

4. Cover and cook on Low for 5 to 7 hours or until peppers are tender. Using a spatula or a large serving spoon, gently remove peppers to a serving dish. Discard cooking liquid.

5. Serve stuffed peppers sprinkled with cheese, pine nuts and cilantro (if using).

Turkey and Pepper Cheese Steak Heroes

Makes 6 servings

Here's an easy-to-make sandwich the whole family will enjoy. Add a tossed Caesar salad and your dinner is done!

Tip

Any prepared oil and vinegar salad dressing can be used in this recipe. For extra flavor, try Greek dressing or sun-dried tomato dressing.

- **3- to 5-quart slow cooker**

3 lbs	turkey thighs, skin removed	1.5 kg
1/3 cup	Italian salad dressing	75 mL
1 tbsp	vegetable oil	15 mL
1	red bell pepper, cut into thin strips	1
1	yellow bell pepper, cut into thin strips	1
1	onion, sliced	1
6	kaiser rolls, split	6
1/2 cup	herb and garlic spreadable cream cheese	125 mL

1. Place turkey in slow cooker stoneware. Pour dressing over turkey.

2. Cover and cook on Low for 6 to 8 hours or on High for 3 to 4 hours, until turkey is falling off the bones.

3. Using a slotted spoon, transfer turkey to a cutting board. Using two forks, pull meat off bones in shreds and discard bones. Return meat to sauce in slow cooker to keep warm. (Turkey mixture will hold on Low, with occasional stirring, for up to 2 hours.)

4. In a skillet, heat oil over medium-high heat. Sauté red pepper, yellow pepper and onion for 6 to 8 minutes or until softened.

5. Spread bottom half of each roll with 1 tbsp (15 mL) of the cream cheese, then top with turkey mixture and pepper mixture. Cover with top half.

Turkey and Cranberry Cobbler

Makes 6 to 8 servings

Some dishes evoke the feeling of home. This old-fashioned favorite has been given an updated twist with the addition of dried cranberries.

Tips

To prepare mushrooms, wipe them with a damp paper towel. Don't rinse or soak them, or they'll absorb water and turn mushy when cooked.

Puff pastry package sizes vary between brands, ranging from 14 to 18 oz (397 to 511 g). If your package is slightly larger or smaller, half a package will still work just fine for this recipe.

It's so easy to use frozen puff pastry dough, and it looks decadently impressive on top of this stew, but you can also serve this stew in puff pastry shells. Bake shells according to package directions and serve stew mixture spooned into shells.

- **4- to 6-quart slow cooker**
- *Large baking sheet*

⅓ cup	all-purpose flour	75 mL
1 tsp	ground dried sage	5 mL
1 tsp	salt	5 mL
¼ tsp	freshly ground black pepper	1 mL
2½ lbs	boneless skinless turkey thighs, cut into 1-inch (2.5 cm) cubes	1.25 kg
2 tbsp	vegetable oil (approx.)	30 mL
8	mushrooms, quartered	8
2	onions, chopped	2
2	carrots, diced	2
2	stalks celery, finely chopped	2
1 tsp	dried thyme	5 mL
1½ cups	chicken broth	375 mL
⅓ cup	dried cranberries	75 mL
1 cup	frozen peas, thawed	250 mL
1	sheet frozen puff pastry (half a 14 oz/397 g package), thawed (see tips, at left)	1

1. In a bowl or a heavy plastic bag, combine flour, sage, salt and pepper. In batches, dredge turkey in flour mixture, shaking off any excess. (Once all the turkey is coated, reserve the remaining flour mixture.)

2. In a large skillet, heat half the oil over medium-high heat. Cook turkey in batches, adding more oil as needed, for 2 to 3 minutes or until browned all over. Using a slotted spoon, transfer to slow cooker stoneware.

3. Add mushrooms, onions, carrots, celery and thyme to skillet; sauté for 5 minutes or until vegetables are tender. Stir in reserved flour mixture until vegetables are coated. Reduce heat to medium. Stir in broth and bring to a boil, stirring and scraping up any brown bits from pan. Pour over turkey. Stir in cranberries.

4. Cover and cook on Low for 6 to 8 hours or on High for 3 to 4 hours, until turkey is tender.

continued on page 138…

5. Stir in peas. Cover and cook on High for 10 to 15 minutes or until heated through.

6. Meanwhile, preheat oven to 375°F (190°C). On a lightly floured surface, roll out pastry to a 15- by 10-inch (38 by 25 cm) rectangle. Cut into 6 or 8 squares (or use a large, round cookie cutter to cut circles) and place at least $\frac{1}{2}$ inch (1 cm) apart on baking sheet.

7. Bake pastry pieces for 15 to 20 minutes or until puffed and golden brown.

8. Ladle cobbler into serving bowls and top each with a pastry crust. Serve immediately.

Turkey, Bacon and Avocado Wraps

Makes 8 wraps

My friend Lisa Gray, who lived in New Zealand for many years, says this is one of the country's most popular sandwich choices. They like to call it a BLAT. In this version, the turkey is cooked slowly in the slow cooker, then shredded and topped with bacon and avocado. Yum! This mixture makes an excellent panini as well.

Tip

If time is a concern, you can place the turkey in the stoneware without browning it first. Cook the bacon separately and layer it on each tortilla just before serving.

- **4- to 6-quart slow cooker**

4	slices bacon, cut into ½-inch (1 cm) pieces	4
2 lbs	turkey drumsticks or thighs, skin removed	1 kg
¾ cup	barbecue sauce	175 mL
2 tbsp	taco seasoning mix	30 mL
8	10-inch (25 cm) flour tortillas	8
1	ripe avocado, mashed	1
2 cups	shredded lettuce	500 mL
½ cup	roasted red bell peppers, drained and chopped	125 mL

1. In a nonstick skillet, cook bacon over medium heat, stirring occasionally, for 4 to 6 minutes or until almost crisp. Add turkey and cook for 3 to 4 minutes per side or until browned all over. Using a slotted spoon or tongs, transfer turkey and bacon to slow cooker stoneware. Discard fat from pan.

2. In a glass measuring cup, combine barbecue sauce and taco seasoning. Pour over turkey and bacon.

3. Cover and cook on Low for 6 to 8 hours or on High for 3 to 4 hours, until turkey is falling off the bones.

4. Using a slotted spoon, transfer turkey to a cutting board. Using two forks, pull meat off bones in shreds and discard bones. Return meat to sauce in slow cooker to keep warm. (Turkey mixture will hold on Low, with occasional stirring, for up to 2 hours.)

5. Preheat oven to 350°F (180°C). Wrap a stack of tortillas in foil and heat for 10 minutes.

6. Spread each tortilla with avocado. Layer lettuce, turkey mixture and peppers on top. Drizzle with sauce, if desired. Fold right side of tortilla over filling. Fold bottom of tortilla up, then fold left side over and continue rolling until the filling is enclosed.

Low and Slow Turkey Joes

Makes 4 to 6 servings

Everyone will love this easy turkey version of sloppy Joes.

Tips

Because ground turkey has such a mild flavor, I often find I need to add extra seasoning to it.

Leftover turkey mixture can be used to top baked potatoes or nachos, for a second-day supper rescue!

- **4- to 5-quart slow cooker**

1 tbsp	vegetable oil	15 mL
1½ lbs	lean ground turkey	750 g
1	small onion, finely chopped	1
1	stalk celery, finely chopped	1
1	can (14 oz/398 mL) diced tomatoes	1
2 tbsp	packed brown sugar	30 mL
1½ tsp	ground cumin	7 mL
1 tsp	chili powder	5 mL
½ tsp	salt	2 mL
3 tbsp	Worcestershire sauce	45 mL
6	whole wheat hamburger buns, split and toasted	6
1 cup	shredded mozzarella or provolone cheese	250 mL
1 cup	shredded carrots	250 mL

1. In a large nonstick skillet, heat oil over medium-high heat. Cook turkey, breaking up with the back of a wooden spoon, for 5 minutes or until no longer pink. Using a slotted spoon, transfer to slow cooker stoneware.

2. Stir in onion, celery, tomatoes, brown sugar, cumin, chili powder, salt and Worcestershire sauce.

3. Cover and cook on Low for 6 to 8 hours or on High for 3 to 4 hours, until bubbling.

4. Spoon turkey mixture over bottom halves of buns. Top with mozzarella and carrot. Cover with top halves.

Beef and Veal

Braised Pot Roast with Caramelized Vegetables

Makes 6 to 8 servings

Use a full-bodied red wine, such as a Shiraz or Bordeaux, to bring out the richest flavor of the gravy in this pot roast. The red wine permeates the meat, adding a robust flavor. You can vary the vegetables, choosing seasonal produce from your local farmer's market. Think about the cooking time, and select vegetables that require the same amount of cooking, so they can all go into the oven at the same time.

Tips

Once the roast is in the slow cooker, it's a good idea to turn it halfway through the cooking time. That way, both sides will evenly braise in the cooking liquid.

You can substitute 1 sprig of fresh rosemary for the dried.

- **Minimum 4-quart slow cooker**
- *Rimmed baking sheet, lined with parchment paper*

3	carrots	3
1/3 cup	all-purpose flour	75 mL
	Salt and freshly ground black pepper	
1	boneless beef cross rib, blade, chuck or shoulder pot roast (about 4 lbs/2 kg)	1
3 tbsp	olive oil, divided	45 mL
1 cup	red wine	250 mL
1 cup	beef broth	250 mL
2 tbsp	tomato paste	30 mL
1 tsp	dried rosemary	5 mL
1	bay leaf	1
8	cloves garlic, smashed	8
2	parsnips, cut into 1-inch (2.5 cm) chunks	2
2	sweet potatoes, cut into 1-inch (2.5 cm) chunks	2
1	celery root, peeled and cut into 1-inch (2.5 cm) chunks	1
1	onion, cut into wedges	1
1	stalk celery, chopped	1
2 tbsp	cold water	30 mL

1. Chop 1 of the carrots into 3 pieces and place in slow cooker stoneware. Cut the remaining carrots into 1-inch (2.5 cm) chunks and set aside.

2. In a bowl, combine flour, 1 tsp (5 mL) salt and 1/2 tsp (2 mL) pepper. Pat roast dry with paper towels and coat all over with flour mixture. Reserve the remaining flour mixture.

3. In a large skillet, heat 2 tbsp (30 mL) of the oil over medium-high heat. Cook roast, turning with two wooden spoons, for 7 to 10 minutes or until browned all over. Transfer to stoneware.

4. Add wine to skillet and bring to a boil, scraping up any brown bits from pan. Stir in broth, tomato paste, rosemary and bay leaf. Pour into stoneware.

5. Cover and cook on Low for 8 to 12 hours or on High for 4 to 6 hours, until roast is fork-tender.

continued on page 146…

Variation

This is a perfect autumn dish. Feel free to use your favorite fall vegetable combination. Be inspired by your local farmer's market, your garden or what you have at home. Other choices could include cubed zucchini, halved small red new potatoes, cubed acorn or butternut squash and sweet Vidalia or red onions.

6. During the last hour of cooking time, preheat oven to 425°F (220°C). On prepared baking sheet, combine reserved carrot chunks, garlic, parsnips, sweet potatoes, celery root, onion and celery. Toss with the remaining oil and season to taste with salt and pepper; spread into a single layer. Roast for 40 minutes, turning once, until vegetables are tender.

7. Transfer beef to a cutting board and tent with foil to keep warm. Strain braising liquid from stoneware into a saucepan. Discard solids.

8. In a bowl, whisk together reserved flour mixture and cold water until a smooth paste forms. Whisk into braising liquid and bring to a boil over medium-high heat. Reduce heat and simmer, stirring often, for about 10 minutes or until liquid is thickened.

9. Slice beef across the grain into 1/2-inch (1 cm) slices. Arrange on a warmed platter, with roasted vegetables alongside. Drizzle beef with some of the gravy and serve the rest in a warmed gravy boat.

Slow Cooker Caramelized Onions

In the stoneware of a 4- to 6-quart slow cooker, toss together 4 large onions, thinly sliced, and 2 tbsp (30 mL) olive oil. Cover and cook on High for 6 to 8 hours, stirring occasionally. Store in an airtight container in the refrigerator for up to 2 weeks.

Braised Brisket with Cranberries

Makes 6 to 8 servings

This festive dish is perfect for the holidays. The brilliant cranberries stand out like jewels, and there is plenty of juice to spoon over creamy mashed potatoes. Make sure you buy fresh brisket (not corned beef). An inside round roast would also work well.

Tips

If you prefer thicker gravy, keep the cooked brisket warm and pour the cooking liquid into a saucepan. Measure 2 tbsp (30 mL) all-purpose flour into a small bowl and add ¼ cup (60 mL) of the cooking liquid, 2 tbsp (30 mL) at a time, stirring to blend thoroughly after each addition. Stir flour mixture into saucepan and cook over medium heat, stirring, until thickened.

If you only have a smaller (4-quart) slow cooker, cut the brisket in half and lay one half on top of the other. It is a good idea to flip the two pieces halfway through the cooking time to ensure even braising in the cooking liquid.

• **Minimum 4-quart slow cooker**

1	double beef brisket (4 to 5 lbs/2 to 2.5 kg), trimmed	1
3 tbsp	all-purpose flour	45 mL
	Salt and freshly ground black pepper	
1 cup	beef broth	250 mL
1 cup	dry red wine, such as Cabernet Sauvignon	250 mL
2 tbsp	light (fancy) molasses	30 mL
24	pearl onions, peeled (see tip, page 182)	24
2 cups	fresh or frozen cranberries, thawed if frozen	500 mL
1	bay leaf	1

1. Rub brisket all over with flour and season with salt and pepper. Place in slow cooker stoneware.

2. In a bowl, combine broth, wine, molasses and ½ cup (125 mL) water. Pour over brisket. Add onions, cranberries and bay leaf.

3. Cover and cook on Low for 10 to 12 hours or on High for 5 to 6 hours, until brisket is very fork-tender. Transfer brisket to a cutting board, tent with foil and let stand for 10 minutes.

4. Slice brisket very thinly across the grain and arrange on a warmed platter. Remove bay leaf from sauce and skim off as much fat as possible. Pour sauce over brisket or serve separately in a gravy boat.

Pot Roast with Dill Sauce

Makes 4 to 6 servings

Beef pot roast is a versatile and economical dish. Thanks to the addition of a creamy dill sauce, this version has a Danish influence. Serve it with egg noodles, which pair well with the dill sauce. If you like, sprinkle the finished dish with minced fresh dill.

Tips

Homemade beef broth is best, but a 10-oz (284 mL) can of condensed beef broth, plus a can of water, will make enough broth for this recipe. Ready-to-use broth in convenient Tetra-Paks is also a handy ingredient and doesn't need to be diluted. Avoid using cubes and powders, which tend to be very salty.

A well-marbled beef cross rib or chuck pot roast is a good choice. The marbling produces a very tender result.

• **Minimum 4-quart slow cooker**

4 tbsp	all-purpose flour, divided	60 mL
1 tsp	salt	5 mL
¼ tsp	freshly ground white pepper	1 mL
1	boneless beef cross rib, blade, chuck or shoulder pot roast (about 2 lbs/1 kg)	1
2 tbsp	vegetable oil	30 mL
4	cloves garlic, finely chopped	4
½ tsp	dried dillweed	2 mL
1 cup	beef broth	250 mL
1 tbsp	Dijon mustard	15 mL
4	Yukon Gold potatoes, cut into 1-inch (2.5 cm) cubes	4
1	large onion, cut into 12 wedges	1
1	bag (12 oz/340 g) baby carrots	1
½ tsp	lemon pepper	2 mL
1 tsp	dried dillweed (or 1 tbsp/15 mL fresh dill)	5 mL
1 cup	regular or light sour cream	250 mL

1. In a bowl or a large sealable plastic bag, combine 2 tbsp (30 mL) of the flour, salt and white pepper. Dredge roast in flour mixture, turning to coat evenly. Discard any excess flour mixture.

2. In a large skillet, heat oil over medium heat. Cook roast, turning with two wooden spoons, for 7 to 10 minutes or until browned all over. Transfer to slow cooker stoneware.

3. In a small bowl, combine garlic, dill, broth and mustard. Pour over roast. Arrange potatoes, onion and carrots around roast. Sprinkle with lemon pepper.

4. Cover and cook on Low for 8 to 10 hours or on High for 4 to 6 hours, until roast and vegetables are fork-tender. Transfer roast to a cutting board and vegetables to a warmed platter and cover to keep warm.

5. In a small bowl, whisk together the remaining flour, dill and 2 tbsp (30 mL) water until smooth. Spoon off any fat from liquid in slow cooker. Pour liquid into a saucepan and bring to a boil over medium-high heat. Stir in flour mixture and cook, stirring constantly, for 2 to 3 minutes or until thickened. Remove from heat and stir in sour cream.

6. Slice meat across the grain and pour sauce over beef and vegetables.

BBQ Pot Roast Sandwiches

Makes 4 to 6 servings

This recipe, featuring the popular sweet and spicy flavor combination, makes the perfect dish for a potluck. Cook the meat in advance, then shred it, return it to the slow cooker and let people help themselves. I recommend it served on thick kaiser rolls, along with flavored mayonnaise.

Tip

To make a flavored mayonnaise for these sandwiches, combine ½ cup (125 mL) mayonnaise and 1 tbsp (15 mL) Dijon mustard or horseradish. You can raid your pantry for other ingredients, such as curry powder, mango chutney, paprika or freshly chopped garlic, to make your own flavor combinations. Double or triple the amounts as needed.

- **Minimum 4-quart slow cooker**

2	cloves garlic, minced	2
1 tbsp	grated gingerroot	15 mL
1 tbsp	chili powder	15 mL
½ tsp	ground cumin	2 mL
¼ tsp	hot pepper flakes	1 mL
¾ cup	root beer	175 mL
⅓ cup	hickory-flavored barbecue sauce	75 mL
2 tbsp	tomato paste	30 mL
1 tbsp	freshly squeezed lemon juice	15 mL
2 tsp	Worcestershire sauce	10 mL
1	beef sirloin tip roast (3 to 3½ lbs/ 1.5 to 1.75 kg)	1
	Salt and freshly ground black pepper	
2 tsp	olive oil	10 mL
1	onion, cut into wedges	1
2 tbsp	cornstarch	30 mL
2 tbsp	cold water	30 mL
4 to 6	crusty kaiser rolls, split and warmed	4 to 6

1. In a saucepan, whisk together garlic, ginger, chili powder, cumin, hot pepper flakes, root beer, barbecue sauce, tomato paste, lemon juice and Worcestershire sauce. Bring to a boil over medium-high heat. Reduce heat and simmer gently, stirring, for 5 minutes. Remove from heat.

2. Pat roast dry with paper towels and sprinkle lightly with salt and pepper. In a large skillet, heat oil over medium-high heat. Cook roast, turning with two wooden spoons, for 7 to 10 minutes or until browned all over. Transfer to slow cooker stoneware. Arrange onion around roast. Pour sauce over top.

3. Cover and cook on Low for 8 to 10 hours or on High for 4 to 6 hours, until roast is fork-tender. Transfer roast to a cutting board and, using a slotted spoon, transfer onion to a bowl.

4. Pour cooking liquid from stoneware into a saucepan and skim off as much fat as possible. In a small bowl, whisk together cornstarch and water until smooth. Whisk into saucepan and bring to a boil over high heat, whisking constantly, until liquid is slightly thickened.

5. Thinly slice roast across the grain (it may be so tender that it falls apart). Top warm kaisers with sliced meat and reserved onions; spoon sauce over top.

Sheila's Mother's Coffee Pot Roast

Makes 8 to 10 servings

This recipe came to me from my friend Sheila McKee-Protopapas, who is a biology professor. She inherited the recipe from her mother, and it's a perfect example of how a recipe evolves, created with pride and joy by one generation after another. Sheila's family has made it for years. She says the flavor is out of this world, and I have to agree!

Tips

Adding vinegar, apple juice or wine to a pot roast helps tenderize the meat while it simmers.

Slow cooking helps tenderize less expensive cuts of meat. Pot roast benefits from long, slow cooking on Low, but if you are short of time you can use the High setting — you'll still create fork-tender meat.

• **Minimum 4-quart slow cooker**

1	boneless beef cross rib, blade, chuck or shoulder pot roast (about 4 lbs/2 kg)	1
1	head garlic, cloves separated (or 1 onion, cut into wedges)	1
1 cup	white or cider vinegar	250 mL
2 tbsp	vegetable oil	30 mL
2 cups	strong brewed coffee	500 mL
2 tbsp	gin or whisky (optional)	30 mL

1. Using the tip of a sharp knife, slit roast all over and insert garlic cloves (or onion wedges). Place roast in a bowl or a large sealable plastic bag and pour vinegar into slits. Cover bowl or seal bag and refrigerate for at least 24 hours or up to 48 hours. Drain off vinegar and discard.

2. In a large skillet, heat oil over medium-high heat. Cook roast, turning with two wooden spoons, for 7 to 10 minutes or until browned all over. Transfer to slow cooker stoneware.

3. Add coffee, gin (if using) and 2 cups (500 mL) water to skillet and stir to scrape up any brown bits from pan. Pour into stoneware.

4. Cover and cook on Low for 8 to 10 hours or on High for 4 to 6 hours, until roast is fork-tender. Transfer roast to a cutting board, tent with foil and let stand for 10 minutes.

5. Skim fat from pan juices. Slice meat across the grain and serve drizzled with juices.

Mexican Brisket

Makes 6 to 8 servings

The brisket is a large, fatty cut of meat from the front of the steer. The slow cooker is the ideal way to cook it, leading to very tender meat. Mexican flavors add heat and give traditional brisket a new twist. Serve with mashed potatoes sprinkled with shredded Cheddar and minced green onions for a Tex-Mex meal.

Tips

If you have leftovers, shred the meat to use for taco filling. Serve it with the traditional taco condiments: salsa, sour cream, shredded cheese and guacamole. You've got two meals!

If you halve this recipe, reduce the cooking time to about 6 hours on Low or 3 hours on High.

Variation

Replace the brisket with a boneless cross rib, blade, chuck or shoulder pot roast (2½ to 3 lbs/1.25 to 1.5 kg). Prepare as directed at right. Cook on Low for 8 to 12 hours or on High for 4 to 6 hours, until fork-tender.

● **Minimum 5-quart slow cooker**

1	double beef brisket (4 to 5 lbs/ 2 to 2.5 kg), trimmed	1
	Freshly ground black pepper	
1 tbsp	vegetable oil	15 mL
4	cloves garlic, minced	4
1	onion, thinly sliced	1
1	can (28 oz/796 mL) diced tomatoes	1
1 tbsp	dried oregano	15 mL
1 tbsp	chili powder	15 mL
1 tbsp	packed brown sugar	15 mL
1 tsp	ground cumin	5 mL
1 tsp	dried thyme	5 mL
1 tbsp	red wine vinegar	15 mL
2 tsp	finely chopped chipotle pepper in adobo sauce	10 mL
2 tbsp	cornstarch	30 mL
2 tbsp	cold water	30 mL
2	green onions, sliced	2

1. If necessary, cut brisket in half to fit slow cooker stoneware. Generously sprinkle pepper all over brisket. In a large skillet, heat oil over medium-high heat. Cook brisket, one piece at a time if necessary, turning with two wooden spoons, for 7 to 10 minutes or until browned all over. Transfer to stoneware.

2. In a bowl, combine garlic, onion, tomatoes, oregano, chili powder, brown sugar, cumin, thyme, vinegar and chipotle pepper. Pour over brisket.

3. Cover and cook on Low for 10 to 12 hours or on High for 5 to 6 hours, until brisket is fork-tender. Transfer brisket to a cutting board, tent with foil and let stand for 10 minutes.

4. Skim off as much fat as possible from cooking liquid and transfer to a saucepan. In a small bowl, whisk together cornstarch and water. Add to saucepan and bring to a boil over high heat, whisking constantly, until liquid is slightly thickened.

5. Slice brisket very thinly across the grain. Spoon some of the sauce onto a warmed platter. Arrange meat on top. Sprinkle with green onions and drizzle with the remaining sauce.

Steak with Mushrooms and Mustard

Makes 4 servings

Steak and mushrooms share a natural affinity. I've given this pairing a contemporary touch by using wild mushrooms. This dish tastes great with polenta or fresh egg noodles.

Tips

Feel free to use your favorite variety of Dijon mustard, such as Provençal, red wine or peppercorn.

Slow cooking helps tenderize less expensive cuts of meat. Braising steak benefits from long, slow cooking on Low, but if you are short of time, count on 6 hours on High to produce fork-tender meat.

Make Ahead

This dish can be assembled up to 24 hours in advance. Prepare through step 2, cover and refrigerate. The next day, place stoneware in slow cooker and proceed with step 3.

- **4- to 6-quart slow cooker**

1	boneless beef blade, shoulder or inside round steak (about 1½ lbs/750 g)	1
1 tbsp	all-purpose flour	15 mL
4 oz	cremini or portobello mushroom caps, coarsely chopped	125 g
4	shallots or small onions, halved	4
3	cloves garlic, thinly sliced, divided	3
1	bay leaf	1
½ tsp	dried thyme	2 mL
1 cup	beef broth	250 mL
3 tbsp	Dijon mustard	45 mL
2 tbsp	brandy or beef broth	30 mL
2 tbsp	butter	30 mL
4 oz	oyster or button mushrooms, sliced	125 g
4 oz	shiitake mushroom caps, sliced	125 g
	Salt and freshly ground black pepper	
¼ cup	crumbled goat cheese (optional)	60 mL

1. Trim steak and cut into 4 pieces. Coat both sides of each piece with flour and place in slow cooker stoneware. Sprinkle cremini mushrooms, shallots, two-thirds of the garlic, bay leaf and thyme over beef.

2. In a bowl, whisk together broth, mustard and brandy. Pour over beef and vegetables.

3. Cover and cook on Low for 8 to 10 hours or on High for 4 to 5 hours, until steak is fork-tender.

4. Just before serving, in a large nonstick skillet, melt butter over medium-high heat. Sauté oyster mushrooms, shiitake mushrooms, the remaining garlic and salt and pepper to taste for 3 to 5 minutes or until mushrooms are softened.

5. Using a slotted spoon, transfer steak and vegetables to a warmed platter. Discard bay leaf. If using goat cheese, stir into cooking liquid until melted. Season sauce to taste with salt and pepper, then spoon over steak. Top with sautéed mushrooms.

Slow Cooker Steak with Creamy Red Wine Gravy

Makes 4 to 6 servings

For best results in this recipe, use a 4- to 6-quart oval slow cooker to ensure that the steak is completely covered with sauce. Serve it with steamed broccoli and lots of crusty baguette slices to soak up the gravy. The next day, you can use leftovers to make open-faced sandwiches. Toast bread or baguette slices, then butter them, pile with steak and drizzle with gravy.

Tips

You will need a large oval slow cooker to cook the steak in one piece. When placed in the stoneware, the meat may extend up the sides, but it will shrink as it cooks. If you are using a smaller slow cooker, cut the steak in half.

You can also use portobello mushrooms in this recipe. You'll need enough to cover the steak; 3 larger mushrooms may be enough.

• **Minimum 4-quart slow cooker (preferably oval)**

1	beef flank steak (1½ to 2 lbs/ 750 g to 1 kg), trimmed	1
	Salt and freshly ground black pepper	
2 tbsp	all-purpose flour	30 mL
12	brown mushrooms, such as cremini or shiitake, stems removed	12
6	green onions, white parts only, thinly sliced	6
4	cloves garlic, minced	4
1 tsp	dried Italian seasoning	5 mL
¼ cup	red wine	60 mL
1	can (10 oz/284 mL) condensed cream of mushroom soup (preferably reduced-sodium)	1

1. Season steak with salt and pepper and coat each side evenly with flour. Transfer to slow cooker stoneware. Arrange mushrooms and green onions on top. Sprinkle with garlic, Italian seasoning and 1 tsp (5 mL) pepper.

2. In a bowl, combine wine, soup and 2 tbsp (30 mL) water. Pour over steak and vegetables.

3. Cover and cook on Low for 8 to 10 hours or on High for 4 to 5 hours, until steak is fork-tender. Transfer steak to a cutting board and mushrooms to a warmed deep platter. Tent steak with foil and let stand for 10 minutes.

4. Slice steak very thinly across the grain and arrange on platter with mushrooms. Season gravy in stoneware with salt and pepper. Pour over steak and mushrooms.

Ranchero Steak and Beans

A cowboy steak is a cut of beef that is usually less expensive and less popular, and one that needs marinating or slow cooking to taste good. This blade steak is cut up, layered with potatoes, onions and baked beans and cooked until the meat is flavorful and very tender. This is a simple and pleasing meal, and it's very economical.

Tips

I like to use baked beans in barbecue sauce, but you can substitute maple-flavored baked beans or beans in tomato sauce.

Save and freeze leftovers from this tasty meal in small plastic containers for a healthy, microwave-ready lunch box filler.

- **Minimum 4-quart slow cooker**

1	boneless beef blade, shoulder or inside round steak (about 2 lbs/1 kg)	1
4	potatoes, cut into 1-inch (2.5 cm) cubes	4
1	onion, chopped	1
1 tsp	salt	5 mL
¼ tsp	freshly ground black pepper	1 mL
1	can (28 oz/796 mL) baked beans in barbecue sauce	1

1. Trim steak and cut into 4 pieces. Place in slow cooker stoneware.

2. Arrange potatoes and onion over beef and sprinkle with salt and pepper. Spread beans over beef mixture.

3. Cover and cook on Low for 8 to 10 hours or on High for 4 to 5 hours, until steak and potatoes are tender and liquid is bubbling.

> **Cut from under the blade or shoulder roast, blade or shoulder steak is a tough piece of meat that is not tender enough to grill, broil or pan-fry, but is very flavorful when slow-cooked or braised.**

Beer-Braised Beef

Makes 6 servings

This recipe is a tribute to one of the national dishes of Belgium: brisket à la carbonnade. Instead of cooking a brisket, this version uses stewing beef but holds onto the beer and lots of onions. It is important to use dark ale, as its deep flavor enhances and adds richness to this dish.

Tips

To prepare mushrooms, first trim off the bottoms of the stems, then wipe off the mushrooms. Don't rinse or soak the mushrooms, or they'll absorb water and turn mushy when you cook them.

Resist the urge to lift the lid and taste or smell whatever is inside the slow cooker as it's cooking. Every peek will increase the cooking time by 20 minutes.

Serve this stew over cooked egg noodles tossed with melted butter and minced fresh dill.

- **Minimum 4-quart slow cooker**

3 tbsp	all-purpose flour	45 mL
	Salt and freshly ground black pepper	
3 lbs	stewing beef, trimmed and cut into 1-inch (2.5 cm) cubes	1.5 kg
3 to 4 tbsp	vegetable oil	45 to 60 mL
4	carrots, quartered lengthwise and cut into 1/2-inch (1 cm) pieces	4
6	onions, sliced	6
4	cloves garlic, minced	4
8 oz	small mushrooms, trimmed	250 g
1 tsp	dried thyme	5 mL
1	bottle (12 oz/341 mL) dark ale, such as Guinness or stout	1
1/2 cup	beef broth, divided	125 mL
1 tbsp	packed brown sugar	15 mL
1 tbsp	red wine vinegar	15 mL
2	bay leaves	2

1. In a heavy plastic bag, combine flour, 1 tsp (5 mL) salt and 1/2 tsp (2 mL) pepper. In batches, add beef to bag and toss to coat with flour mixture. Reserve the remaining flour mixture.

2. In a large nonstick skillet, heat half the oil over medium-high heat. Cook beef in batches, adding more oil as needed, for 5 minutes or until browned all over. Using a slotted spoon, transfer to slow cooker stoneware. Stir in carrots.

3. Reduce heat to medium. Add onions to skillet and sauté for 3 to 4 minutes or until tender and translucent. Add garlic, mushrooms, thyme, 1/2 tsp (2 mL) pepper and the reserved flour mixture; sauté for 1 minute. Stir in ale, broth, brown sugar and vinegar; cook, stirring, for 1 minute or until thickened. Pour over beef mixture. Add bay leaves.

4. Cover and cook on Low for 8 to 10 hours or on High for 4 to 6 hours, until vegetables are tender and stew is bubbling. Discard bay leaves. Season to taste with salt and pepper.

Steak Fajitas with Tomato Corn Relish

**Makes
6 servings**

....

This is a good meal for a casual get-together with friends. Have everything ready and let your guests assemble the fajitas themselves. Make it a Mexican party and throw together some lime margaritas!

Tips

If you like heat, add a minced jalapeño to the relish.

How to fill and fold tortillas: Spoon filling along the center of the warm tortilla. Fold the right side of the tortilla over the filling, then fold up the bottom. Fold the left side over the filling and wrap it around to form a tight roll. To prevent drips, wrap a small piece of foil, waxed paper or parchment paper around the bottom of the fajita.

• **Minimum 4-quart slow cooker**

1	beef flank steak (about 2 lbs/1 kg), trimmed	1
2	onions, thinly sliced	2
2	cloves garlic, finely chopped	2
1 cup	thick and chunky salsa	250 mL
1 1/2 tsp	smoked paprika	7 mL
1 tsp	salt, divided	5 mL
1/2 tsp	ground cumin	2 mL
1	red bell pepper, cut into strips	1
1	yellow bell pepper, cut into strips	1
12	10-inch (25 cm) cheese-flavored flour tortillas	12
1/2 cup	sour cream	125 mL
2 cups	shredded Monterey Jack cheese	500 mL
1	large tomato, diced	1
1	can (14 oz/398 mL) corn kernels, drained	1
3 tbsp	finely chopped fresh cilantro	45 mL
1 tbsp	freshly squeezed lime juice	15 mL
1/4 tsp	freshly ground black pepper	1 mL

1. Place steak in slow cooker stoneware. Spread onions on top.

2. In a bowl, combine garlic, salsa, paprika, 1/2 tsp (2 mL) of the salt and cumin. Pour over steak and onions.

3. Cover and cook on Low for 6 to 8 hours or on High for 3 to 4 hours, until steak is tender. Transfer steak to a cutting board or bowl and, using two forks, shred meat. Return to stoneware.

4. Stir in red and yellow bell peppers. Cover and cook on High for 30 to 45 minutes or until peppers are tender-crisp.

5. Meanwhile, in a bowl, combine tomato, corn, cilantro, lime juice, the remaining salt and pepper. Let stand at room temperature for 20 to 30 minutes before serving.

6. Just before serving, preheat oven to 350°F (180°C). Wrap a stack of tortillas in foil and heat in oven for 10 minutes.

7. Spoon about 1/2 cup (125 mL) of the steak mixture along the center of each tortilla. Top with relish, sour cream and cheese. Fold tortilla around filling (see tip, at left).

Madras Beef

**Makes
6 servings**

This is a simple, delicious recipe cooked in an easy sauce that's full of Indian flavorings. Using a can of tomato soup speeds up the preparation time. Serve over steamed basmati rice, with steamed green beans and warm naan (an Indian flatbread). Garnish the beef with minced fresh cilantro, if you like.

Tip

When browning meat in hot oil, avoid overfilling the skillet. If the pan is too full, the meat will steam rather than brown. Turn the meat frequently and cook it as quickly as possible, then use a slotted spoon to remove it.

- **4- to 6-quart slow cooker**

2 tbsp	vegetable oil (approx.)	30 mL
2 lbs	stewing beef, trimmed and cut into 1-inch (2.5 cm) cubes	1 kg
2	onions, thinly sliced	2
1	can (10 oz/284 mL) condensed tomato soup	1
2 tbsp	Madras curry paste	30 mL
½ tsp	garam masala or curry powder	2 mL
½ tsp	paprika	2 mL
½ cup	plain yogurt	125 mL

1. In a large nonstick skillet, heat half the oil over medium-high heat. Cook beef in batches, adding more oil as needed, for 5 minutes or until browned all over. Using a slotted spoon, transfer to slow cooker stoneware.

2. Reduce heat to medium. Add onions to skillet and sauté for 3 to 4 minutes or until tender and translucent. Spoon over beef.

3. In a bowl, combine soup, curry paste, garam masala and paprika. Stir into beef mixture.

4. Cover and cook on Low for 8 to 10 hours or on High for 4 to 5 hours, until beef is tender. Stir in yogurt.

> Garam masala is a blend of ground spices commonly used in Indian and other South Asian cuisines. It is not necessarily hot, but it adds intense flavor. Good commercial brands of garam masala are now widely available in supermarkets.

Hoisin Slivered Slow Cooker Beef

Makes 4 to 6 servings

There's no need to order Chinese takeout! This Asian-inspired dish uses some unusual ingredients, but they're all available at the supermarket. Steamed rice or cooked vermicelli noodles, along with steamed chopped baby bok choy, will complete the meal. Garnish with thinly sliced green onions and chopped peanuts, if you like. If you have extra sauce left over, toss it with noodles for a quick lunch the next day.

Tip

You can also serve this dish with rice and green beans.

- **3- to 5-quart slow cooker**

1 tbsp	vegetable oil (approx.)	15 mL
1 tsp	sesame oil (optional)	5 mL
1½ lbs	boneless beef outside round, blade or shoulder steak, trimmed and cut into 1-inch (2.5 cm) cubes	750 g
3	cloves garlic, minced	3
2 tsp	grated gingerroot	10 mL
¼ cup	soy sauce	60 mL
2 tbsp	fish sauce	30 mL
2 tbsp	sweet Thai chili sauce	30 mL
2 tbsp	hoisin sauce	30 mL
1 tbsp	rice vinegar	15 mL
½ tsp	sambal oelek (optional)	2 mL

1. In a large nonstick skillet, heat half the vegetable oil and the sesame oil (if using) over medium-high heat. Cook beef in batches, adding more oil as needed, for 5 minutes or until browned all over. Using a slotted spoon, transfer to slow cooker stoneware.

2. Stir in garlic, ginger, soy sauce, fish sauce, chili sauce, hoisin sauce, vinegar and sambal oelek (if using).

3. Cover and cook on Low for 6 to 8 hours or on High for 3 to 4 hours, until beef is fork-tender.

> **Sambal oelek is an Indonesian-inspired chili sauce. Even a small spoonful adds heat and character to a dish. It can be found with the Asian foods in the grocery store or in Asian supermarkets.**

Italian Pot Pie with Parmesan Mashed Potatoes

Makes 6 to 8 servings

Warm, traditional comfort food takes on an Italian twist. If you have leftover mashed potatoes, this recipe is a great way to use them up.

Tips

Store mushrooms in a paper bag, with the top loosely folded over once or twice, or place them in a glass container and cover it with a tea towel or moist paper towel. Be sure to allow air circulation. Store in the refrigerator (but not in the crisper) and use within a few days — or a week, if they are packaged and unopened.

To prepare mushrooms, first trim off the bottoms of the stems, then wipe off the mushrooms. Don't rinse or soak the mushrooms, or they'll absorb water and turn mushy when you cook them.

- **4- to 6-quart slow cooker**

2 tbsp	vegetable oil (approx.)	30 mL
2 lbs	stewing beef, trimmed and cut into 1-inch (2.5 cm) cubes	1 kg
1	onion, chopped	1
1	clove garlic, minced	1
2	carrots, cut into 1-inch (2.5 cm) chunks	2
1½ cups	sliced mushrooms	375 mL
½ tsp	dried basil	2 mL
½ tsp	dried oregano	2 mL
¼ tsp	freshly ground black pepper	1 mL
1	jar (28 oz/796 mL) tomato pasta sauce	1

Parmesan Mashed Potatoes

1½ lbs	baking potatoes (3 or 4 large), peeled and quartered	750 g
1	egg, lightly beaten	1
1 cup	freshly grated Parmesan cheese, divided	250 mL
	Salt and freshly ground black pepper	
2 tbsp	chopped fresh parsley	30 mL

1. In a large nonstick skillet, heat half the oil over medium-high heat. Cook beef in batches, adding more oil as needed, for 5 minutes or until browned all over. Using a slotted spoon, transfer to slow cooker stoneware.

2. Reduce heat to medium. Add onion and garlic to skillet and sauté for about 5 minutes or until onion is tender and translucent. Add carrots, mushrooms, basil, oregano and pepper; sauté for about 5 minutes or until mushrooms are softened. Pour over beef mixture, along with pasta sauce, stirring to combine.

3. Cover and cook on Low for 6 to 8 hours or on High for 3 to 4 hours, until beef is almost tender and stew is bubbling.

continued on page 164...

Authentic Italian Parmesan cheese (Parmigiano-Reggiano) is expensive, but its flavor is certainly worth the price. Well-wrapped in the refrigerator, a block keeps for months, and it goes a long way when you freshly grate it as you need it.

If using leftover mashed potatoes for the topping, you'll need about 3 cups (750 mL). Warm in the microwave on High for 5 minutes, then add the egg, cheese and parsley as directed. (Warm mashed potatoes mix a little more easily than cold.)

4. *Parmesan Mashed Potatoes:* Meanwhile, place potatoes in a large pot. Add enough cold water to cover and bring to a boil over medium-high heat. Reduce heat and boil gently for 20 minutes or until tender. Drain well and mash until smooth. Stir in egg and ¾ cup (175 mL) of the cheese. Season to taste with salt and pepper. Stir in parsley.

5. Spoon potatoes evenly over beef in stoneware and sprinkle with the remaining cheese. Cover and cook on Low for 1 to 2 hours or until potatoes are light golden brown.

Make Ahead

You can make the mashed potato topping up to 12 hours before preparing this dish. Transfer to an airtight container and refrigerate until ready to use.

Step 2 can be completed up to 2 days in advance. Transfer the sautéed vegetable mixture to an airtight container, stir in the pasta sauce and refrigerate. When you are ready to cook, complete step 1, add the vegetable mixture and proceed with step 3.

> **The fluffiness of your mash depends on the type of potatoes used. The creamy yellow Yukon gold variety has a wonderful buttery flavor and makes delicious mashed potatoes. Russet potatoes (baking potatoes) also work well. Regular white potatoes, while not as flavorful, still mash well. In fact, the only type that don't really fluff up is new potatoes, as they don't have a very high starch content.**

Philly Cheese and Beef Casserole

The taste of this casserole is reminiscent of a good Philadelphia cheese steak. Even though it breaks my normal condiment rules, ketchup is a must alongside. This dish is not exactly low in fat, but then, neither is its namesake.

Tip

Always use a large, deep pot to boil pasta. You need at least 1 quart (1 L) water per 3½ oz (100 g) dry pasta. And always salt the water, because this seasons the pasta internally as it absorbs the liquid and swells. You'll need about 1 tbsp (15 mL) salt for a large pot of boiling water. Chefs prefer to use sea salt or kosher salt because it is easier to control the amount you add and it dissolves faster than table salt.

- **4- to 6-quart slow cooker, stoneware greased**

3 cups	short pasta, such as penne, rigatoni or rotini	750 mL
1 lb	lean ground beef	500 g
2	onions, finely chopped	2
2	cloves garlic, minced	2
1	small green bell pepper, finely chopped	1
8 oz	mushrooms, chopped	250 g
½ tsp	dried thyme	2 mL
1	can (12 oz/370 mL) evaporated milk	1
8 oz	herb and garlic spreadable cream cheese	250 g
1 tbsp	Dijon mustard	15 mL
2 cups	shredded sharp (old) Cheddar cheese	500 mL
Topping		
1 cup	dry bread crumbs	250 mL
3 tbsp	melted butter	45 mL
½ cup	shredded sharp (old) Cheddar cheese	125 mL

1. In a large pot of boiling salted water, cook pasta for about 8 minutes or until tender but firm (al dente). Drain and place in prepared slow cooker stoneware.

2. In a large nonstick skillet, cook beef over medium-high heat, breaking it up with the back of a wooden spoon, for 7 minutes or until no longer pink. Using a slotted spoon, transfer to stoneware.

3. Reduce heat to medium. Add onions, garlic, green pepper, mushrooms and thyme to skillet and sauté for 3 to 4 minutes or until softened. Transfer to stoneware.

4. Add milk, cream cheese and mustard to skillet and cook, stirring gently, for 3 to 4 minutes or until thickened. Stir into pasta mixture, along with cheese.

5. Cover and cook on Low for 8 hours or on High for 4 hours, until bubbling.

6. *Topping:* In a bowl, toss together bread crumbs, butter and cheese. Sprinkle over pasta mixture. Cover and cook on High for 20 minutes or until cheese is melted.

Family-Style Chili Mac and Cheese

Makes 4 to 6 servings

An old family favorite takes a new turn with the addition of tomatoes. This dish is exceptionally easy and fast by slow cooker standards! My son likes the cheesy version, but you can also make it without cheese. This is a great weeknight supper for those busy months that are filled with lots of after-school activities. It's calming to know that dinner will be ready when you get home.

Tip

To avoid tears when chopping onions, put the onions in the freezer for a few minutes first.

- **3- to 5-quart slow cooker**

1 lb	lean ground beef or turkey	500 g
1	onion, finely chopped	1
2	cloves garlic, minced	2
1	can (14 oz/398 mL) diced tomatoes, drained	1
1	can (8 oz/227 mL) tomato sauce	1
2 tbsp	chili powder	30 mL
½ tsp	ground cumin	2 mL
¼ tsp	hot pepper flakes	1 mL
¼ tsp	freshly ground black pepper	1 mL
1 cup	elbow macaroni	250 mL
1 cup	shredded Cheddar cheese	250 mL

1. In a large nonstick skillet, cook beef, onion and garlic over medium-high heat, breaking up beef with the back of a wooden spoon, for about 7 minutes or until beef is no longer pink. Using a slotted spoon, transfer to slow cooker stoneware.

2. Stir in tomatoes, tomato sauce, chili powder, cumin, hot pepper flakes and black pepper.

3. Cover and cook on Low for 4 hours or on High for 2 hours, until bubbling.

4. In a pot of boiling salted water, cook macaroni for 7 to 8 minutes or until tender but firm (al dente). Drain and stir into beef mixture, along with cheese. Cover and cook on Low for 1 hour.

Make Ahead

This dish can be assembled up to 12 hours in advance. Prepare through step 2, cover and refrigerate overnight. The next day, place stoneware in slow cooker and proceed with step 3.

Fiesta Tamale Pie

Makes 4 to 6 servings

....

The entire family will enjoy this economical and tasty main course pie. You can serve leftovers as a dip with nacho chips or use them to fill tortillas for quick burritos!

Tips

Buy ground beef when it's on special. Divide it into 1-lb (500 g) portions, flatten each into a thin disc and seal tightly in a freezer bag, then freeze to have on hand for spur-of-the-moment casseroles. A thin disc thaws much more easily, right in a skillet, than a thick clump.

It is always best to brown ground meat thoroughly before adding it to the slow cooker. This ensures that the meat reaches the recommended cooked temperature of 160°F (71°C), or 165°F (74°C) for ground poultry. If you have a good nonstick skillet, you will not need to add cooking oil unless you are browning ground turkey or chicken, which is generally very lean.

- **4- to 6-quart slow cooker**

1 tbsp	vegetable oil	15 mL
1 lb	lean ground beef	500 g
1	onion, chopped	1
1 tbsp	chili powder	15 mL
1 tbsp	dried oregano	15 mL
1 tsp	ground cumin	5 mL
1	can (10 oz/284 mL) enchilada sauce	1
2 cups	cooked or canned red kidney beans (see page 84), drained and rinsed	500 mL
1	package (6½ oz/184 g) cornbread and muffin mix	1
1	egg, lightly beaten	1
⅓ cup	milk	75 mL
2 tbsp	butter, melted	30 mL
½ cup	shredded Monterey Jack cheese	125 mL
1	can (4½ oz/127 mL) chopped mild green chiles, with juice	1
¼ cup	sour cream	60 mL
4	green onions, chopped	4

1. In a large nonstick skillet, heat oil over medium-high heat. Cook ground beef and onion, breaking up beef with the back of a wooden spoon, for about 7 minutes or until beef is no longer pink. Add chili powder, oregano and cumin; sauté for 1 to 2 minutes or until fragrant. Using a slotted spoon, transfer to slow cooker stoneware. Stir in enchilada sauce and beans.

2. Place cornbread mix in a bowl and make a well in the center. Pour egg, milk and butter into well and stir just until blended (the batter will be lumpy). Stir in cheese and chiles with juice. Spread cornbread mixture evenly over beef mixture.

3. Place two clean, dry tea towels over top of stoneware, then place lid on top of towels (this will allow the topping to rise without getting soggy). Cook on Low for 6 to 8 hours or on High for 3 to 4 hours, until cornbread mixture has risen and is crusty and meat mixture is bubbling.

4. Top each serving with a dollop of sour cream and sprinkle with green onions.

Curried Beef with Mashed Sweet Potatoes

Makes 4 to 6 servings

Mashed sweet potatoes add both sweetness and color to the curried beef. It's a nice alternative to mashed potatoes or rice.

Tips

It's important to fully cook ground meat before adding it to the slow cooker. Cook ground meat until no longer pink inside. Use the back of a wooden spoon to break up the meat as it cooks; otherwise, you will end up with large chunks of meat.

Broth (or stock) is one of the most indispensable pantry staples. Commercial broth cubes and powders are loaded with salt and just don't deliver the flavor of homemade stock or prepared broth. I like to keep 32-oz (1 L) Tetra Paks on hand, especially the sodium-reduced variety.

Tomato paste is now available in tubes in many supermarkets and delis. It keeps for months in the refrigerator.

- **3- to 5-quart slow cooker**

5	cloves garlic, finely chopped	5
1	onion, coarsely chopped	1
1	2-inch (5 cm) piece gingerroot, roughly chopped	1
2 tbsp	vegetable oil	30 mL
1½ lbs	lean ground beef or lamb	750 g
1 tbsp	curry powder	15 mL
1 tsp	ground cumin	5 mL
1 tsp	ground coriander	5 mL
½ tsp	cayenne pepper	2 mL
2 cups	beef broth	500 mL
2 tbsp	tomato paste	30 mL
4	large sweet potatoes	4
2 tbsp	butter	30 mL
	Salt and freshly ground black pepper	
1 tbsp	chopped fresh parsley	15 mL
1 cup	frozen peas, thawed	250 mL
⅓ cup	slivered almonds	75 mL
⅓ cup	raisins	75 mL
1 tbsp	chopped fresh cilantro	15 mL
	Chopped cashews	

1. In a food processor, process garlic, onion and ginger into paste (or finely chop by hand).

2. In a large nonstick skillet, heat oil over medium heat. Sauté garlic mixture for 5 minutes or until fragrant and starting to turn golden. Add beef and cook, breaking up beef with the back of a wooden spoon, for about 7 minutes or until beef is no longer pink. Stir in curry powder, cumin, coriander and cayenne; sauté for 1 to 2 minutes or until fragrant. Using a slotted spoon, transfer to slow cooker stoneware. Stir in broth and tomato paste.

3. Cover and cook on Low for 6 to 8 hours or on High for 3 to 4 hours, until bubbling.

continued on page 170…

4. Meanwhile, preheat oven to 400°F (200°C). Using a fork, pierce sweet potatoes several times. Bake for about 1 hour or until tender. Let cool slightly, then peel off skins. In a bowl, mash with butter, 1 tsp (5 mL) salt and ½ tsp (2 mL) black pepper. Stir in parsley. Keep warm.

5. Stir peas, almonds and raisins into stoneware. Cover and cook on High for 10 to 15 minutes. Season to taste with salt and black pepper.

6. Spoon sweet potato mixture onto a warmed platter. Make a well in the center and spoon in curried beef. Sprinkle with cilantro and cashews.

Make Ahead

The mashed sweet potatoes can be prepared as directed in step 4, then covered and refrigerated for up to 1 day or frozen for up to 2 months. Let thaw in the refrigerator, if necessary, then let stand at room temperature for 30 minutes before reheating.

The curried beef can be assembled up to 2 days in advance. Prepare through step 2, cool immediately, then cover and refrigerate. When ready to cook, place stoneware in slow cooker and proceed with step 3.

Pizza Meatloaf

Makes 4 servings

This is any kid's favorite! Serve it with linguine tossed with butter and grated Parmesan cheese. Instead of using ground beef, chicken or turkey, you can use a combination of the three, or use some ground pork or veal. Look for a combination package of ground beef, veal and pork at the grocery store or ask your butcher for a portion of each.

Tip

Make your own bread crumbs: In a food processor, process leftover bread to fine crumbs. Transfer to a ziplock bag, date it and freeze for up to 3 months. To dry or toast, spread bread crumbs on a large rimmed baking sheet and toast in a 350°F (180°C) oven, stirring occasionally, for 10 to 12 minutes or until golden brown.

• **Minimum 4-quart slow cooker**

1 lb	lean ground beef, chicken or turkey	500 g
1	egg, lightly beaten	1
1	clove garlic, minced	1
1½ cups	shredded mozzarella or Cheddar cheese, divided	375 mL
⅔ cup	tomato pasta sauce, divided	150 mL
¼ cup	dry bread crumbs	60 mL
1 tsp	dried basil	5 mL
½ tsp	salt	2 mL
¼ tsp	dried oregano	1 mL
¼ tsp	freshly ground black pepper	1 mL

1. Cut a 2-foot (60 cm) length of foil in half lengthwise to make two strips. Fold each strip in half lengthwise. Crisscross the strips on the bottom of the slow cooker stoneware, bringing the ends up the sides and over the rim.

2. In a large bowl, using your hands, combine beef, egg, garlic, half the cheese, half the pasta sauce, bread crumbs, basil, salt, oregano and pepper. Press evenly into prepared stoneware.

3. Tucking strip ends under lid, cover and cook on Low for 8 to 10 hours or on High for 4 to 6 hours, until a meat thermometer inserted into center of meatloaf registers 170°F (77°C). Spread the remaining pasta sauce over meatloaf and sprinkle with the remaining cheese. Cover and cook on Low for 20 minutes or until cheese has melted.

4. Remove lid and grasp strip ends to lift out meatloaf, draining off any accumulated fat from top. Transfer to a cutting board and let cool for 10 minutes before slicing.

Variation
Add ½ cup (125 mL) sliced pepperoni to the ground beef mixture.

Stuffed Mediterranean Meatloaf

Makes 6 to 8 servings

This flavorful filled loaf is delicious served with rice and a chunky Greek salad. Slice any leftover meatloaf and stuff it into a pocket pita for lunch. Add shredded lettuce and slices of tomato and cucumber, and sprinkle with crumbled feta cheese. Wrap the pita and take it to school or work. It sure beats the traditional sandwich.

Tip

If using a large, oval slow cooker, press beef mixture into an oval shape, ensuring that each layer is at least 1 inch (2.5 cm) thick. Thinner layers will cook too quickly.

- **Minimum 4-quart slow cooker**

1½ lbs	lean ground beef	750 g
8 oz	lean ground pork	250 g
2	cloves garlic, minced	2
1	egg, lightly beaten	1
¼ cup	fine dry bread crumbs	60 mL
1 tsp	dried oregano	5 mL
¼ tsp	freshly ground black pepper	1 mL
	Chopped fresh parsley	

Stuffing

½ cup	crumbled feta cheese	125 mL
¼ cup	chopped drained oil-packed sun-dried tomatoes	60 mL
½ tsp	dried oregano	2 mL
1	clove garlic, minced	1

1. Cut a 2-foot (60 cm) length of foil in half lengthwise to make two strips. Fold each strip in half lengthwise. Crisscross the strips on the bottom of the slow cooker stoneware, bringing the ends up the sides and over the rim.

2. In a large bowl, using your hands, combine beef, pork, garlic, egg, bread crumbs, oregano and pepper. Set aside.

3. *Stuffing:* In a small bowl, combine cheese, sun-dried tomatoes, oregano and garlic. Press half the beef mixture evenly into slow cooker stoneware. Spread cheese mixture over beef mixture, leaving a border on all sides so stuffing doesn't ooze out. Top with the remaining beef mixture and press edges together.

4. Tucking strip ends under lid, cover and cook on Low for 8 to 10 hours or on High for 4 to 6 hours, until a meat thermometer inserted into center of meatloaf registers 170°F (77°C).

5. Remove lid and grasp strip ends to lift out meatloaf, draining off any accumulated fat from top. Transfer to a cutting board and let cool for 10 minutes before slicing. Serve sprinkled with parsley.

Variation

Ground pork adds flavor to the meatloaf, but you can replace it with ground chicken or more ground beef.

Short Ribs Barolo

Settle in for meltingly tender ribs that are long on flavor but short on effort. Look for small, thick bone-in short ribs, which are meatier than flanken-style ribs (cut long and thin). Each rib weighs about 4 oz (125 g). Before serving, pull out the bones, if you like. Serve this dish with steamed broccoli.

Tip

You can use an 8-oz (227 mL) can of tomato sauce instead of the 1 cup (250 mL).

Variation

If you can't find pancetta, use thickly sliced bacon. Even sodium-reduced side bacon will work well.

- **4- to 6-quart slow cooker**

2 tbsp	vegetable oil (approx.)	30 mL
2 lbs	beef short ribs or braising ribs, cut into 3-inch (7.5 cm) sections	1 kg
	Salt and freshly ground black pepper	
2	Spanish onions, diced	2
2	stalks celery, cut into ½-inch (1 cm) slices	2
1	carrot, cut into ½-inch (1 cm) rounds	1
4 oz	pancetta, diced	125 g
1 cup	Barolo wine or other hearty red wine	250 mL
1 cup	tomato sauce	250 mL

1. In a large Dutch oven, heat half the oil over high heat until smoking. Generously season beef with salt and pepper. Cook beef in batches, adding more oil as needed, for 4 to 5 minutes per side or until browned all over. Using a slotted spoon, transfer to slow cooker stoneware.

2. Pour any excess oil out of the pot. Reduce heat to medium-high. Add onions, celery, carrot and pancetta; sauté for about 8 minutes or until vegetables are lightly browned and starting to soften. Transfer to stoneware, arranging around beef.

3. In a bowl, combine wine and tomato sauce. Pour over beef and vegetable mixture.

4. Cover and cook on Low for 8 to 12 hours or on High for 4 to 6 hours, until beef is falling off the bones and vegetables are tender. Using a slotted spoon, transfer beef to a platter and keep warm.

5. Strain cooking liquid through a fine-mesh sieve into a saucepan. Discard solids. Bring to a boil over medium-high heat. Reduce heat and simmer, stirring often, for 10 to 12 minutes or until slightly thickened and reduced to about 2½ cups (625 mL). Season to taste with salt and pepper. Pour over beef. Serve immediately.

Make Ahead

Making this dish a day ahead and reheating it enhances the flavors. Prepare through step 5, adding the beef to the sauce, let cool slightly, then cover and refrigerate for up to 1 day. For best results, reheat in a covered ovenproof casserole dish at 350°F (180°C) for about 30 minutes or until heated through.

Diner Red Brick

Makes 4 to 6 servings

There has been a recent rebirth of comfort food, and meatloaf is making a comeback! It not only transports us back to many a childhood supper, it's a satisfying and economical meal. In the days of the diner, a meatloaf was called a "red brick" on the menu. This updated version uses lean ground beef, with turkey and pork for extra flavor. Serve with steamed green beans and mashed potatoes.

Tips

You can add a little heat to this meatloaf by using hot salsa instead of mild.

When making your mashed potatoes, substitute buttermilk for milk or cream, to add a bit of tang. Once you try it, you will use buttermilk every time.

- **4- to 6-quart slow cooker**

1 lb	lean ground beef	500 g
8 oz	ground turkey	250 g
8 oz	lean ground pork	250 g
2	eggs, lightly beaten	2
1 cup	fine dry bread crumbs	250 mL
1½ cups	mild salsa, divided	375 mL
1 tbsp	Worcestershire sauce	15 mL
1 tsp	dry mustard	5 mL
½ tsp	salt	2 mL
¼ tsp	freshly ground black pepper	1 mL

1. Cut a 2-foot (60 cm) length of foil in half lengthwise to make two strips. Fold each strip in half lengthwise. Crisscross the strips on the bottom of the slow cooker stoneware, bringing the ends up the sides and over the rim.

2. In a large bowl, using your hands, combine beef, turkey, pork, eggs, bread crumbs, 1 cup (250 mL) of the salsa, Worcestershire sauce, mustard, salt and pepper. Press evenly into prepared stoneware.

3. Tucking strip ends under lid, cover and cook on Low for 8 to 10 hours or on High for 4 to 6 hours, until a meat thermometer inserted into center of meatloaf registers 170°F (77°C). Spread the remaining salsa over meatloaf. Cover and cook on High for 10 minutes.

4. Remove lid and grasp strip ends to lift out meatloaf, draining off any accumulated fat from top. Transfer to a cutting board and let cool for 10 minutes before slicing.

Spicy Meatball Sandwiches with Coleslaw

Makes 4 to 6 servings

These fun, easy sandwiches are great at a casual get-together with friends, a football party or a meal with the family. The tangy coleslaw offsets the heat of the spicy meatballs. These sandwiches combine crunch (the bun), tang (the coleslaw) and heat (the meatballs) in every bite!

Tips

When rolling the meat mixture into meatballs, don't overmix. Meatballs should be springy and firm enough to hold their shape, yet still tender. In other words, don't handle the meat too much or pack it too densely.

To keep my hands from getting sticky when rolling meatballs, I moisten my hands with water or give them a light coating of oil or flour.

- **4- to 6-quart slow cooker**

Meatballs

1½ lbs	lean ground beef	750 g
2	cloves garlic, minced	2
2 tsp	celery seeds	10 mL
½ tsp	salt	2 mL
¼ tsp	freshly ground black pepper	1 mL
2 tbsp	vegetable oil (approx.)	30 mL

Spicy Tomato Sauce

6	thin lemon slices	6
¼ cup	packed brown sugar	60 mL
1 cup	ketchup	250 mL
⅔ cup	chili sauce	150 mL
2 tbsp	Worcestershire sauce	30 mL
2 tbsp	spicy mustard	30 mL

6 to 8	small submarine rolls or hot dog buns	6 to 8
12 to 16	thin red or white onion slices	12 to 16
1 lb	coleslaw or broccoli slaw mix	500 g
½ cup	coleslaw dressing	125 mL

1. *Meatballs:* In a bowl, using your hands, combine beef, garlic, celery seeds, salt and pepper. Form mixture into 1-inch (2.5 cm) meatballs.

2. In a skillet, heat half the oil over medium-high heat. Cook meatballs in batches, adding more oil as needed, for about 3 minutes or until browned all over. Using a slotted spoon, transfer to slow cooker stoneware.

The ideal meatball for soups and sandwiches is just one or two bites in diameter: about 1 inch (2.5 cm). Keep your eye on your work as you roll — meatballs tend to get bigger as your mind wanders!

You can also use kaiser buns or lightly toasted baguette slices to hold the meatballs.

3. *Spicy Tomato Sauce:* Reduce heat to medium. Add lemon slices, brown sugar, ketchup, chili sauce, Worcestershire sauce, mustard and $\frac{1}{2}$ cup (125 mL) water to skillet and bring to a boil, stirring. Pour sauce over meatballs.

4. Cover and cook on Low for 8 hours or on High for 4 hours, until meatballs are no longer pink inside. Discard lemon slices.

5. Split rolls in half horizontally and hollow out some of the bread from each half, leaving them about $\frac{1}{2}$ inch (1 cm) thick around the edges. Separate red onion slices into rings. Set aside. In a bowl, combine coleslaw and dressing.

6. Place 2 or 3 meatballs on bottom half of each roll. Evenly divide onion rings and coleslaw over top and drizzle with sauce, if desired.

Make Ahead

Split and hollow out the buns in advance, then store them in a plastic bag until you're ready to assemble the sandwiches. Dress the coleslaw and refrigerate it at the beginning of the day to let the raw vegetables absorb the dressing and become slightly more tender.

Veal Shanks with Spicy Black Bean Sauce

Makes 6 to 8 servings

Veal shanks traditionally get an Italian treatment. I have given them a Chinese twist instead, using bottled black bean sauce. Serve them with steamed rice and sautéed Chinese greens, such as baby bok choy or snow peas. Toss any leftover sauce with noodles the next day.

Tips

Veal shanks are readily available at supermarkets and butcher shops. They have a piece of connective tissue around the outer edge that helps keep the meat connected to the bone. During long, slow cooking, this tissue can be broken down, causing the meat to come away from the bone and fall apart in the stew, so it's important to secure shanks with butcher's twine. Before browning, wrap a piece of twine around the circumference of the meat and tie it with a tight knot. You can also ask the butcher to do this for you.

If you can't find an Anaheim chile pepper, you can substitute a jalapeño pepper.

- **4- to 6-quart slow cooker**

2 tbsp	vegetable oil (approx.)	30 mL
6 to 8	veal shanks (each about 12 oz/375 g), ticd (scc tip, at left)	6 to 8
4	green onions, sliced, white and light green parts separated	4
1	red Anaheim chile pepper, minced	1
1/2 cup	black bean sauce with garlic	125 mL
1 tsp	minced gingerroot	5 mL
1/2 tsp	freshly ground black pepper	2 mL
	Grated zest and juice of 1 orange	

1. In a large skillet, heat half the oil over medium heat. Cook veal in batches, adding more oil as needed, for 4 minutes or until lightly browned on all sides. Transfer to slow cooker stoneware.

2. In a bowl, combine white parts of green onions, chile pepper, black bean sauce, ginger, pepper, half the orange zest and the orange juice. Pour over veal and stir to combine.

3. Cover and cook on Low for 10 hours or on High for 6 hours, until veal is very tender. Serve garnished with the remaining green onions and orange zest.

Veal and Leek Ragoût in Herbed Popovers

Makes 6 servings

This simple stew reminds me of Sunday dinners at my Nanna McClaren's house. She came from fine English stock, so roast beef with Yorkshire pudding was the standard fare. I have used veal, leeks and mushrooms, but the dish has that same rich taste.

Tips

Leeks contain a lot of sand and must be cleaned carefully. Remove most of the green part and halve the white part lengthwise. Rinse thoroughly under cold running water, spreading leaves apart, and drain in a colander, then slice.

Store mushrooms in a paper bag, with the top loosely folded over once or twice, or place them in a glass container and cover it with a tea towel or moist paper towel. Be sure to allow air circulation. Store in the refrigerator (but not in the crisper) and use within a few days — or a week, if they are packaged and unopened.

- **4- to 6-quart slow cooker**
- *12-cup muffin tin, well greased*

2 tbsp	vegetable oil (approx.)	30 mL
2 lbs	stewing veal, cut into 1-inch (2.5 cm) cubes	1 kg
4	leeks (white and light green parts only), thickly sliced	4
8 oz	mushrooms, chopped	250 g
2 tbsp	all-purpose flour	30 mL
	Salt and freshly ground black pepper	
2 cups	veal or chicken broth	500 mL
2 tbsp	white balsamic vinegar or cider vinegar	30 mL
1 tsp	dried thyme	5 mL
½ cup	heavy or whipping (35%) cream	125 mL

Herbed Popovers

2	eggs	2
1 cup	all-purpose flour	250 mL
1 cup	milk	250 mL
1 tbsp	snipped fresh chives	15 mL
1 tbsp	chopped fresh parsley	15 mL
½ tsp	dried rosemary	2 mL
½ tsp	salt	2 mL

1. In a large skillet, heat half the oil over medium-high heat. Cook veal in batches, adding more oil as needed, for about 4 minutes or until browned all over. Using a slotted spoon, transfer to slow cooker stoneware.

2. Add leeks and mushrooms to skillet and sauté for 5 to 10 minutes or until softened. Sprinkle with flour, 1 tsp (5 mL) salt and ½ tsp (2 mL) pepper; stir to coat. Stir in broth, vinegar, thyme and ½ cup (125 mL) water; bring to a boil, scraping up any brown bits from pan. Pour over veal.

3. Cover and cook on Low for 8 hours or on High for 4 hours, until veal is tender. Stir in cream and season to taste with salt and pepper.

4. *Herbed Popovers:* Meanwhile, in a large bowl, beat eggs until frothy. Stir in flour, milk, chives, parsley, rosemary and salt until just blended. (Leave a few lumps and don't overmix.) Divide batter evenly among prepared muffin cups.

5. Place muffin tin in cold oven. Set oven temperature to 450°F (230°C) and bake for 25 minutes. Using the tip of a sharp knife, prick each popover to let steam escape. Bake for 5 to 10 minutes or until golden brown and puffed.

6. Split open popovers, place in serving bowls and ladle stew over top.

Make Ahead

The popovers can be baked, removed from muffin cups and placed on a baking sheet, covered with a clean tea towel and set aside at room temperature for up to 8 hours. Reheat in a 350°F (180°C) oven for 5 to 10 minutes.

Veal Marengo

I love this simple but rustic veal dish. When my Swiss friend Thomas heads to his vacation home in the Piedmont area of Italy, he likes to go truffle hunting with his neighbor, then he cooks up a dish similar to this one. I have substituted regular mushrooms for the truffles, but you can finish with a drizzle of truffle oil before serving, for an authentic twist.

Tips

Pearl onions come in red, white and golden varieties. They are found in the produce section of the supermarket, loose or in small mesh bags. If you purchase a bag of onions, there are about 24 inside.

For ease of preparation, use frozen pearl onions. If you can't find them, it is quite easy to prepare fresh onions. Simply cut an X into the base of each onion. Bring a pot of water to a boil over high heat. Drop onions (with skins) into boiling water and cook for 1 minute. Drain and immediately immerse in ice-cold water. Let cool, then squeeze onions out of their skins.

- **4- to 6-quart slow cooker**

3 tbsp	all-purpose flour	45 mL
1 tsp	salt	5 mL
½ tsp	freshly ground black pepper	2 mL
2 lbs	stewing veal, cut into 1-inch (2.5 cm) cubes	1 kg
2 tbsp	vegetable oil (approx.)	30 mL
2	cloves garlic, minced	2
1	onion, finely chopped	1
1 cup	diced tomatoes	250 mL
2 tbsp	tomato paste	30 mL
⅔ cup	dry white wine	150 mL
1 cup	veal or chicken broth	250 mL
8 oz	small mushrooms	250 g
24	pearl onions, peeled (see tips, at left)	24
12 to 15	kalamata olives	12 to 15
	Hot cooked farfalle or penne pasta	
	Chopped fresh parsley (optional)	
	White truffle oil (optional)	

1. In a heavy plastic bag, combine flour, salt and pepper. In batches, add veal to bag and toss to coat with flour mixture.

2. In a large nonstick skillet, heat half the oil over medium-high heat. Cook veal in batches, adding more oil as needed, for about 4 minutes or until browned all over. Using a slotted spoon, transfer to slow cooker stoneware.

3. Add garlic, chopped onion, tomatoes and tomato paste to skillet; stir to combine. Add wine and boil until sauce is reduced by half. Add to stoneware, along with broth, mushrooms and pearl onions; stir to combine.

4. Cover and cook on Low for 6 to 8 hours or on High for 3 to 4 hours, until meat is tender.

5. Stir in olives. Cover and cook on High for 15 minutes or until heated through.

6. Divide farfalle among serving bowls and spoon stew over top. Sprinkle with parsley (if using) and drizzle with truffle oil (if using).

Roast Pork Loin with Port and Fig Sauce

Makes 4 to 6 servings

Pork is enhanced by many kinds of fruit, but the subtle sweetness of fresh figs with port wine makes an especially seductive combination.

Tip

If your liquid honey has crystallized (or if you are using solid creamed honey instead), place the jar (or as much as you need in a small heatproof bowl) in a saucepan of hot water and let warm until the crystals dissolve and the honey is melted. Or heat in the microwave on Medium-High (70%) for about 1 minute, stirring after 30 seconds, until melted.

• **Minimum 4-quart slow cooker**

1	boneless pork loin rib roast (about 2½ lbs/1.25 kg), trimmed	1
1 tbsp	olive oil	15 mL
1 tsp	dried rosemary	5 mL
½ tsp	freshly ground black pepper	2 mL
¾ cup	chopped dried Mission figs	175 mL
1	shallot, diced	1
1 cup	port wine	250 mL
½ cup	chicken broth	125 mL
1 tbsp	liquid honey	15 mL
2	3-inch (7.5 cm) cinnamon sticks	2
2 tbsp	butter	30 mL

1. Place pork in slow cooker stoneware. Brush with oil and sprinkle with rosemary and pepper. Arrange figs around pork.

2. In a bowl, stir together shallot, port, broth and honey. Pour around pork. Immerse cinnamon sticks in port mixture.

3. Cover and cook on Low for 4 to 6 hours or until pork is fork-tender. Transfer pork to a warmed platter and tent loosely with foil.

4. Remove cinnamon sticks from cooking liquid. Using an immersion blender, or in a food processor or blender, purée cooking liquid until smooth. Stir in butter until melted.

5. Slice pork across the grain and serve sauce in a gravy boat on the side.

Make Ahead

This dish can be assembled up to 12 hours in advance. Prepare through step 2, cover and refrigerate overnight. The next day, place stoneware in slow cooker and proceed with step 3.

> **Mission figs are small black figs grown in California. Dried Mission figs have a complex smoky flavor, which makes them a good ingredient for savory stews.**

Italian Pork Roast Braised with Beans

Makes 6 to 8 servings

As it cooks, this Italian-inspired pork roast fills the house with the scent of garlic, rosemary and sage. The pork roast is coated with a dry rub, then braised in a tangy tomato sauce.

Tips

Crush dried rosemary between your thumb and fingers before adding it to a dish. This helps release the full aromatic flavor of the herb.

There are three types of pork loin roast: sirloin, rib and center-cut. I prefer the rib roast for slow cooking because it has a little more marbling, which suits the long, moist heat of the slow cooker.

While this recipe calls for a boneless roast, you can also use a bone-in rib roast, which slices easily into individual portions.

- **Minimum 4-quart slow cooker**
- *Food processor*

1	clove garlic, minced	1
1 tsp	dried sage	5 mL
1 tsp	dried rosemary	5 mL
2 tbsp	olive oil, divided	30 mL
1	boneless pork loin roast (2½ to 3 lbs/1.25 to 1.5 kg), trimmed	1
	Salt and freshly ground black pepper	
1	onion, finely chopped	1
1	can (14 oz/398 mL) tomato sauce	1
4 cups	cooked or canned white kidney beans (see page 84), drained and rinsed	1 L
¼ cup	dry white wine	60 mL
1	clove garlic	1
¼ cup	chopped fresh sage	60 mL
¼ cup	chopped fresh flat-leaf (Italian) parsley	60 mL
1 tsp	chopped fresh rosemary	5 mL
2 tbsp	toasted pine nuts (see tip, page 196)	30 mL

1. In a bowl, combine minced garlic, dried sage, dried rosemary and 1 tbsp (15 mL) of the oil. Rub all over pork and season to taste with salt and pepper. Place pork in slow cooker stoneware.

2. In a bowl, combine onion, tomato sauce, beans and wine. Set aside.

3. In food processor, process garlic clove, fresh sage, fresh parsley and fresh rosemary until finely chopped. Add the remaining oil and pine nuts; process until well combined. Stir half the fresh herb mixture into the reserved bean mixture and pour around pork. Cover and refrigerate the remaining fresh herb mixture.

Resist the urge to lift the lid and taste or smell whatever is inside the slow cooker as it's cooking. Every peek will increase the cooking time by 20 minutes.

4. Cover and cook on Low for 5 to 6 hours or until pork is fork-tender. Transfer pork to a warmed platter and tent loosely with foil.

5. Transfer bean mixture to a saucepan and bring to a boil over medium-high heat. Reduce heat and simmer for 5 minutes or until slightly thickened. Stir in the reserved fresh herb mixture.

6. Slice pork across the grain and spoon bean mixture around pork.

Make Ahead

This dish can be assembled up to 12 hours in advance. Prepare through step 2, cover and refrigerate overnight. The next day, place stoneware in slow cooker and proceed with step 3.

Saucy Pepper Pork

Makes 4 to 6 servings

Sweet peppers and flavorful (but not spicy) sauce combine with tender, moist rib-end chops for a delicious weeknight family dinner. Served over quick-cooking egg noodles, it's a complete meal. If you like, tuck some apple wedges among the chops during the last half-hour or so of cooking.

Tips

Ready-to-use broth in convenient Tetra-Paks is a handy ingredient and doesn't need to be diluted. Avoid using cubes and powders, which tend to be very salty.

You can use pork shoulder blade (butt) chops in this recipe, but you will need to increase the cooking time to 6 to 8 hours on Low or 3 to 4 hours on High.

- **4- to 6-quart slow cooker**

2 tbsp	all-purpose flour	30 mL
½ tsp	dried thyme	2 mL
½ tsp	paprika	2 mL
½ tsp	salt	2 mL
¼ tsp	freshly ground black pepper	1 mL
4 to 6	pork loin rib chops (about 1 inch/ 2.5 cm thick), trimmed	4 to 6
2 tbsp	vegetable oil (approx.)	30 mL
1 cup	chicken broth	250 mL
2	red bell peppers, thinly sliced	2
2	cloves garlic, minced	2
1	onion, thinly sliced	1
2 tbsp	chopped fresh parsley	30 mL

1. On a plate, combine flour, thyme, paprika, salt and pepper. Gently coat both sides of each pork chop with flour mixture. Discard excess flour mixture.

2. In a large nonstick skillet, heat half the oil over medium-high heat. Cook pork chops in batches, adding more oil as needed, for about 3 minutes per side or until browned on both sides. Transfer to slow cooker stoneware.

3. Add broth to skillet and cook, scraping up any brown bits from pan. Add to stoneware, along with red peppers, garlic and onion.

4. Cover and cook on Low for 4 to 5 hours or on High for 2 to 2½ hours, until pork chops are fork-tender and sauce is bubbling.

5. Place pork chops on plates and spoon sauce over top. Sprinkle with parsley.

Pizza Mia Pork Chops

**Makes
6 servings**

The simplest recipes are sometimes the best. This dish was named after my friend and assistant, Leslie Huber. Her youngest daughter, Mia, is a huge pizza fan. (Are there any kids that aren't?) I like to use ready-made pasta or pizza sauce, since all of the seasoning has been added. You can serve these chops over any shape of pasta, but orzo soaks up some of the extra sauce.

Tips

Be as creative as you wish with your toppings. Imagine the pork chops as your pizza crust and garnish with your favorite pizza toppings, such as pepperoni, pineapple, hot peppers or olives.

You can use pork shoulder blade (butt) chops, instead of the pork loin chops, but you will need to increase the cooking time to 6 to 8 hours on Low or 3 to 4 hours on High.

- **4- to 6-quart slow cooker (preferably oval)**

6	pork loin rib chops (about 1 inch/2.5 cm thick)	6
½ tsp	salt	2 mL
¼ tsp	freshly ground black pepper	1 mL
2 tbsp	vegetable oil (approx.)	30 mL
1	onion, chopped	1
1	green bell pepper, chopped	1
1 cup	sliced mushrooms	250 mL
2 cups	pizza sauce	500 mL
1 cup	shredded mozzarella cheese	250 mL
4 cups	hot cooked orzo	1 L

1. Season both sides of pork chops with salt and pepper. In a large nonstick skillet, heat half the oil over medium-high heat. Cook pork chops in batches, adding more oil as needed, for about 3 minutes per side or until browned on both sides. Transfer to slow cooker stoneware.

2. Arrange onion, green pepper and mushrooms over pork chops. Pour pizza sauce over top.

3. Cover and cook on Low for 4 to 5 hours or on High for 2 to 2½ hours, until pork chops are fork-tender.

4. Sprinkle cheese over top, cover and cook for 10 minutes or until cheese is melted.

5. Divide orzo evenly among individual serving plates. Top each with a pork chop and sauce.

Pork Chop, Bean and Potato Bake

Makes 4 servings

This all-in-one dinner makes life so much easier. I love hash browns, especially the casserole version that seems to show up at every potluck. For smaller households, this recipe can easily be cut in half.

Tip

You can use pork shoulder blade (butt) chops in this recipe, but you will need to increase the cooking time to 6 to 8 hours on Low or 3 to 4 hours on High.

- **4- to 6-quart slow cooker**

2 cups	fresh or frozen lima beans, thawed if frozen	500 mL
1	onion, finely chopped	1
1 tbsp	dried parsley	15 mL
1 tbsp	packed brown sugar	15 mL
1 tsp	dry mustard	5 mL
2 tbsp	vegetable oil (approx.)	30 mL
4	pork loin rib chops (about 1 inch/2.5 cm thick)	4
3 cups	frozen hash brown potatoes, thawed	750 mL
1 cup	shredded Cheddar cheese, divided	250 mL
½ cup	sour cream	125 mL
	Chopped fresh parsley (optional)	

1. In a pot of boiling salted water, cook beans for about 5 minutes or until slightly tender. Drain, reserving ½ cup (125 mL) of the cooking water. Transfer beans to slow cooker stoneware.

2. In a bowl, stir together the reserved cooking water, onion, dried parsley, brown sugar and mustard. Pour over beans.

3. In a large nonstick skillet, heat half the oil over medium-high heat. Cook pork chops in batches, adding more oil as needed, for about 3 minutes per side or until browned on both sides. Place over beans.

4. In a bowl, combine hash browns, half the cheese and sour cream. Spoon over pork chops.

5. Cover and cook on Low for 4 to 5 hours or on High for 2 to 2½ hours, until pork chops are fork-tender.

6. Sprinkle the remaining cheese over the hash brown mixture. Cover and cook on High for 10 minutes or until cheese is melted. Garnish with fresh parsley, if desired.

Make Ahead

This dish can be partially assembled up to 2 days in advance. Prepare through step 2, cover and refrigerate. When ready to cook, place stoneware in slow cooker and proceed with step 3.

Pork Chops with Horseradish Apples

**Makes
4 servings**

....

This home-style dish delivers the wonderful flavors of fall. Granny Smith apples add their special tartness, and the horseradish ups the ante.

Tips

When choosing pork chops for slow cooking, select chops that are at least 1 inch (2.5 cm) thick. Chops that are too thin will overcook and dry out, making them tough and tasteless. I find that shoulder blade (butt) chops, sirloin chops or rib chops give the best results.

You can use pork loin rib chops in this recipe, but you will need to reduce the cooking time to 4 to 5 hours on Low or 2 to 2½ hours on High.

A flour and liquid combination added to a dish to thicken it is called a slurry. To prevent lumps in soups and stews when adding a slurry, combine the liquid and flour in a jar with a tight-fitting lid, then shake well until blended and smooth before pouring it into hot cooking liquid or sauce.

- **4- to 6-quart slow cooker**

4	pork shoulder blade (butt) chops (about 1 inch/2.5 cm thick), trimmed	4
1 tbsp	paprika	15 mL
1 tsp	dried thyme	5 mL
1 tsp	salt	5 mL
½ tsp	freshly ground black pepper	2 mL
2 tbsp	vegetable oil (approx.)	30 mL
2	Granny Smith apples, peeled and cut into ½-inch (1 cm) wedges	2
1	onion, thinly sliced	1
⅓ cup	dry white wine	75 mL
⅓ cup	chicken broth	75 mL
½ cup	heavy or whipping (35%) cream	125 mL
2 tbsp	all-purpose flour	30 mL
2 tbsp	creamed horseradish (approx.)	30 mL
1 tbsp	Dijon mustard	15 mL
2 tbsp	snipped fresh chives (optional)	30 mL

1. Season both sides of pork chops with paprika, thyme, salt and pepper. In a large nonstick skillet, heat half the oil over medium-high heat. Cook pork chops in batches, adding more oil as needed, for about 3 minutes per side or until browned on both sides. Transfer to a plate lined with paper towels and let drain. Transfer to slow cooker stoneware. Arrange apples and onion over pork chops. Pour in wine and broth.

2. Cover and cook on Low for 6 to 8 hours or on High for 3 to 4 hours, until pork chops are fork-tender. Using a slotted spoon, transfer pork chops to a warmed platter and tent loosely with foil.

3. In a jar with a tight-fitting lid, combine cream and flour, shaking until well combined. Stir into liquid in stoneware, along with horseradish and mustard. Cover and cook on High for 15 to 20 minutes or until liquid is slightly thickened. Pour over pork chops. Garnish with chives (if using).

Pulled Pork Taco Supper

Makes 6 to 8 servings

I couldn't choose, so this dish has the makings of a taco with the seasonings of a fajita. It's easy on the cook *and* on the budget.

Tips

To warm hard taco shells, place on a baking sheet in a 350°F (180°C) oven for 5 minutes. If using soft tortillas, wrap in foil and warm in a 350°F (180°C) oven for 15 to 20 minutes.

To avoid tears when chopping onions, put them in the freezer for a few minutes beforehand.

- **Minimum 4-quart slow cooker**

1	boneless pork shoulder blade (butt) roast (about 3½ lbs/1.75 kg), trimmed	1
½ tsp	salt	2 mL
½ tsp	freshly ground black pepper	2 mL
6	cloves garlic, minced	6
2	onions, finely chopped	2
1 cup	chicken broth	250 mL
1 tbsp	chili powder	15 mL
1 cup	frozen corn kernels, thawed	250 mL
1 cup	salsa	250 mL
2 tbsp	tomato paste	30 mL
¼ cup	finely chopped fresh cilantro or parsley	60 mL
16	hard or soft taco shells, warmed (see tip, at left)	16
2 cups	chopped iceberg lettuce	500 mL
1 cup	chopped tomatoes	250 mL
1 cup	shredded Cheddar cheese	250 mL
¼ cup	light sour cream	60 mL

1. Place pork in slow cooker stoneware and sprinkle with salt and pepper. Add garlic, onions, broth and chili powder.

2. Cover and cook on Low for 8 to 10 hours or on High for 4 to 5 hours, until pork is fork-tender. Transfer pork to a cutting board and let cool slightly.

3. Remove any butcher's string holding the roast together. Using two forks, shred pork.

4. Skim fat from cooking liquid in stoneware. Return pork to cooking liquid. Stir in corn, salsa and tomato paste. Cover and cook on High for 15 minutes or until pork is heated through and sauce is thickened. Stir in cilantro.

5. Ladle into a bowl and serve alongside taco shells, with lettuce, tomatoes, cheese and sour cream for toppings.

Make Ahead

This dish can be assembled up to 2 days in advance. Prepare through step 1, cover and refrigerate. When ready to cook, place stoneware in slow cooker and proceed with step 2.

Pork Marrakesh

**Makes
4 servings**

These pork chops are succulent and full of flavor. The aromatic dried and fresh herbs, combined with the fruit, stimulate your senses, inviting you to indulge. Serve over hot couscous.

Tips

Browning the pork before placing it in the stoneware gives the dish an extra-rich flavor and eliminates some of the fat. But if you're pressed for time, you can season the meat and add it directly to the slow cooker without browning it first.

To toast pine nuts, place the nuts in a dry nonstick skillet over low heat and toast, stirring gently, for 2 to 3 minutes or until fragrant and light golden brown. Be careful: they can burn in an instant!

- **4- to 6-quart slow cooker**

4	pork loin rib chops (about 1 inch/2.5 cm thick), trimmed	4
½ tsp	salt	2 mL
¼ tsp	freshly ground black pepper	1 mL
2 tbsp	olive oil (approx.), divided	30 mL
1	large red onion, thinly sliced	1
12	dried apricots, sliced	12
¾ cup	unsweetened apple juice	175 mL
2 tsp	minced gingerroot	10 mL
½ tsp	dried thyme	2 mL
1	3-inch (7.5 cm) cinnamon stick	1
¼ cup	chopped fresh cilantro	60 mL
	Toasted pine nuts (see tip, at left)	

1. Season both sides of pork chops with salt and pepper. In a large nonstick skillet, heat 1 tbsp (15 mL) of the oil over medium-high heat. Cook pork chops in batches, adding more oil as needed, for about 3 minutes per side or until browned on both sides. Transfer to a plate.

2. Reduce heat to medium and add the remaining 1 tbsp (15 mL) oil to skillet. Sauté red onion for about 3 minutes or until tender and translucent.

3. Arrange half the onion and half the apricots in slow cooker stoneware. Place pork chops on top. Spread the remaining onion and apricots on top. Add apple juice, ginger, thyme and cinnamon stick.

4. Cover and cook on Low for 4 to 5 hours or on High for 2 to 2½ hours, until pork chops are fork-tender. Discard cinnamon stick. Sprinkle with cilantro and pine nuts.

Pork and Potato Poutine

What teenager doesn't like poutine? This version uses roasted fingerling potatoes, rather than deep-fried french fries, and traditional cheese curds. If you can't find the curds, replace them with shredded white Cheddar or mozzarella cheese.

Tips

While many pork dishes use chicken broth to make the gravy, I like to use beef broth for this one, to add richness. For a lighter-flavored gravy, you can use chicken or veal broth.

Broth (or stock) is one of the most indispensable pantry staples. Commercial broth cubes and powders are loaded with salt and just don't deliver the flavor of homemade stock or prepared broth. I like to keep 32-oz (1 L) Tetra Paks on hand, especially the sodium-reduced variety.

- **4- to 5-quart slow cooker**
- *Rimmed baking sheet, lined with parchment paper*

6	slices bacon, chopped	6
1	boneless pork shoulder blade (butt) roast (about 3 lbs/1.5 kg), trimmed and cut into 1-inch (2.5 cm) cubes	1
1 tbsp	vegetable oil (optional)	15 mL
3	cloves garlic, minced	3
2	carrots, diced	2
2	stalks celery, diced	2
1	large onion, chopped	1
1 tbsp	dried thyme	15 mL
1 tbsp	dried parsley	15 mL
1 tsp	paprika	5 mL
1/2 tsp	salt	2 mL
1/4 tsp	freshly ground black pepper	1 mL
1 1/2 cups	beef broth (see tips, at left)	375 mL
1	bay leaf	1
2 tbsp	cornstarch	30 mL
2 tbsp	cold water	30 mL

Potato Poutine

3 lbs	fingerling potatoes, halved lengthwise	1.5 kg
3 tbsp	olive oil	45 mL
2 tsp	kosher salt	10 mL
1/4 tsp	freshly ground black pepper	1 mL
8 oz	fresh white cheese curds	250 g
	Chopped fresh parsley	

1. In a large nonstick skillet, cook bacon over medium-high heat, stirring, for about 5 minutes or until crisp. Transfer to a plate lined with paper towels. Set aside.

2. In batches, add pork to skillet and cook, adding oil if needed, for about 4 minutes or until browned all over. Using a slotted spoon, transfer to slow cooker stoneware.

Variations

This recipe also works well with beef. Use a braising roast, such as a blade, cross rib, chuck or shoulder, and cut it into 1-inch (2.5 cm) cubes.

Reduce the beef broth to 1 cup (250 mL) and add ½ cup (125 mL) dry red wine.

For an upscale version of the poutine, use a soft melting cheese, such as Brie, cut into chunks.

3. Add garlic, carrots, celery, onion, thyme, parsley, paprika, salt and pepper to skillet and sauté for about 5 minutes or until fragrant. Add onion mixture and bacon to stoneware.

4. Add broth to skillet, bring to a boil and cook for about 5 minutes, scraping up any brown bits from pan. Pour over pork mixture. Add bay leaf.

5. Cover and cook on Low for 8 to 10 hours or on High for 4 to 5 hours, until pork is fork-tender.

6. *Potato Poutine:* Meanwhile, preheat oven to 400°F (200°C). In a large bowl, toss potatoes with oil, salt and pepper. Spread in a single layer on prepared baking sheet. Bake for 40 to 50 minutes, stirring once or twice, until browned and tender.

7. In a bowl, whisk together cornstarch and water. Stir into stoneware. Cover and cook on High for 10 minutes or until gravy is thickened. Discard bay leaf.

8. Divide potatoes evenly among individual serving plates. Ladle pork mixture on top and top with cheese curds and parsley. Serve immediately.

Make Ahead

This dish can be assembled up to 2 days in advance, as long as the pork is left out. Complete steps 1, 3 and 4. Cover and refrigerate. When ready to cook, add vegetable oil to the skillet and brown the pork as directed in step 2. Place stoneware in slow cooker, add pork and proceed with step 5.

Vietnamese Sticky Pork Chops

Makes 4 to 6 servings

These chops are cooked slowly with spices and a little bit of sugar to create a dish that is sweet, with a hint of heat.

Tips

Rice stick noodles can be prepared in a number of different ways. For this dish, the easiest way is to cook them in boiling water until they are wilted, then drain and rinse. Don't let them boil for too long (only about 2 or 3 minutes) or they will turn to mush.

You can substitute boneless pork shoulder blade (butt) chops for the pork loin rib chops, but you will need to increase the cooking time to 6 to 8 hours on Low or 3 to 4 hours on High.

Hoisin sauce is a thick, reddish brown sauce made from soybeans and used primarily in Thai and Chinese dishes. It can be found in the Asian aisle of the supermarket.

- **4- to 5-quart slow cooker**

2 tbsp	vegetable oil (approx.)	30 mL
4 to 6	pork loin rib chops (about 1 inch/2.5 cm thick), trimmed	4 to 6
3	cloves garlic, minced	3
3	star anise pods (or 1 tsp/5 mL Chinese five-spice powder)	3
1 tbsp	minced gingerroot	15 mL
1 tbsp	granulated sugar	15 mL
1/4 tsp	freshly ground black pepper	1 mL
1/2 cup	hoisin or black bean sauce	125 mL
2 tbsp	rice vinegar	30 mL
1 tbsp	Sriracha chili sauce	15 mL
4	carrots, cut into 1-inch (2.5 cm) pieces	4
1 tbsp	cornstarch	15 mL
2 tbsp	cold water	30 mL
1	green onion, finely chopped	1
	Cooked rice stick noodles	
2 tbsp	chopped fresh cilantro	30 mL
	Toasted sesame seeds (optional)	

1. In a large nonstick skillet, heat half the oil over medium-high heat. Cook pork chops in batches, adding more oil as needed, for about 3 minutes per side or until browned on both sides. Transfer to a plate.

2. In a bowl, combine garlic, star anise, ginger, sugar, pepper, hoisin sauce, vinegar and chili sauce.

3. Arrange carrots in slow cooker stoneware. Place pork chops on carrots. Pour garlic mixture over pork chops.

4. Cover and cook on Low for 4 to 5 hours or on High for 2 to 2 1/2 hours, until pork chops are fork-tender. Using a slotted spoon, transfer pork chops and carrots to a plate. Cover to keep warm.

continued on page 202…

5. Pour cooking liquid into a saucepan and bring to a boil over medium-high heat. In a bowl, whisk together cornstarch and water. Stir into saucepan and return to a boil. Reduce heat and boil gently, stirring, until sauce is thickened. Stir in green onion.

6. Place noodles on a platter and arrange pork chops on top. Drizzle with sauce and serve additional sauce on the side, if desired. Sprinkle with cilantro and sesame seeds (if using).

> Sriracha chili sauce is a purée of chiles, sugar, vinegar, garlic and salt. It is to Thai cuisine what ketchup is to North American cuisine. It is used in cooking and as a condiment to add heat to a dish. You can find it in Asian grocery stores and at many well-stocked supermarkets.

Liki Tiki Pork

**Makes
6 servings**

This delicious sweet-and-sour pork evokes thoughts of warm tropical breezes, swaying palm trees and the smell of sand and surf. It is elegant enough to serve on festive occasions or whenever you want to make something special for your family. Serve over rice.

Tip

Hoisin sauce has a sweet, tangy flavor and is available in the Asian foods section of the supermarket.

- **3- to 4-quart slow cooker**

2 tbsp	vegetable oil (approx.)	30 mL
1	boneless pork shoulder blade (butt) roast (about 2 lbs/1 kg), trimmed and cut into 1-inch (2.5 cm) cubes	1
2	stalks celery, chopped	2
1	onion, finely chopped	1
2 tbsp	white wine vinegar	30 mL
1 tbsp	Dijon mustard	15 mL
1 tbsp	hoisin sauce	15 mL
1 tsp	salt	5 mL
1/2 tsp	freshly ground black pepper	2 mL
1	can (8 oz/227 mL) pineapple chunks, drained, reserving juice	1
2 tbsp	cornstarch	30 mL
2 tbsp	cold water	30 mL
1	ripe mango, cut into chunks	1
1 cup	macadamia nuts or blanched almonds	250 mL
1/2 cup	unsweetened shredded coconut	125 mL

1. In a large nonstick skillet, heat half the oil over medium-high heat. Cook pork in batches, adding more oil as needed, for about 4 minutes or until browned all over. Using a slotted spoon, transfer to slow cooker stoneware. Stir in celery and onion.

2. In a bowl, combine vinegar, mustard, hoisin sauce, salt, pepper and pineapple juice. Stir into stoneware.

3. Cover and cook on Low for 6 to 8 hours or on High for 3 to 4 hours, until pork is fork-tender and stew is bubbling. Using a slotted spoon, transfer pork to a bowl.

4. In a small bowl, whisk together cornstarch and water. Stir into cooking liquid in stoneware. Cover and cook on High for 10 to 15 minutes or until thickened.

5. Return pork to stoneware, along with pineapple chunks, mango, macadamia nuts and coconut. Stir until warmed through.

BBQ Pork Sandwiches with Five-Vegetable Slaw

Makes 4 to 6 servings

Start the ingredients in the slow cooker in the morning, so dinner simmers during the day. Spicy roast pork and crisp coleslaw add up to down-home sandwiches with uptown taste.

Tips

The most flavorful paprika comes from Hungary. Types range from mild to hot. Use the type that suits your taste.

Tomato paste is now available in tubes in many supermarkets and delis. It keeps for months in the refrigerator.

• **Minimum 4-quart slow cooker**

4	large garlic cloves, minced	4
1 tsp	ground cumin	5 mL
½ tsp	paprika	2 mL
½ tsp	ground coriander	2 mL
½ tsp	salt	2 mL
¼ tsp	freshly ground black pepper	1 mL
¼ tsp	cayenne pepper	1 mL
⅓ cup	dark (cooking) molasses	75 mL
⅓ cup	cider vinegar	75 mL
¼ cup	tomato paste	60 mL
1	boneless pork shoulder blade (butt) roast (about 2 lbs/1 kg), trimmed	1
2	bay leaves	2
4 to 6	crusty kaiser rolls, split	4 to 6

Five-Vegetable Slaw

4 cups	coleslaw or broccoli slaw mix	1 L
½ cup	thinly sliced red bell pepper	125 mL
½ cup	thinly sliced green bell pepper	125 mL
½	cucumber, peeled, halved lengthwise, seeded and thinly sliced	½
3	green onions, thinly sliced on the diagonal	3
⅓ cup	mayonnaise	75 mL
1 tbsp	cider vinegar	15 mL
¼ tsp	salt	1 mL
¼ tsp	freshly ground black pepper	1 mL

1. In a bowl, whisk together garlic, cumin, paprika, coriander, salt, black pepper, cayenne, molasses, vinegar and tomato paste.

2. Arrange pork and bay leaves in slow cooker stoneware. Stir in molasses mixture until pork is coated.

3. Cover and cook on Low for 8 to 10 hours or on High for 4 to 5 hours, until pork is fork-tender. Transfer pork to a cutting board and let cool slightly.

4. Remove any butcher's string holding the roast together. Using two forks, shred pork.

5. Skim fat from cooking liquid in stoneware. Discard bay leaves. Return pork to cooking liquid.

6. *Five-Vegetable Slaw:* In a large bowl, toss together coleslaw mix, red pepper, green pepper, cucumber and green onions. Add mayonnaise, vinegar, salt and pepper; toss to coat.

7. Heap pork mixture on bottom halves of rolls, place a heaping serving of slaw on top and cover with tops of rolls. Serve immediately.

Make Ahead

You can make the vegetable slaw up to 2 days in advance. Cover and refrigerate until ready to use.

This dish can be assembled up to 2 days in advance. Prepare through step 2, cover and refrigerate. When ready to cook, place stoneware in slow cooker and proceed with step 3.

Mexican Fiesta Pork

Makes 4 to 6 servings

It's hard to believe this dish could taste so great with so few ingredients. But that's its appeal! Use mild, medium or hot salsa depending on the level of heat you like.

Tips

To save yourself the work, ask the butcher to cut a roast into cubes for you. If that's not possible, trim and cube a piece of pork shoulder for this dish. If the pork shoulder is bone-in, be sure to buy enough to yield 2 lbs (1 kg) once the bone is removed.

Many independent butchers sell pork stew meat, which is fine to use in this recipe.

• **Minimum 4-quart slow cooker**

1	boneless pork shoulder blade (butt) roast (about 2 lbs/1 kg), trimmed and cut into 1-inch (2.5 cm) cubes	1
1	can (4½ oz/127 mL) chopped mild green chiles, drained	1
4½ cups	thick and chunky salsa	1.125 L
2 cups	cooked or canned black beans (see page 84), drained and rinsed	500 mL
	Mexican Rice (see recipe, page 208) or flour tortillas, warmed	
1 cup	shredded Monterey Jack cheese	250 mL
	Guacamole or sour cream (optional)	

1. In slow cooker stoneware, combine pork, chiles and salsa.

2. Cover and cook on Low for 6 to 8 hours or until fork-tender.

3. Stir in beans. Cover and cook on Low for 5 to 10 minutes or until beans are heated through.

4. Spoon pork mixture over Mexican Rice or into warm tortillas. Sprinkle with cheese. Top each portion with a dollop of guacamole (if using).

Make Ahead

This dish can be assembled up to 12 hours in advance. Prepare through step 1, cover and refrigerate overnight. The next day, place stoneware in slow cooker and proceed with step 2.

Mexican Rice

I like to make this
authentic Mexican
rice recipe as a side
dish when I am serving
Mexican food. The
keys are cooking the
rice properly and using
good-quality chicken
broth.

Tip

Jalapeño peppers
contain volatile oils
that can burn your
skin and eyes if they
come into direct
contact. It is best
to wear plastic or
rubber gloves when
chopping jalapeños,
and take care not to
touch your face or
eyes while you work.
If your bare hands do
touch the peppers,
wash your hands and
nails well with hot,
soapy water.

- *Preheat oven to 350°F (180°C)*
- *Large ovenproof skillet, with lid*

1	white onion, finely chopped	1
1	can (19 oz/540 mL) diced tomatoes, with juice	1
2 cups	long-grain white rice	500 mL
$\frac{1}{3}$ cup	vegetable oil	75 mL
4	cloves garlic, minced	4
3	jalapeño peppers, seeded and minced, divided	3
2 cups	chicken broth	500 mL
$1\frac{1}{2}$ tsp	salt	7 mL
$\frac{1}{2}$ cup	finely chopped fresh cilantro	125 mL
1	lime, cut into wedges	1

1. In a bowl, combine onion and tomatoes with juice. Set aside.

2. In a fine-mesh strainer, rinse rice under cold running water until water runs clear. Drain well.

3. In ovenproof skillet, heat oil over medium-high heat for about 2 minutes. (Add a few grains of rice; if they sizzle, the oil is hot enough.) Stir-fry rice for 6 to 8 minutes or until light golden and translucent.

4. Reduce heat to medium. Add garlic and two-thirds of the jalapeños to skillet and sauté for about $1\frac{1}{2}$ minutes or until fragrant. Stir in reserved onion mixture, broth and salt. Increase heat to high and bring to a boil.

5. Cover and bake in preheated oven for 30 to 35 minutes, stirring once halfway through, until liquid is absorbed and rice is tender. Stir in cilantro and the remaining jalapeño to taste. Serve with lime wedges on the side.

Unstuffed Sweet-and-Sour Cabbage

**Makes
4 servings**

Making Eastern European–style cabbage rolls is a time-consuming endeavor. This unorthodox method, which uses dried cranberries and ground pork, is much easier — and, I like to think, tastes even better.

Tip

I like to use savoy cabbage for this dish. With its flavorful crinkled leaves, this cabbage is one of the best for cooking. Its loose leaves have lace-patterned veins and vary in color from dark to light green. They are tender and have a milder, sweeter flavor than those of green cabbage. You can also use red cabbage.

- **Minimum 5-quart slow cooker (preferably oval)**

1	head green cabbage (about 2 lbs/1 kg), quartered lengthwise and cored	1
¼ cup	sodium-reduced chicken broth	60 mL
3	cloves garlic, thinly sliced, divided	3
1 tsp	salt, divided	5 mL
1 tbsp	olive oil	15 mL
1	large onion, thinly sliced	1
1 lb	lean ground pork or turkey (or 8 oz/250 g of each)	500 g
½ tsp	freshly ground black pepper	2 mL
1	can (28 oz/796 mL) diced tomatoes, with juice	1
⅓ cup	dried cranberries or cherries	75 mL
1 tbsp	packed dark brown sugar	15 mL
3 tbsp	red wine vinegar	45 mL
2 tbsp	chopped fresh flat-leaf (Italian) parsley	30 mL

1. Place cabbage in slow cooker stoneware. Add broth, one-third of the garlic and ¼ tsp (1 mL) of the salt.

2. Meanwhile, in a large nonstick skillet, heat oil over medium-high heat. Sauté onion for about 3 minutes or until tender and translucent. Add the remaining garlic and sauté for 1 minute. Add pork, the remaining salt and pepper; cook, breaking up pork with the back of a wooden spoon, for about 3 minutes or until pork is no longer pink. Stir in tomatoes with juice, cranberries, brown sugar and vinegar. Pour into stoneware.

3. Cover and cook on Low for 8 to 10 hours or on High for 4 to 5 hours, until bubbling. Transfer to a serving dish and sprinkle with parsley.

Make Ahead

This dish can be assembled up to 12 hours in advance. Prepare through step 2, letting pork mixture cool before adding it to stoneware. Cover and refrigerate overnight. The next day, place stoneware in slow cooker and proceed with step 3.

Pork Curry with Apples and Chinese Noodles

**Makes
6 servings**

. . . .

This tasty curry looks as good as it tastes. Offer a dish of mango chutney alongside, to complement the flavors of the fruit. You can also serve this curry over hot cooked rice.

Tip

It's easy to grate gingerroot if you keep an unpeeled nub of it in the freezer, wrapped in a plastic freezer bag. (Ginger tends to quickly get moldy and soft when it's stored in the fridge.) Use a Microplane-style rasp grater, available at good kitchenware and department stores, for best results. These have tiny razor-like edges that make quick and easy tasks of grating and cleaning.

- **3½- to 5-quart slow cooker**

2 tbsp	vegetable oil (approx.)	30 mL
1	boneless pork shoulder blade (butt) roast (about 2 lbs/1 kg), trimmed and cut into 1-inch (2.5 cm) cubes	1
1	large onion, sliced	1
2	cloves garlic, minced	2
1 tbsp	grated gingerroot	15 mL
1	3-inch (7.5 cm) cinnamon stick	1
1 tsp	ground coriander	5 mL
1 tsp	ground cumin	5 mL
1 tsp	ground turmeric	5 mL
½ tsp	hot pepper flakes	2 mL
½ tsp	fennel seeds	2 mL
½ tsp	salt	2 mL
¼ tsp	freshly ground black pepper	1 mL
½ cup	chicken broth	125 mL
1 tbsp	all-purpose flour	15 mL
1 cup	plain yogurt (not fat-free)	250 mL
1 tbsp	liquid honey	15 mL
2	red-skinned apples, cut into cubes	2
1	package (12 oz/350 g) fresh lo mein noodles	1
⅓ cup	chopped fresh cilantro or parsley	75 mL
¼ cup	raisins	60 mL
¼ cup	chopped roasted peanuts	60 mL

1. In a large nonstick skillet, heat half the oil over medium-high heat. Cook pork in batches, adding more oil as needed, for about 4 minutes or until browned all over. Using a slotted spoon, transfer to slow cooker stoneware.

2. Reduce heat to medium. Add onion to skillet and sauté until tender and translucent. Add garlic, ginger, cinnamon stick, coriander, cumin, turmeric, hot pepper flakes, fennel seeds, salt and black pepper; sauté for about 3 minutes or until fragrant. Stir in broth. Pour into stoneware.

It is best to use lo mein noodles for this dish since they can be cooked in boiling water, which is easier than frying the noodles to serve with the curry. If Chinese egg noodles aren't available, thin Italian pasta, such as fettuccini or linguini, makes a handy substitute.

Cooking times can vary a great deal between slow cooker manufacturers. Always let your food cook for the minimum amount of time before testing for doneness.

3. Cover and cook on Low for 8 to 10 hours or on High for 4 to 5 hours, until pork is fork-tender.

4. In a bowl, stir together flour, yogurt and honey. Stir into stoneware, along with apples. Cover and cook on High for 20 minutes or until pork mixture is thickened and apples are warmed through and slightly softened. Discard cinnamon stick.

5. Meanwhile, in a large pot of boiling salted water, cook noodles for 3 to 4 minutes or until tender. Drain and toss into pork mixture. Transfer to a large platter and sprinkle with cilantro, raisins and peanuts.

> In Chinese, *mein* means "noodles," and the two most popular types are lo mein and chow mein. Lo mein are tossed noodles, which are added to a stir-fry at the end of the cooking process so they stay soft and absorb the sauce. Chow mein are fried first so they are crunchy and crisp.

Ham, Barley and Sweet Potato Jambalaya

Makes 6 servings

It's time for a little history lesson. Listen well. Some say the word "jambalaya" came from the French *jambon*, meaning "ham," the French phrase *à la*, meaning "in the style of," and the African *ya*, meaning "rice." However the word originated, jambalaya is a traditional Louisiana one-pot meal — but you can serve it with a nice green salad and French bread.

Tips

Cajun seasoning is available at most supermarkets and specialty food stores. If you can't find it, substitute 1½ tsp (7 mL) ground cumin, 1 tsp (5 mL) each ground thyme and paprika, ¼ tsp (1 mL) cayenne pepper and a pinch of ground allspice.

Rinse the barley in a fine-mesh sieve under cold running water, stirring to make sure it is thoroughly rinsed, then drain well.

- **3½- to 5-quart slow cooker**

1 tbsp	vegetable oil	15 mL
2 cups	cubed Black Forest ham	500 mL
2	cloves garlic, minced	2
2	stalks celery, chopped	2
1	onion, chopped	1
2 tsp	Cajun seasoning	10 mL
1 tsp	dried oregano	5 mL
1 tsp	salt	5 mL
½ tsp	freshly ground black pepper	2 mL
1	can (28 oz/796 mL) diced tomatoes, with juice	1
3 cups	chicken broth	750 mL
1 cup	pearl barley, rinsed	250 mL
2	large sweet potatoes, peeled and cut into ½-inch (1 cm) cubes	2
2	bay leaves	2
1	green bell pepper, finely chopped	1
8 oz	large cooked peeled shrimp (optional)	250 g
2 tbsp	chopped fresh parsley	30 mL
	Hot pepper sauce	

1. In a large skillet, heat oil over medium heat. Sauté ham, garlic, celery, onion, Cajun seasoning, oregano, salt and pepper for about 5 minutes or until ham is browned all over and onion is tender and translucent. Stir in tomatoes with juice, broth and barley; bring to a boil. Transfer to slow cooker stoneware. Stir in sweet potatoes and bay leaves.

2. Cover and cook on Low for 6 to 8 hours or on High for 3 to 4 hours, until most of the liquid is absorbed.

continued on page 214...

3. Using a fork, stir in green pepper and shrimp (if using). Cover and cook on High for 20 minutes or until green pepper is tender and shrimp are heated through. Discard bay leaves. Sprinkle with parsley. Serve with hot pepper sauce (you can add a few dashes directly to the jambalaya if you know all your diners like heat).

Make Ahead

This dish can be assembled up to 2 days in advance. Complete step 1, omitting the barley, cover and refrigerate. When ready to cook, place stoneware in slow cooker, add barley and proceed with step 2.

> **Pearl barley is a popular grain and a great alternative to rice. It has been hulled, steamed and polished, meaning the bran has been removed. It has an oval shape with a dull white color. When cooked, it has a creamy, chewy texture. Barley can be found near the dried peas and beans in the supermarket.**

Stuffed Zucchini with Ham and Rice

**Makes
4 servings**

This dish is best made in a large oval slow cooker, which will hold both of the zucchini. Look for smaller zucchini, but if you can't find them, trim and cut the zucchini into smaller chunks and spoon the rice mixture over the chunks.

Variation

In place of the ham, you can use smoked turkey or chicken.

- **Minimum 5-quart slow cooker (preferably oval)**

2	zucchini (about 7 inches/18 cm long)	2
	Salt	
2	thick slices Black Forest ham, finely chopped	2
1	small onion, finely chopped	1
1	can (14 oz/398 mL) diced tomatoes, with juice	1
1 cup	cooked long-grain white rice	250 mL
½ tsp	paprika	2 mL
½ tsp	dried oregano	2 mL
½ cup	crumbled feta cheese	125 mL

1. Remove ends of zucchini, then cut each in half lengthwise, scoop out seedy pulp and discard. Sprinkle zucchini with salt and set aside.

2. Meanwhile, in a large bowl, combine ham, onion, tomatoes with juice, rice, paprika and oregano. Mound rice mixture in scooped-out zucchini and place in slow cooker stoneware.

3. Cover and cook on Low for 4 to 5 hours or until zucchini are tender. Sprinkle with cheese. Cover and cook for 5 to 10 minutes or until cheese has melted.

Make Ahead

This dish can be assembled up to 12 hours in advance. Prepare through step 2, cover and refrigerate overnight. The next day, place stoneware in slow cooker and proceed with step 3.

Uptown Pork and Beans

**Makes 4 to
6 servings**

Residents of the city of Waterloo, Ontario, call our downtown area "Uptown." We are also famous for our sausages, served frequently during autumn, when we celebrate Canada's largest Bavarian festival, Oktoberfest, which celebrates the German heritage of many of the region's settlers. This recipe is a nod to our world-renowned festival and great city!

Tip

Leftovers from this tasty meal can be served over spaetzle noodles or on soft kaiser rolls. (You could call the latter "Sloppy Johanns"!)

- **4- to 6-quart slow cooker**

1 lb	fresh Oktoberfest-style sausages or other mild fresh sausages	500 g
6	thick slices bacon, chopped	6
2	cans (each 14 oz/398 mL) baked beans in tomato sauce	2
2	cloves garlic, minced	2
2	carrots, cut into ½-inch (1 cm) chunks	2
1	onion, finely chopped	1
1	stalk celery, chopped	1
1 cup	ketchup	250 mL
1 cup	unsweetened apple cider or apple juice	250 mL
2 tbsp	cider vinegar	30 mL
2 tbsp	Oktoberfest-style mustard or honey mustard	30 mL
2 tbsp	pure maple syrup	30 mL

1. In a large skillet, cook sausage over medium-high heat, turning often, for 10 minutes or until browned all over. Remove from heat and cut into 1-inch (2.5 cm) slices. Transfer to slow cooker stoneware.

2. Stir in bacon, beans, garlic, carrots, onion, celery, ketchup, apple cider, vinegar, mustard and maple syrup.

3. Cover and cook on Low for 6 to 8 hours or on High for 3 to 4 hours, until bubbling.

Make Ahead

This dish can be assembled up to 12 hours in advance. Prepare through step 2, letting sausage cool before adding it to stoneware. Cover and refrigerate overnight. The next day, place stoneware in slow cooker and proceed with step 3.

> **Oktoberfest mustard is a traditional Russian-style sweet mustard. While some mustards have a sharp, pungent flavor, this mustard is tangy, with a touch of sweetness. A sweet brown mustard or honey mustard is a good alternative. Independent butcher shops and gourmet food shops usually have a good selection of specialty mustards.**

Seven-Layer Sausage Rigatoni Casserole

**Makes
8 servings**

A slow cooker is ideal for pasta casseroles. During the long cooking, the flavors blend and the sauce melts into every corner of the pasta. If you're letting it cook for longer than 6 hours, you'll want to make sure your slow cooker switches to Warm mode when it should, so the pasta doesn't overcook.

Tip

A generous amount of salt in the cooking water seasons the pasta internally as it absorbs the water and swells. The claim that salted water cooks food faster (because the salt increases the boiling temperature) is exaggerated: you're not adding enough salt to raise the boiling temperature by more than about 1°F (1°C).

- **4- to 6-quart slow cooker, stoneware greased**

3 cups	rigatoni pasta	750 mL
1 lb	mild or hot fresh Italian sausage, casings removed	500 g
3	cloves garlic, minced	3
1	can (28 oz/796 mL) crushed tomatoes	1
1	can (10 oz/284 mL) condensed cream of mushroom soup	1
1 tbsp	dried basil	15 mL
1	jar (13 oz/370 mL) roasted red bell peppers, drained and chopped (see tip, page 261)	1
2	zucchini, coarsely chopped	2
2½ cups	shredded mozzarella cheese	625 mL
½ cup	freshly grated Parmesan cheese	125 mL
½ cup	fresh bread crumbs	125 mL
2 tbsp	melted butter	30 mL

1. In a large pot of boiling salted water, cook rigatoni for 7 to 8 minutes or until firm but tender (al dente). Drain.

2. Meanwhile, in a large skillet, cook sausage over medium-high heat, breaking it up with the back of a wooden spoon, for about 6 to 8 minutes or until browned. Remove from heat.

3. In a bowl, combine garlic, tomatoes, soup and basil.

4. Place half the pasta in bottom of prepared slow cooker stoneware. Top with half the sausage, then half the red peppers and zucchini. Spread with half the tomato mixture. Sprinkle with half the mozzarella. Repeat the layers with the remaining ingredients.

5. In a bowl, combine Parmesan and bread crumbs. Sprinkle evenly over pasta mixture. Drizzle with butter.

6. Cover and cook on Low for 4 to 6 hours or on High for 2 to 3 hours, until bubbling.

Sausage Lasagna

**Makes
8 servings**

....

This meat sauce starts quickly on the stove, but hours in the slow cooker add a real depth of flavor. Use sheets of fresh lasagna; that way, you can trim them easily with scissors to fit either oval or round slow cookers.

Tips

To fit lasagna noodles into a round slow cooker, break off corners as needed. You don't have to precook the noodles. When the lasagna's done, they'll be ready too.

Cooking times are approximate and can vary among slow cookers. Lasagna can be prone to overcooking, so begin to check for doneness at the minimum cooking time, if possible.

• **Minimum 5-quart slow cooker (preferably oval)**

1 lb	mild or hot fresh Italian sausage, casings removed	500 g
2	carrots, finely chopped	2
2	cloves garlic, minced	2
1	onion, finely chopped	1
2 tsp	dried basil leaves	10 mL
1/2 tsp	salt	2 mL
1/4 tsp	freshly ground black pepper	1 mL
1	can (28 oz/796 mL) tomato pasta sauce	1
2 cups	shredded mozzarella cheese, divided	500 mL
1 cup	ricotta cheese	250 mL
1 cup	freshly grated Parmesan cheese	250 mL
1/4 cup	basil pesto	60 mL
4 to 6	sheets fresh lasagna (or 15 oven-ready lasagna noodles)	4 to 6

1. In a large pot or Dutch oven, cook sausage over medium-high heat, breaking it up with the back of a wooden spoon, for 6 to 8 minutes or until browned. Add carrots, garlic, onion, basil, salt and pepper; sauté for 3 to 5 minutes or until onion is tender and translucent. Stir in pasta sauce. Set aside.

2. In a bowl, combine 1 cup (250 mL) of the mozzarella, ricotta, Parmesan and pesto.

3. Spoon one-quarter of the sausage mixture into slow cooker stoneware. Top with 1 fresh lasagna sheet (or 5 oven-ready noodles, broken into pieces to fit), breaking an extra lasagna sheet into pieces if necessary to cover sausage mixture completely. Spread with half the cheese mixture, then one-quarter of the sausage mixture. Repeat the layers twice more, ending with sausage mixture.

4. Cover and cook on Low for 4 to 6 hours or until lasagna is tender and heated through.

5. Sprinkle the remaining mozzarella over lasagna in stoneware. Turn off heat, cover and let stand for about 10 minutes or until cheese is melted.

Abruzzi-Style Spaghetti

Makes 6 to 8 servings

One night while watching a cooking show on television, my kitchen assistant Leslie saw a celebrity chef prepare a rustic pasta sauce with pork ribs and sausage. "Why don't we try making something similar in the slow cooker?" she asked. When I developed this hearty Italian-style dinner, it was a huge hit with everyone, including my household's hungry teenagers. Serve bowls of this pasta with fresh bread and a green salad.

Tips

Tomato paste is now available in tubes in many supermarkets and delis. These tubes are great, because you can just use as much as you need and the rest keeps for months in the refrigerator.

To prevent soft, mushy pasta, do not allow it to be in the water any longer than necessary. Add it only when the water is at a full boil, and keep it at a steady boil while it cooks.

• **Minimum 4-quart slow cooker**

1½ lbs	pork spareribs	750 g
1 lb	mild fresh Italian sausage	500 g
4	cloves garlic, minced	4
¾ cup	freshly grated Parmesan cheese	175 mL
½ cup	Italian-seasoned dry bread crumbs	125 mL
2 tbsp	dried basil	30 mL
1 tbsp	granulated sugar	15 mL
½ tsp	freshly ground black pepper	2 mL
1	can (48 oz/1.42 L) tomato juice	1
1	can (5½ oz/156 mL) tomato paste	1
1½ lbs	spaghetti	750 g
	Chopped fresh flat-leaf (Italian) parsley	
	Grated Parmesan cheese (optional)	

1. Cut spareribs into two- or three-rib portions. Cut sausage into 3-inch (7.5 cm) lengths. Set aside.

2. In slow cooker stoneware, combine garlic, cheese, bread crumbs, basil, sugar and pepper. Whisk in tomato juice and tomato paste until blended. Add spareribs and sausage, spooning sauce evenly over meat.

3. Cover and cook on Low for 4 to 6 hours or on High for 8 to 10 hours, until pork is falling off the bones.

4. Meanwhile, in a large pot of boiling salted water, cook spaghetti for 8 to 10 minutes or until tender but firm (al dente). Drain.

5. Using a slotted spoon, transfer spareribs and sausage to a platter, arranging them around the edge. Skim off fat from sauce. Toss spaghetti with 2 cups (500 mL) of the sauce, then transfer to center of platter. Sprinkle spaghetti with parsley and additional cheese, if desired. Serve the remaining sauce on the side.

Make Ahead

This dish can be assembled up to 12 hours in advance. Cut the spareribs and sausage as described in step 1 and refrigerate each separately. Prepare the cheese mixture and refrigerate it separately. The next day, assemble ingredients in slow cooker stoneware and proceed with step 3.

Mexican Pork Ribs

Makes 4 to 6 servings

Tomatillos are small green fruits surrounded by papery husks, and they are a staple in Mexican cuisine. Green tomatoes or firm plum (Roma) tomatoes seasoned with lemon juice can be used as a substitute. Serve with Mexican Rice (page 208).

Tips

Store fresh ripe tomatillos with their husks on in a paper bag in the refrigerator for up to 1 month. Just make sure they don't get wet, or the inside of the husk may become a little slimy. When you are ready to use them, peel off the husks and wash the tomatillos to remove any stickiness.

Tomatillos may also be frozen whole or sliced. Thawed tomatillo will be soft, but fine for use in this sauce.

- **3- to 5-quart slow cooker**
- *Preheat broiler, with rack set 6 inches (15 cm) below heat source*
- *Blender*
- *Broiler pan or rimmed baking sheet, lined with foil*

1 lb	tomatillos, husks removed, washed (or one 11-oz/325 mL can, drained)	500 g
4 lbs	country-style pork ribs, cut into individual ribs, if possible	2 kg
2 tbsp	olive oil	30 mL
	Salt and freshly ground black pepper	
3	cloves garlic, minced	3
2	jalapeño peppers, seeded and finely chopped	2
1	onion, finely chopped	1
2	cans (each 4½ oz/127 mL) diced mild green chiles	2
1 tbsp	dried oregano	15 mL
⅓ cup	chopped fresh cilantro (approx.)	75 mL
	Shredded Cheddar cheese	
	Lime wedges	
	Fresh cilantro leaves (optional)	

1. In blender, purée tomatillos until smooth. Set aside.

2. Rub ribs with oil and place in prepared broiler pan. Season with salt and pepper. Broil, turning once, for 10 to 15 minutes or until browned. Drain and transfer to slow cooker stoneware.

3. Stir in tomatillos, garlic, jalapeños, onion, chiles, oregano, ½ tsp (2 mL) salt, ¼ tsp (1 mL) pepper and ½ cup (125 mL) water.

4. Cover and cook on Low for 5 hours or on High for 2½ hours, stirring twice to coat ribs, until ribs are tender.

5. Stir in cilantro. Serve sprinkled with cheese, and with lime wedges to squeeze over top. Garnish with additional cilantro leaves, if desired.

> The term "country-style ribs" is a bit confusing, as they are not really ribs at all. This cut comes from the rib end of the loin. The butcher cuts across and through the loin, then opens up the loin like a book. The "ribs" are sold as a slab with bones on the end, but sometimes they come in small chunks. Either way, they will cook up perfectly in the slow cooker.

Rubbed 'n' Dipped Caribbean Spiced Ribs

**Makes
4 servings**

....

This recipe uses a traditional dry rub spice blend to flavor the ribs, followed by a slow simmer in a sweet yet tangy barbecue sauce.

Tips

Look for well-trimmed ribs at the market or grocery store. Ask the butcher to remove the silverskin (the membrane at the back of the ribs) to save you time. But if you purchase untrimmed cuts, which can be quite a cost savings, it is easy enough to do this yourself. The membrane is located on the underside (the concave side) of the rack of ribs. Holding a piece of paper towel to help you grip, wiggle your fingers underneath the membrane and gently pull it away from the meat.

You can also use 2 lbs (1 kg) country-style ribs, cut into individual rib portions, for this recipe. Country-style ribs are the meatiest cut of pork ribs.

- **Minimum 5-quart slow cooker, stoneware greased**

3 lbs	pork back ribs	1.5 kg
2 tbsp	dried minced onion	30 mL
1 tsp	dry mustard	5 mL
1 tsp	hot pepper flakes	5 mL
½ tsp	ground allspice	2 mL
½ tsp	ground cinnamon	2 mL
½ tsp	garlic powder	2 mL
1	onion, sliced	1
1½ cups	barbecue sauce	375 mL

1. Cut ribs into three- or four-rib portions. Remove silverskin from underside of ribs, if necessary (see tip, at left).

2. In a small bowl, combine onion, mustard, hot pepper flakes, allspice, cinnamon and garlic powder. Rub onion mixture into ribs. Place ribs in prepared slow cooker stoneware, then tuck onion slices between ribs. Pour ½ cup (125 mL) water around ribs.

3. Cover and cook on Low for 8 to 9 hours, until ribs are tender. Using a slotted spoon, gently remove ribs from stoneware, draining well. Discard cooking liquid.

4. Pour barbecue sauce into a shallow bowl. Dip ribs in sauce, then return to stoneware. Pour any remaining sauce over ribs. Cover and cook on Low for 1 hour or until ribs are glazed.

Make Ahead

This dish can be assembled up to 12 hours in advance. Prepare through step 2, cover and refrigerate overnight. The next day, place stoneware in slow cooker and proceed with step 3.

Boneless Pork Ribs Braised with Fennel and Olives

Makes 6 to 8 servings

Because country-style pork ribs are meaty and thick, they don't really lend themselves to being eaten with your hands, like back ribs do. They are, however, beautifully suited to braising in the slow cooker. Fragrant with fennel and olives, this dish works well for an evening with guests. Serve it with risotto or roasted garlic potatoes, and have a warm loaf of crusty French bread nearby, for soaking up the extra sauce.

Tip

Flat-leaf (Italian) parsley is more fragrant and less bitter than the curly variety.

- **Minimum 5-quart slow cooker**

¼ cup	all-purpose flour	60 mL
2 tsp	ground fennel seeds	10 mL
1 tsp	coarse salt	5 mL
¼ tsp	freshly ground black pepper	1 mL
3 lbs	country-style pork ribs, cut into individual ribs, if possible	1.5 kg
⅓ cup	olive oil (approx.), divided	75 mL
1	large fennel bulb, stems and fronds removed, cut lengthwise into ½-inch (1 cm) slices	1
1	onion, sliced	1
6	cloves garlic, minced	6
1 tsp	dried rosemary	5 mL
1 cup	chicken broth	250 mL
1 cup	diced tomatoes	250 mL
1 tsp	grated orange zest	5 mL
½ cup	freshly squeezed orange juice	125 mL
½ cup	pitted kalamata olives	125 mL
2 tbsp	chopped fresh flat-leaf (Italian) parsley	30 mL

1. On a plate, combine flour, fennel seeds, salt and pepper. Dredge ribs in flour mixture to coat, brushing off excess. Reserve the remaining flour mixture.

2. In a large nonstick skillet, heat 2 tbsp (30 mL) of the oil over medium-high heat. Cook ribs in batches, adding more oil as necessary, for about 3 minutes per side or until browned all over. Transfer to a plate.

3. Dredge fennel slices in the reserved flour mixture. Reserve any remaining flour mixture. Add the remaining oil to skillet. Cook fennel slices for about 2 minutes per side or until lightly browned. Arrange in slow cooker stoneware. Place ribs over fennel.

4. Reduce heat to medium. Add onion to skillet and cook for about 3 minutes or until tender and translucent. Stir in garlic, rosemary and the reserved flour mixture until onions are coated. Stir in broth and bring to a boil. Add tomatoes and orange juice; cook, stirring, for about 5 minutes or until slightly thickened. Pour over ribs.

continued on page 226…

Tip

To zest an orange,
use a Microplane-
style rasp grater
or citrus zester,
ensuring that you
don't grate the white
pith underneath.
Microplanes have
tiny razor-like edges,
which make quick
and easy tasks of
grating and cleaning.
If you use a zester,
finely chop the
zest before adding
it to the recipe.
Microplanes and
zesters are widely
available at specialty
kitchenware shops.

5. Cover and cook on Low for 5 hours or on High for 2½ hours, until ribs are tender.

6. Sprinkle with olives, parsley and orange zest. Cover and cook for 6 to 8 minutes or until olives are heated though.

> Fennel bulb, a vegetable commonly found in Mediterranean-style dishes, has a licorice flavor that is mellowed by cooking. It has a grapefruit-size bulb with stalks and fronds poking out from the top. To prepare fennel bulb, simply trim the hard, hollow stalks from the top (saving the feathery fronds for garnish, if you like). Cut the bulb in half lengthwise, then slice it vertically.

Jerk Pork Ribs and Sweet Potatoes

**Makes
6 servings**

Jerk seasoning, a fiery spice blend, comes to us from the island of Jamaica. While some purist "jerks" may crave the heat, it is actually the flavor notes of thyme and allspice you want to capture in this dish.

Tips

I used a dry jerk rub for this recipe, but a liquid seasoning would work well too.

Country-style ribs are the meatiest cut of pork ribs, but side ribs or spareribs will also work in this recipe. To help reduce the fat in the finished dish, cut the slab into five- or six-rib portions, place in a large pot of water and bring to a boil, then reduce heat and simmer for 30 to 45 minutes. Continue with step 1 as directed.

- **Minimum 4-quart slow cooker**
- *Preheat broiler, with rack set 6 inches (15 cm) below heat source*
- *Broiler pan or rimmed baking sheet, lined with foil*

3 lbs	country-style pork ribs, cut into individual ribs, if possible	1.5 kg
1 tsp	salt	5 mL
1/2 tsp	freshly ground black pepper	2 mL
2 tbsp	Jamaican jerk seasoning	30 mL
1/4 cup	dark rum	60 mL
2 tbsp	vegetable oil	30 mL
2 tbsp	butter, softened	30 mL
2 lbs	sweet potatoes, peeled and cut into 1/2-inch (1 cm) slices	1 kg
1	onion, sliced	1
2 tbsp	packed brown sugar	30 mL
3	green onions, sliced	3
1	tomato, finely chopped	1

1. Place ribs on prepared broiler pan and season with salt and pepper. Broil, turning once, for 10 to 15 minutes or until browned. Transfer to a plate lined with paper towels and let drain.

2. In a bowl, combine jerk seasoning, rum and oil. Set aside.

3. Spread butter over bottom of slow cooker stoneware. Arrange potatoes and onion on top. Sprinkle with brown sugar. Place ribs on top. Spoon jerk mixture over ribs.

4. Cover and cook on Low for 6 to 8 hours or on High for 3 to 4 hours, until ribs are tender. Using a slotted spoon, transfer potatoes and ribs to a warmed platter and tent with foil to keep warm.

5. Skim fat from cooking liquid, then stir in green onions and tomato. Spoon over ribs.

> **Originating in Jamaica, jerk seasoning is used to season meat for grilling. The ingredients vary from cook to cook, but it is generally a combination of hot chile peppers and allspice, with additional seasonings such as cinnamon, cloves, thyme, garlic and onions.**

African Lamb Tagine

Makes 4 to 6 servings

The stews of North Africa are traditionally made in a conical vessel called a tagine. The lid of the tagine is tall, and it causes the steam to build up and precipitate back down to the stew so that none of the aroma or flavor is lost during cooking. The slow cooker uses basically the same principal. Crunchy peanut butter thickens the broth at the end of the cooking time, and the couscous soaks up the wonderful flavors.

Tips

For the best flavor, start with whole cumin seeds and allspice berries. Toast them in a dry skillet over medium-high heat, stirring constantly, for about 3 minutes or until fragrant. Then grind them as finely as you can in a spice grinder or using a mortar and pestle.

When browning meat in hot oil, avoid overfilling the skillet. If the pan is too full, the meat will steam rather than brown. Turn the meat frequently and cook it as quickly as possible, then use a slotted spoon to remove it.

- **Minimum 4-quart slow cooker**

2 tbsp	vegetable oil (approx.)	30 mL
2 lbs	boneless stewing lamb, cut into 1-inch (2.5 cm) cubes	1 kg
4	parsnips, diced	4
2	sweet potatoes, peeled and diced	2
1	onion, finely chopped	1
4	cloves garlic, finely chopped	4
1 tbsp	curry powder	15 mL
1/2 tsp	ground cumin	2 mL
1/4 tsp	ground allspice	1 mL
1 cup	beef broth	250 mL
1	can (14 oz/398 mL) diced tomatoes, with juice	1
1	3-inch (7.5 cm) cinnamon stick	1
1/2 tsp	hot pepper flakes	2 mL
2 tbsp	crunchy peanut butter	30 mL
	Salt	
	Hot cooked couscous	
	Chopped fresh parsley or cilantro	

1. In a large skillet, heat half the oil over medium-high heat. Cook lamb in batches, adding more oil as needed, for 4 minutes or until browned all over. Using a slotted spoon, transfer to slow cooker stoneware, leaving fat in pan.

2. Reduce heat to medium-low. Add parsnips, sweet potatoes and onion to skillet and sauté for about 4 minutes or until starting to soften. Add garlic, curry powder, cumin and allspice; sauté for about 1 minute or until vegetables are coated and spices are fragrant. Using a slotted spoon, transfer to stoneware.

3. Add broth to skillet and bring to a boil, scraping up any brown bits from pan. Pour over lamb mixture. Stir in tomatoes with juice, cinnamon stick and hot pepper flakes.

4. Cover and cook on Low for 6 to 8 hours or on High for 3 to 4 hours, until lamb is tender and stew is bubbling.

continued on page 230...

5. Discard cinnamon stick. Stir in peanut butter until thoroughly combined. Season to taste with salt.

6. Place couscous on a serving platter. Top with stew and sprinkle with parsley.

Couscous, a North African granular pasta, is available in a precooked instant form in most grocery stores. Unless the box instructions tell you otherwise, for 4 servings, bring 1½ cups (375 mL) water to a boil, then stir in 1 cup (250 mL) couscous. Cover, remove from heat and let stand for 5 minutes. Fluff with a fork, then stir in chopped fresh cilantro or parsley. Couscous, enlivened with any fresh herb, is a good complement for most stews.

Mediterranean "Pulled" Lamb with Mint Vinegar

Makes 6 to 8 servings

I love the flavor combination of lemon, garlic and herbs with lamb, and this recipe fulfills my taste buds' expectations! This is not meant to be a roast, but it is meant to be fall-apart soft — almost like "pulled" lamb. Serve it over plain couscous with a tomato and cucumber salad.

Tips

Fresh lamb shoulder roasts are sometimes hard to find if you don't have a farmer's market nearby. Ask your butcher to order it in for you, if possible, or look for a frozen roast and thaw it in the refrigerator (it'll take 1 to 2 days).

Fresh mint in the vinegar is what really elevates this lamb dish and finishes it beautifully. I would not recommend substituting dried mint. Take the extra time to chop the fresh herb. Look for small containers of fresh herbs in the produce aisle of the supermarket.

- **Minimum 4-quart slow cooker**

1	boneless lamb shoulder roast (3 to 4 lbs/1.5 to 2 kg), tied	1
½ tsp	salt	2 mL
¼ tsp	freshly ground black pepper	1 mL
4 to 6	cloves garlic, crushed	4 to 6
½ cup	freshly squeezed lemon juice	125 mL
¼ cup	olive oil	60 mL
1 tsp	dried oregano	5 mL
1 tsp	ground nutmeg	5 mL

Mint Vinegar

¼ cup	white balsamic vinegar	60 mL
1 tbsp	finely chopped fresh mint leaves	15 mL
1 tsp	granulated sugar	5 mL

1. Place lamb in slow cooker stoneware and sprinkle with salt and pepper.

2. In a bowl, combine garlic, lemon juice, oil, oregano and nutmeg. Pour over lamb.

3. Cover and cook on Low for 10 to 12 hours or on High for 5 to 6 hours, until lamb is fork-tender. Transfer lamb to a bowl and cut off strings. Using two forks, pull lamb apart into chunky shreds, discarding excess fat. Arrange on a deep serving platter.

4. *Mint Vinegar:* In a small saucepan, combine vinegar, mint and sugar; bring to a boil. Reduce heat and simmer, stirring, for 1 minute or until sugar is dissolved. Drizzle over lamb.

Lamb Shanks with Oranges and Olives

Makes 4 to 6 servings

The trick to all braised dishes is the very first step: carefully browning the meat to a deep golden brown. This not only ensures delicious, full-flavored meat, but also contributes to a rich and complex sauce. In this recipe, lamb shanks are slowly simmered with rosemary, white wine, onions and orange juice until the meat falls from the bone. Serve over hot mashed potatoes to sop up the sauce.

Tip

You can find the popular Greek black kalamata olives in most large grocery stores or gourmet food shops. Look for the fresh ones in the deli, rather than the canned variety. They're salty and very flavorful.

- **Minimum 4-quart slow cooker**

¼ cup	all-purpose flour	60 mL
1 tsp	salt	5 mL
½ tsp	freshly ground black pepper	2 mL
4 lbs	large meaty sliced or whole lamb shanks	2 kg
2 tbsp	olive oil (approx.)	30 mL
4	cloves garlic, minced	4
1	large red onion, finely chopped	1
1 tbsp	dried rosemary	15 mL
1 cup	tomato pasta sauce	250 mL
½ cup	dry white wine	125 mL
½ cup	chicken broth	125 mL
	Grated zest and juice of 1 navel orange	
½ cup	kalamata olives	125 mL

1. On a plate, combine flour, salt and pepper. Dredge lamb shanks in flour mixture to lightly coat, shaking off any excess. Reserve the remaining flour mixture.

2. In a skillet, heat half the oil over medium-high heat. Cook lamb in batches, adding more oil as needed, for 10 to 15 minutes or until lightly browned all over. Using tongs, transfer to slow cooker stoneware, leaving fat in the pan.

3. Reduce heat to medium. Add garlic, red onion, rosemary and the reserved flour mixture to skillet and sauté for about 2 minutes or until garlic is softened. Add pasta sauce, wine, broth and orange juice; cook, stirring, until thickened. Pour over lamb shanks.

4. Cover and cook on Low for 10 to 12 hours or on High for 5 to 6 hours, until lamb is falling off the bone. Turn off heat and let stand for 10 minutes. Transfer to a warmed platter and sprinkle with orange zest and olives.

> The shank is the lower portion of the leg. It is almost always sold bone-in. It's not a very tender cut of meat, so it is ideally suited to slow cooking, which allows the ample collagen in the shank to melt, producing a velvety sauce.

Big-Batch Dinners
for a Crowd

Layered Cheese Ravioli Lasagna

Makes 10 to 12 servings

To give you great lasagna without as much layering, this recipe uses fresh cheese ravioli, topped with loads of cheese and red peppers. It is the perfect pasta for cheese lovers, a perfect potluck take-along and an easy-to-make entrée that friends and family will find hard to resist.

Tip

The size of the ravioli will vary depending on the brand, but don't worry, it doesn't really matter: with smaller ravioli, the layers will be more pasta than cheese; with larger ones, the dish will be cheesier.

Variation

To lower the carbohydrate content (glycemic load) of this dish, you can substitute whole wheat spinach and cheese ravioli, which also delivers more nutrition and fewer calories.

- **Minimum 6-quart slow cooker, stoneware greased**

Pasta Sauce

1 tbsp	olive oil	15 mL
1	onion, chopped	1
2	cloves garlic, minced	2
1	carrot, shredded	1
1 tsp	dried Italian seasoning	5 mL
1	jar (28 oz/796 mL) tomato pasta sauce	1
1	can (28 oz/796 mL) diced tomatoes, with juice	1

Ravioli Lasagna

2 cups	shredded provolone cheese	500 mL
1 cup	shredded mozzarella cheese	250 mL
2 tbsp	freshly grated Parmesan cheese	30 mL
1	jar (14 oz/398 mL) sliced roasted red peppers, drained	1
1	package (2 lbs/1 kg) fresh cheese ravioli	1

1. *Pasta Sauce:* In a large nonstick skillet, heat oil over medium-high heat. Sauté onion for 4 to 6 minutes or until tender and translucent. Add garlic, carrot and Italian seasoning; sauté for 1 to 2 minutes or until fragrant. Stir in pasta sauce and tomatoes with juice; bring to a boil. Reduce heat and simmer, stirring occasionally, for about 10 minutes or until slightly thickened. Remove from heat.

2. *Ravioli Lasagna:* In a large bowl, combine provolone, mozzarella and Parmesan. Set aside.

3. Spread 1 cup (250 mL) of the pasta sauce evenly over bottom of prepared slow cooker stoneware. Spread one-third of the ravioli evenly over sauce. Spread one-third of the red peppers evenly over ravioli. Top with one-third of the remaining sauce and sprinkle with one-third of the cheese mixture. Repeat layers two more times with the ravioli, red peppers, sauce, then cheese.

4. Cover and cook on Low for 4 to 5 hours or until bubbling. Remove stoneware from slow cooker and let stand for 10 minutes before serving.

Smoky Chicken Chipotle Soft Tacos

Makes 14 to 16 servings

These perfect party tacos make a great excuse to gather friends and family for a Friday night appetizer. I love the rich, smoky flavor the peppers add to the chicken. Serving the tacos with guacamole and sour cream helps combat the heat of the peppers. Leftovers can be served over nachos or as a topping for baked potatoes or cooked pasta.

Tip

After opening canned chipotle chiles, transfer the peppers and their sauce to a glass jar with an airtight lid, close tightly and store in the refrigerator for up to 1 month. For longer storage, transfer peppers and sauce to a freezer bag and gently press out the air, then seal the bag. Manipulate the bag to separate the peppers so that it will be easy to break off a frozen section of pepper and sauce without thawing the whole package. Freeze for up to 6 months.

• **5- to 6-quart slow cooker**

5 lbs	boneless skinless chicken thighs	2.5 kg
2	onions, chopped	2
2	chipotle peppers in adobo sauce, minced, with 1 tbsp (15 mL) sauce	2
1	Cubanelle pepper, seeded and finely chopped	1
1	can (5½ oz/156 mL) tomato paste	1
¾ cup	chili sauce	175 mL
2 tbsp	unsweetened cocoa powder	30 mL
1 tsp	ground cumin	5 mL
¾ tsp	salt	3 mL
½ tsp	ground cinnamon	2 mL
Pinch	ground nutmeg	Pinch
Pinch	ground coriander	Pinch
14 to 16	6- or 7-inch (15 or 18 cm) flour tortillas, warmed (see tip, at right)	14 to 16

Toppings

Shredded Cheddar cheese or Tex-Mex cheese blend

Diced tomatoes

Diced onions

Sour cream

Guacamole

Shredded lettuce

Salsa

Lime wedges

1. Place chicken in slow cooker stoneware. Stir in onions, chipotle peppers with sauce, Cubanelle pepper, tomato paste, chili sauce, cocoa powder, cumin, salt, cinnamon, nutmeg and coriander.

2. Cover and cook on Low for 6 to 7 hours or until juices run clear when chicken is pierced with a fork.

3. Using two forks, shred chicken in stoneware. Stir with sauce to combine. (Chicken mixture will hold on Low or Warm heat for up to 2 hours; stir occasionally.)

4. Spoon $\frac{1}{3}$ cup (75 mL) of the chicken mixture along the center of each tortilla. Sprinkle with desired toppings, squeeze lime juice over top, if desired, and roll up.

Tex-Mex Chicken and Beans

This memorable fix-and-forget casserole feeds a crowd after a full day of activities. Use good-quality salsa to save time without skimping on flavor. Serve with nacho chips or cornbread for scooping or sopping up every last bit from the bottom of the bowl.

Tips

If you like food with a little kick, adjust the heat level by using a hotter salsa.

Yes, you really do add all the ingredients to the slow cooker at once. The water and juice from the chicken help cook the beans so they won't have a pasty mouth feel.

- **Minimum 6-quart slow cooker**

2 cups	dried pinto beans, rinsed	500 mL
3 cups	mild or medium salsa	750 mL
2 to 3	chipotle peppers in adobo sauce, minced, with 1 tbsp (15 mL) sauce	2 to 3
1/4 cup	all-purpose flour	60 mL
3 lbs	boneless skinless chicken thighs	1.5 kg
	Salt and freshly ground black pepper	
1	red onion, chopped	1
1	red bell pepper, chopped	1
	Sour cream	
	Chopped fresh cilantro	

1. In slow cooker stoneware, stir together beans, 2 cups (500 mL) water, salsa, chipotle peppers and flour. Sprinkle chicken with salt and pepper and arrange on salsa mixture. Sprinkle with red onion and red pepper.

2. Cover and cook on Low for 8 hours or until beans are tender and juices run clear when chicken is pierced with a fork. (Do not lift lid or stir.)

3. Using a slotted spoon, transfer chicken to a plate. Using two forks, shred into large pieces. Stir back into stew. Divide evenly among individual serving bowls. Top each with a dollop of sour cream and sprinkle with cilantro.

10-Alarm Turkey Chili

**Makes 8 to
10 servings**

Heads up! This chili
is crazy spicy — in a
good way! If you like a
little less heat, use only
2 chipotle peppers.

Tips

If you've purchased
good-quality
chocolate, don't
worry if you add a
little too much — it
will only add to the
richness of the sauce.

This dish tastes
especially good if
you toast and grind
cumin seeds yourself
rather than using
ground cumin. Toast
the seeds in a dry
skillet over medium-
high heat, stirring,
for about 3 minutes
or until fragrant. Use
a mortar and pestle
or a spice grinder to
grind the seeds as
finely as you can.

Because ground
turkey has such a mild
flavor, I often find I
need to add extra
seasoning to it.

- **Minimum 5-quart slow cooker**

2 tbsp	vegetable oil	30 mL
4 lbs	lean ground turkey or chicken	2 kg
4	cloves garlic, minced	4
1	large onion, chopped	1
4	chipotle peppers in adobo sauce, minced, with 1 tbsp (15 mL) sauce	4
2	red and/or yellow bell peppers, chopped	2
2	carrots, chopped	2
1	can (28 oz/796 mL) crushed tomatoes	1
1	can (28 oz/796 mL) diced tomatoes, drained	1
2 cups	cooked or canned pinto beans (see page 84), drained and rinsed	500 mL
2 cups	cooked or canned red kidney beans (see page 84), drained and rinsed	500 mL
1 cup	corn kernels, thawed if frozen	250 mL
2 tbsp	chili powder	30 mL
2 tsp	ground cumin	10 mL
1 tbsp	Worcestershire sauce	15 mL
1 oz	dark chocolate (at least 70% cacao), broken into small pieces	30 g
	Salt	
	Sour cream (optional)	

1. In a large nonstick skillet, heat oil over medium-high heat. Cook turkey, garlic and onion, breaking up meat with the back of a wooden spoon, for 3 to 5 minutes or until turkey is no longer pink. Using a slotted spoon, transfer to slow cooker stoneware.

2. Stir in chipotle peppers with sauce, red and/or yellow peppers, carrots, crushed tomatoes, diced tomatoes, pinto beans, kidney beans, corn, chili powder, cumin and Worcestershire sauce.

3. Cover and cook on Low for 6 to 8 hours or on High for 3 to 4 hours, until bubbling. Stir in chocolate until melted. Season to taste with salt.

4. Spoon into individual serving bowls and top each with a dollop of sour cream (if using).

Polish Pierogies with Caramelized Onions

Makes 8 to 10 servings

This is the next best thing to making your own pierogies and so much better than buying frozen ones. It's a meatless affair that uses lasagna noodles instead of pierogi dough, layering them with mashed potatoes and cottage cheese. In Poland, pierogies were a traditional peasant food, but in time, their popularity spread to all social classes. This is a perfect potluck dish.

Tip

If you use sweet onions, such as Spanish or Vidalia, there's no need to add sugar when caramelizing the onions. If your onions are strong and not sweet, stir in some granulated or raw sugar about 10 minutes after cooking starts. Use about 1 tbsp (15 mL) sugar per onion. Watch closely throughout cooking and stir occasionally, reducing the heat if necessary to ensure that the sugar does not burn.

• **Minimum 6-quart slow cooker, stoneware greased**

2 tbsp	olive oil	30 mL
4	large onions, thinly sliced	4
	Salt and freshly ground black pepper	
3	large baking potatoes, peeled and diced	3
1 cup	shredded Cheddar cheese	250 mL
2 cups	4% cottage cheese	500 mL
1	egg, lightly beaten	1
1/4 tsp	onion salt	1 mL
1	package (12 oz/340 g) fresh lasagna sheets (or 12 oven-ready lasagna noodles)	1
	Chopped fresh dill	
	Sour cream	

1. In a large skillet, heat oil over medium-high heat. Reduce heat to medium-low and cook onions, stirring occasionally, for 30 to 45 minutes or until golden and just beginning to caramelize. Season to taste with salt and pepper. Set aside.

2. Meanwhile, in a large pot, cover potatoes with cold water and season with salt. Bring to a boil over high heat. Reduce heat to medium and boil gently for 12 to 15 minutes or until tender. Drain and mash. Stir in Cheddar, 1 tsp (5 mL) salt and 1/2 tsp (2 mL) pepper. Set aside.

3. In a bowl, combine cottage cheese, egg and onion salt.

4. Spread half the onions over bottom of prepared slow cooker stoneware. Cover with 1 lasagna sheet, breaking another sheet if necessary to cover onions completely (or use 3 oven-ready noodles). Spread potato mixture evenly on top. Cover with another lasagna sheet. Spread cottage cheese mixture evenly on top. Cover with another lasagna sheet. Spread the remaining onions evenly on top.

5. Cover and cook on Low for 4 to 6 hours or until bubbling. Remove stoneware from slow cooker and let stand for 10 minutes before serving. Serve with chopped fresh dill and a dollop of sour cream.

Make Ahead

Prepare the caramelized onions in advance. See box, page 146.

Nationals Chili Dogs

My husband is on a quest to visit every major-league ballpark across the country. When I get to tag along, I look for the ballpark food specialty. At Nationals Park, we were served a Cincinnati-style chili over steamed hot dogs, which was my inspiration for this recipe. Kids love them, and they make a great choice for tailgate parties. Enjoy some laughs, beer and good dogs. What could be better than that?

Tip

Any type of hot dog wiener will work, but slightly firmer all-beef or turkey hot dogs are best.

- **5- to 6-quart slow cooker**

Chili Sauce

2 lbs	lean ground beef	1 kg
1	large onion, chopped	1
3	cloves garlic, minced	3
1	can (14 oz/398 mL) diced tomatoes, with juice	1
1	can (4½ oz/127 mL) diced mild green chiles	1
1 tbsp	chili powder	15 mL
1 tsp	granulated sugar	5 mL
1 tsp	paprika	5 mL
½ tsp	ground cumin	2 mL
½ tsp	celery seeds	2 mL
¼ tsp	salt	1 mL
¼ tsp	freshly ground black pepper	1 mL
1 tbsp	prepared mustard	15 mL
1 tsp	Worcestershire sauce	5 mL
20	hot dog wieners (or 10 jumbo-size), warmed	20
20	hot dog buns (or 10 jumbo-size), split and toasted	20
	Shredded Cheddar cheese (optional)	
	Chopped onion (optional)	
	Prepared mustard (optional)	

1. *Chili Sauce:* In a large skillet, cook beef, onion and garlic over medium-high heat, breaking up beef with the back of a wooden spoon, for 6 to 8 minutes or until vegetables are tender and beef is no longer pink. Drain off excess fat. Stir in tomatoes with juice, chiles, chili powder, sugar, paprika, cumin, celery seeds, salt, pepper, mustard and Worcestershire sauce.

2. Arrange wieners in slow cooker stoneware. Spoon beef mixture over top.

3. Cover and cook on Low for 4 to 5 hours or on High for 2 to 2½ hours, until bubbling.

4. Using tongs, transfer wieners to buns. Top each with about ⅓ cup (75 mL) sauce and garnish with cheese, onion and mustard (if using).

Barbecue Burger Sliders

"If you can do meatballs in the slow cooker, why not burgers?" I asked myself. Now you can have a great barbecue-flavored burger without the hassle of making your way out to the grill, especially, if like me, you live somewhere with long, snowy winters.

Tip

If you don't want to make barbecue sauce, simply use 2 cups (500 mL) bottled barbecue sauce.

Makes 2 cups (500 mL)

There are plenty of store-bought barbecue sauces, but nothing compares to this lip-smacking sauce. The chipotle pepper gives it a little kick.

• **Minimum 6-quart slow cooker**

4 lbs	lean ground beef or turkey	2 kg
4	eggs, lightly beaten	4
2	onions, finely chopped	2
2 cups	fine dry bread crumbs	500 mL
2 tbsp	Dijon mustard	30 mL
2 tbsp	Worcestershire sauce	30 mL
2 tsp	dried oregano	10 mL
2 cups	Barbecue Sauce (see recipe, below)	500 mL
24	mini hamburger buns, split	24

1. In a large bowl, combine beef, eggs, onions, bread crumbs, mustard, Worcestershire sauce and oregano. Using your hands, gently form about ¼ cup (60 mL) of the beef mixture into a 1-inch (2.5 cm) thick patty. Make 24 of these mini patties and layer them in slow cooker stoneware. Pour barbecue sauce over top.

2. Cover and cook on Low for 4 to 6 hours or until burgers are firm and an instant-read thermometer inserted in the center registers at least 160°F (71°C).

3. Transfer each burger to a bun. Skim fat off sauce. Spoon a little sauce on each burger and serve the remaining sauce on the side.

Barbecue Sauce

2 tbsp	olive oil	30 mL
1	onion, finely chopped	1
2	cloves garlic, minced	2
1½ cups	ketchup	375 mL
1 cup	beef broth or beer	250 mL
¼ cup	light (fancy) molasses	60 mL
½	chipotle pepper in adobo sauce, seeded and minced (see tip, page 88)	½
1 tbsp	mustard	15 mL

1. In a small skillet, heat oil over medium-high heat. Sauté onion for about 5 minutes or until tender and translucent. Add garlic and sauté for 1 to 2 minutes or until fragrant. Stir in ketchup, broth, molasses, chipotle pepper and mustard; bring to a boil. Reduce heat and simmer, stirring occasionally, for about 40 minutes or until thickened to consistency of bottled barbecue sauce.

2. Remove from heat and let cool. Refrigerate in a tightly sealed jar for up to 2 weeks.

Pass-the-Hot-Potato Bar

**Makes
12 servings**

. . . .

The potato-bar choices in this recipe elevate the standard baked potato to a whole new level. This is a great way to bring people together to talk, eat and have fun. This bar creates a lot of excitement, as everyone gets to choose their own topping combos.

Tips

If these toppings seem too adult-friendly, choose toppings you know everyone will enjoy. Try leftover chili, salsa, ranch dressing, sour cream, shredded Cheddar cheese, crumbled goat cheese, shredded cooked chicken, sliced black olives or chopped fresh parsley or cilantro.

Keep in mind that the more potatoes you have in the cooker, the longer the cooking time.

• **Minimum 6-quart slow cooker**

12	baking potatoes	12
¼ cup	olive oil	60 mL
	Salt	

Red Onion Jam

2 tbsp	butter	30 mL
2	large red onions, thinly sliced	2
½ cup	red wine	125 mL
3 tbsp	granulated sugar	45 mL
3 tbsp	balsamic or red wine vinegar	45 mL
2 tbsp	grenadine (optional)	30 mL

Chopped chives

Crumbled crisply cooked bacon

Chopped pistachios

1. Using a fork or the tip of a sharp knife, prick potatoes all over and rub with oil. Sprinkle each with salt, wrap in foil and place in slow cooker stoneware. (Do not add water.)

2. Cover and cook on Low for 6 to 7 hours or on High for 3 to 4 hours, until tender. Reduce heat to Low, if necessary, or Warm, if possible. (Potatoes will hold for up to 2 hours before serving.)

3. *Red Onion Jam:* Meanwhile, in a large skillet, melt butter over medium-low heat. Sauté onions for 12 to 15 minutes or until tender but not browned. Add wine, sugar, vinegar and grenadine (if using). Reduce heat to low and cook, stirring occasionally, for 10 to 12 minutes or until thickened and jammy.

4. Open corners of foil to expose the tops of potatoes. Slice an X in each, then squeeze the bottom of the potato to open the cuts. Top each potato with jam, chives, bacon and pistachios.

Baba's Russian Mennonite Borscht

Makes 8 to 10 servings

My friend Sheila received this recipe from her old college roommate. It was a favorite from his grandmother, a Russian immigrant who would make it for her family when they were homesick. In Mennonite cuisine, borscht is a soup with cabbage, beef, potato and tomato, but no beets, and, unlike in many cultures, it is served hot. Baba's borscht is an economical, tasty and filling soup. Serve it with thick, dark bread, such as pumpernickel.

Tip

When browning meat in hot oil, avoid overfilling the skillet. If the pan is too full, the meat will steam rather than brown. Turn the meat frequently and cook it as quickly as possible, then use a slotted spoon to remove it.

- **Minimum 6-quart slow cooker**

1/4 cup	all-purpose flour	60 mL
1 tsp	dried basil	5 mL
1 tsp	dried dillweed	5 mL
1/2 tsp	dried savory	2 mL
2 lbs	stewing beef, cut into 1-inch (2.5 cm) cubes	1 kg
2 tbsp	vegetable oil (approx.)	30 mL
2 cups	chicken or vegetable broth	500 mL
6	carrots, sliced	6
4	potatoes, peeled and diced	4
4	tomatoes, chopped	4
3	onions, chopped	3
1/2	small head cabbage, chopped (about 5 cups/1.25 L)	1/2
1	envelope (1 1/2 oz/45 g) onion soup mix	1
1	can (14 oz/398 mL) tomato sauce	1
1 tbsp	Worcestershire sauce	15 mL
	Sour cream	
	Finely chopped fresh dill (optional)	

1. In a heavy plastic bag, combine flour, basil, dill and savory. In batches, add beef to bag and toss to coat with flour mixture. Discard any excess flour mixture.

2. In a large nonstick skillet, heat half the oil over medium-high heat. Cook beef in batches, adding more oil as needed, for 5 minutes or until browned all over. Using a slotted spoon, transfer to slow cooker stoneware.

3. Add broth to skillet and bring to a boil, scraping up any brown bits from pan. Transfer to stoneware. Stir in carrots, potatoes, tomatoes, onions, cabbage, onion soup mix, tomato sauce and Worcestershire sauce.

4. Cover and cook on Low for 10 to 12 hours or on High for 5 to 6 hours, stirring once if possible, until beef and vegetables are tender.

5. Ladle into individual serving mugs. Top each with a dollop of sour cream and sprinkle with fresh dill (if using).

Pulled Pork Sammies with Radish Slaw

Makes 8 to 10 servings

Forget any worries about feeding a large crowd when you make this slow cooker all-time favorite. It starts with a dry rub to season the meat, then slow-cooks it in tangy apple juice to tenderize it. A Habitat for Humanity group conducting a local build were the lucky recipients of my recipe test, and everyone gave it a "hammers up" rating!

Tips

A boneless pork shoulder is an inexpensive cut of pork that turns into a tender, juicy and succulent piece of meat after low and slow cooking.

Tomato paste is now available in tubes in many supermarkets and delis. It keeps for months in the refrigerator.

● **Minimum 6-quart slow cooker**

¼ cup	garlic powder	60 mL
¼ cup	paprika	60 mL
2 tbsp	chili powder	30 mL
2 tbsp	dried oregano	30 mL
2 tbsp	coarse salt	30 mL
1 tbsp	freshly ground black pepper	15 mL
1 tbsp	celery seeds	15 mL
3 lbs	boneless pork shoulder blade (butt) roast, trimmed	1.5 kg
1	large onion, sliced	1
5	cloves garlic, minced	5
4	sprigs fresh thyme	4
1	bay leaf	1
2 cups	unsweetened apple juice	500 mL

Barbecue Sauce

½ cup	smoky-flavored barbecue sauce	125 mL
1 tbsp	tomato paste	15 mL
1	clove garlic, minced	1
1	chipotle pepper in adobo sauce, minced (optional)	1

Radish Slaw

⅓ cup	light mayonnaise	75 mL
1 tbsp	granulated sugar	15 mL
3 tbsp	white wine vinegar	45 mL
3 tbsp	freshly squeezed lime juice	45 mL
	Salt and freshly ground black pepper	
1	small green cabbage (about 2 lbs/1 kg), halved, cored and thinly sliced	1
1	bunch radishes, halved and thinly sliced (about 1½ cups/375 mL)	1
24	small hamburger buns, toasted	24

continued on page 254...

To get the most juice from a lime, let it warm to room temperature, then roll it on the counter, pressing down with the palm of your hand, before squeezing it. Or microwave a whole lime on High for 30 seconds, then roll, cut and squeeze it. Juice can be frozen in ice cube trays, then kept in the freezer in sealable plastic bags for later use. Zest can also be wrapped and frozen for later use.

Cooking times can vary a great deal between slow cooker manufacturers. Always let your food cook for the minimum amount of time before testing for doneness.

1. In a small bowl, combine garlic powder, paprika, chili powder, oregano, salt, pepper and celery seeds. Place pork in a bowl and rub all over with spice mixture. Let marinate at room temperature for 15 to 30 minutes.

2. Arrange onion over bottom of slow cooker stoneware. Place pork on top. Add garlic, thyme, bay leaf and apple juice.

3. Cover and cook on Low for 8 to 10 hours or on High for 4 to 6 hours, until pork is fork-tender and falling apart. Transfer pork to a cutting board and let cool slightly.

4. Remove any butcher's string holding the roast together. Using two forks, shred pork.

5. Skim fat from cooking liquid. Reserve 1 cup (250 mL) cooking liquid and set aside. Discard bay leaf and the remaining cooking liquid. Return pork to stoneware.

6. *Barbecue Sauce:* In a bowl, combine the reserved cooking liquid, barbecue sauce, tomato paste, garlic and chipotle pepper (if using). Stir into pork. Keep warm on Low heat.

7. *Radish Slaw:* Meanwhile, in a large bowl, whisk together mayonnaise, sugar, vinegar and lime juice. Season to taste with salt and pepper. Add cabbage and radishes; toss to coat. Cover and refrigerate for at least 1 hour.

8. Spoon pork mixture on the bottom half of each bun and top with a big scoop of slaw. Cover with top half of bun.

Make Ahead
The radish slaw can be prepared up to 1 day ahead.

Pork Carnitas

Makes 10 to 12 servings

Enter any taqueria in California and you'll find carnitas on the menu, usually pork shoulder (butt) roast, slow-braised, pulled apart, then roasted over high heat to caramelize it. This is a great way to use the slow cooker and the oven to create an authentic Mexican dish to feed a crowd. Add some sangría or margaritas, and you'll have a Mexican party-in-a-pot!

Tip

Carnitas means "little meats," a type of Mexican braised or roasted pork. Carnitas are sometimes served with refried beans and thinly sliced radishes. You can add the radishes to this recipe, if you choose.

- **Minimum 6-quart slow cooker**
- *Rimmed baking sheet*

4 lbs	boneless pork shoulder blade (butt) roast, trimmed and cut into large cubes	2 kg
8	cloves garlic, minced	8
1 tsp	salt	5 mL
1/2 tsp	freshly ground black pepper	2 mL
1 cup	freshly squeezed orange juice	250 mL
2 tbsp	olive oil	30 mL
1	can (14 oz/398 mL) refried beans, warmed (optional)	1
20 to 24	6- or 7-inch (15 or 18 cm) corn or flour tortillas, warmed	20 to 24
	Fresh cilantro leaves	
1	large white onion, thinly sliced	1
4	avocados, peeled and diced	4
20 to 24	lime wedges	20 to 24

1. In slow cooker stoneware, combine pork, garlic, salt, pepper and 8 cups (2 L) water.

2. Cover and cook on Low for 10 to 12 hours or on High for 5 to 6 hours, until pork is fork-tender. Discard cooking liquid.

3. Preheat oven to 400°F (200°C). Break pork into smaller chunks and spread on baking sheet. Drizzle with orange juice and oil. Roast, stirring occasionally, for 15 to 20 minutes or until browned and crisp.

4. Spread a layer of refried beans (if using) on each tortilla. Top with pork, cilantro, onion and avocado. Serve with a lime wedge to squeeze over top.

Make Ahead

This dish can be assembled up to 12 hours in advance. Prepare through step 1, cover and refrigerate overnight. The next day, place stoneware in slow cooker and proceed with step 2.

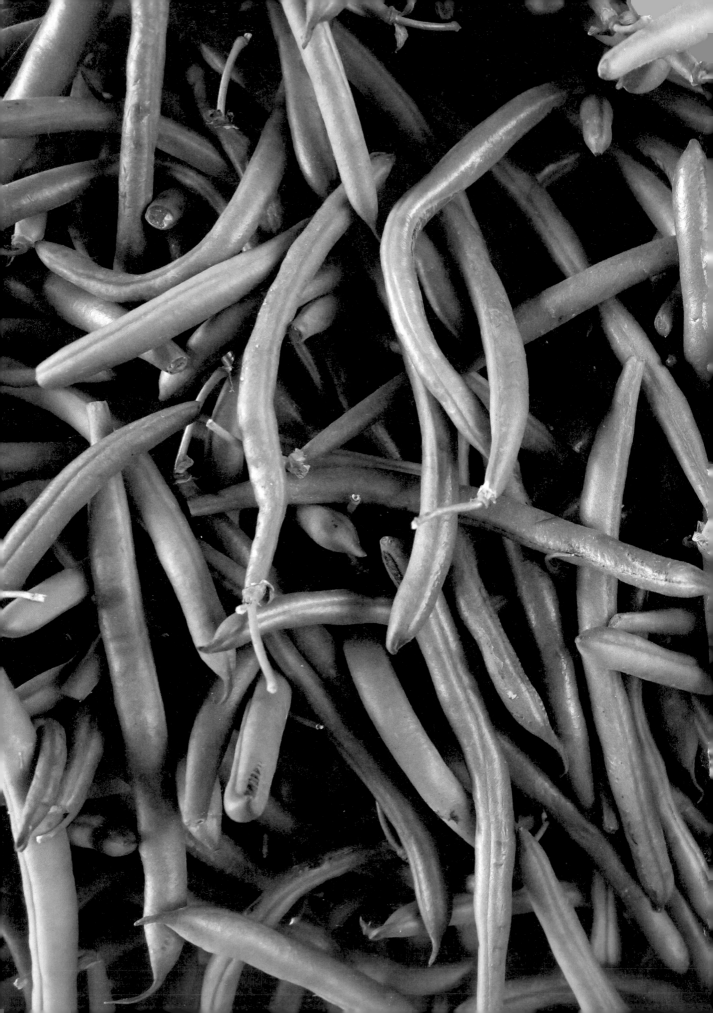

Meals for Two

Pantry Corn Chowder

Makes 2 servings

There is nothing more satisfying on a cool evening than a steaming bowl of this hearty classic. It's so simple to prepare, using basic pantry essentials: frozen corn, potatoes, bacon and cream. In this recipe, evaporated milk replaces the cream, with the same creamy results.

Tips

If you have not thawed the corn, quickly defrost it in the microwave.

Most leftover canned and jarred ingredients can be transferred to an airtight container, covered and stored in the refrigerator. Transfer the remaining evaporated milk to a glass jar with a tight-fitting lid and refrigerate for up to 7 days. Freezing is not recommended, as the solids tend to separate from the water, and no amount of stirring, shaking or blending will help blend it back together. Be sure to mark the date and amount on the jar for easy use next time.

- **3- to 4-quart slow cooker**

2 cups	frozen corn kernels, thawed	500 mL
¾ cup	evaporated milk	175 mL
3	slices bacon, minced	3
1	small onion, minced	1
3	small red potatoes, diced	3
2	cloves garlic, minced	2
2 cups	chicken broth	500 mL
1	bay leaf	1
⅛ tsp	dried thyme	0.5 mL
	Salt and freshly ground black pepper	

1. In a food processor or blender, process 1 cup (250 mL) of the corn and the evaporated milk until fairly smooth. Set aside.

2. In a nonstick skillet, sauté bacon and onion over medium heat for 5 to 7 minutes or until onion is tender and translucent. Using a slotted spoon, transfer to slow cooker stoneware.

3. Stir in puréed corn mixture, the remaining corn, potatoes, garlic, broth, bay leaf and thyme.

4. Cover and cook on Low for 8 to 10 hours or on High for 4 to 6 hours, until bubbling and potatoes are tender. Discard bay leaf. Season to taste with salt and pepper.

> Evaporated milk holds up extremely well in the slow cooker and will not curdle when it is cooked over a long period of time. Don't confuse evaporated milk with the sweetened condensed milk used in desserts and candies.

Mediterranean Minestrone

Makes
2 servings

Ground lamb gives this soup extra flavor. The topping of fresh mint and feta cheese adds to its Mediterranean essence.

Tips

If you can only purchase 1 lb (500 g) of ground lamb or more, divide it into 8-oz (250 g) portions. Use one for this recipe. Wrap the other portions and freeze in heavy-duty freezer bags.

To prevent soft, mushy pasta, do not allow it to be in the water any longer than necessary. Add it only when the water is at a full boil, and keep it at a steady boil while it cooks.

- **3- to 4-quart slow cooker**

8 oz	lean ground lamb	250 g
3	cloves garlic, minced	3
1/2	stalk celery, finely chopped	1/2
1/4 cup	chopped onion	60 mL
1/4 cup	finely chopped carrot	60 mL
1	tomato, chopped	1
2 cups	cooked or canned white kidney beans (see page 84), drained and rinsed	500 mL
2 cups	beef broth	500 mL
3/4 cup	coarsely chopped zucchini	175 mL
2 tsp	freshly squeezed lemon juice	10 mL
1/2 tsp	dried oregano	2 mL
1/2 tsp	hot pepper flakes	2 mL
1/8 tsp	freshly ground black pepper	0.5 mL
1	bay leaf	1
1/4 cup	elbow macaroni or other small pasta	60 mL
1 tbsp	snipped fresh mint	15 mL
2 tbsp	crumbled feta cheese	30 mL

1. In a nonstick skillet, cook lamb, garlic, celery, onion and carrot over medium-high heat, breaking up lamb with the back of a wooden spoon, for 4 minutes or until onion is translucent and tender and lamb is no longer pink. Using a slotted spoon, transfer to slow cooker stoneware.

2. Stir in tomato, beans, broth, zucchini, lemon juice, oregano, hot pepper flakes, black pepper and bay leaf.

3. Cover and cook on Low for 4 to 6 hours or on High for 2 to 3 hours, until bubbling and vegetables are tender. Discard bay leaf.

4. Meanwhile, cook pasta according to package directions until tender but firm (al dente). Drain. About 10 minutes before the end of cooking, stir pasta into lamb mixture.

5. Just before serving, stir in mint. Ladle into individual serving bowls and sprinkle with cheese.

Make Ahead

This dish can be assembled up to 12 hours in advance. Prepare through step 2, cover and refrigerate overnight. The next day, place stoneware in slow cooker and proceed with step 3.

Roasted Red Pepper Soup

**Makes
2 servings**

Using roasted red peppers from a jar makes putting this soup together quick and easy. It has a slightly smoky, sweet flavor from the peppers and is a knock-'em-dead start to any meal. For a complete meal, serve with a simple grilled cheese sandwich or panini.

Tip

For convenience, roasted red bell peppers are available in jars or can be found fresh in the deli section of some supermarkets. To make your own, preheat broiler. Cut peppers in half and remove stem and seeds. Place cut side down on rimmed baking sheet. Broil until skins have blackened. Transfer to a paper bag, close it, and let peppers sweat for about 30 minutes. Peel off skins and chop flesh. Roasted peppers can be stored in plastic freezer bags in the freezer for up to 3 months. You will need 4 or 5 whole roasted peppers for this recipe.

- **3- to 4-quart slow cooker**

1 tsp	butter	5 mL
1	onion, finely chopped	1
1	clove garlic, minced	1
1	jar (13 oz/370 mL) roasted red peppers, drained and chopped	1
1 cup	vegetable broth	250 mL
1/2 cup	freshly squeezed orange juice	125 mL
1/8 tsp	salt	0.5 mL
1/2 cup	half-and-half (10%) cream	125 mL
1 tbsp	chopped fresh basil	15 mL
1/4 cup	crumbled blue cheese	60 mL

1. In a small skillet, melt butter over medium heat. Sauté onion and garlic for about 5 minutes or until onion is tender and translucent. Transfer to slow cooker stoneware. Stir in roasted peppers, broth, orange juice and salt.

2. Cover and cook on Low for 4 to 6 hours or on High for 2 to 2 1/2 hours, until bubbling.

3. Using an immersion blender, or in a food processor or blender, in batches as necessary, purée soup until smooth. (If using food processor or blender, return purée to stoneware.)

4. Stir in cream and basil. Cover and cook on High for 10 minutes or until heated through.

5. Ladle into bowls and sprinkle with cheese.

Hearty Drumstick "Stoup" with Parsley Dumplings

Makes 2 servings

I couldn't decide whether this satisfying recipe was a soup or a stew, so I settled on calling it "stoup." You can cheat and substitute prepared refrigerated biscuits for the Parsley Dumplings.

Tips

Turkey drumsticks can vary in size. Oval slow cookers easily fit an elongated cut of meat such as a drumstick. Round slow cookers may be more challenging. If you have difficulty fitting a drumstick into the stoneware, substitute a meaty turkey thigh.

A mini food processor is perfect for smaller portions. It takes up less storage space, uses less energy, is easier to clean and holds just the right amount of ingredients for one or two.

- **3- to 4-quart slow cooker (preferably oval)**
- *Food processor*

1	turkey drumstick (about 12 oz/375 g)	1
2	cloves garlic, minced	2
1	carrot, diced	1
1	stalk celery, diced	1
1	small onion, finely chopped	1
1	bay leaf	1
½ tsp	poultry seasoning	2 mL
½ tsp	dried thyme	2 mL
2 cups	chicken broth	500 mL
2 tbsp	chopped fresh parsley	30 mL
	Salt and freshly ground black pepper	

Parsley Dumplings

1	slice white bread, quartered	1
1 tbsp	chopped fresh parsley	15 mL
¼ cup	all-purpose flour	60 mL
¼ tsp	baking powder	1 mL
⅛ tsp	salt	0.5 mL
2 tbsp	milk	30 mL
1 tbsp	butter, melted	15 mL

1. In slow cooker stoneware, combine turkey, garlic, carrot, celery, onion, bay leaf, poultry seasoning and thyme. Pour in broth and 1 cup (250 mL) water.

2. Cover and cook on High for 5 to 6 hours or until meat is falling off the bones. Discard bay leaf. Using a slotted spoon, transfer turkey to a cutting board and let cool.

3. Remove and discard turkey skin and bones. Using two forks, shred turkey and return to stoneware, along with parsley. Season to taste with salt and pepper.

4. *Parsley Dumplings:* Meanwhile, in food processor, pulse bread and parsley to medium-size crumbs. Add flour, baking powder and salt; process until just combined. Add milk and butter; pulse until just blended.

5. Drop mounded spoonfuls of batter into soup. Cover and cook on High for 12 to 15 minutes or until a tester inserted in the center of a dumpling comes out clean.

Creamy Herbed Chicken Stew

....

I have a soft spot for this creamy stew. It reminds me of chicken pot pie without the crust. Creamy sauce and juicy chunks of chicken and vegetables combine to make it the ultimate comfort food.

Tip

You can substitute boneless skinless chicken breasts for the chicken thighs, but you will need to reduce the cooking time to 3 to 4 hours on Low. Cooking times for poultry may be shorter for smaller slow cookers and/or when there is a relatively high proportion of white to dark meat. When cooking mostly white-meat dishes, be sure to avoid overcooking.

- **3- to 4-quart slow cooker**

6	white mushrooms, quartered	6
1 cup	baby carrots	250 mL
¼ cup	chopped onion	60 mL
¼ cup	sliced celery	60 mL
½ tsp	dried thyme, divided	2 mL
¼ tsp	dried sage	1 mL
⅛ tsp	salt	0.5 mL
⅛ tsp	freshly ground black pepper	0.5 mL
8 oz	boneless skinless chicken thighs (about 4)	250 g
¾ cup	chicken broth	175 mL
¼ cup	frozen peas, thawed	60 mL
¼ cup	heavy or whipping (35%) cream	60 mL
2 tbsp	all-purpose flour	30 mL
	Chopped fresh parsley	

1. In slow cooker stoneware, combine mushrooms, carrots, onion and celery. Sprinkle with half the thyme, sage, salt and pepper. Place chicken on top. Pour broth over chicken.

2. Cover and cook on Low for 6 to 8 hours or until vegetables are tender and juices run clear when chicken is pierced.

3. Stir in peas. Cover and cook for 10 to 15 minutes or until heated through.

4. Using a slotted spoon, transfer chicken and vegetables to a serving bowl and keep warm.

5. In a bowl, whisk together cream, flour and the remaining thyme. Stir into cooking liquid in stoneware. Cover and cook on High for about 10 minutes or until thickened into sauce. Pour over chicken and vegetables. Sprinkle with parsley.

Beef Stew for Two

Soups and stews don't always have to feed a crowd. This heartwarming dish was designed just for two. Serve it with a crisp green salad and a few crusty rolls for soaking up the extra juice.

Tips

Select lean stewing beef or trim any excess fat from the meat. Trimming takes a little extra time, but it's worth it.

Store any leftovers in an airtight container in the refrigerator for up to 3 days or freeze for up to 3 months. If the consistency of leftover stew seems too thick, reheat it first, as it can thin considerably once it is warmed. If the warmed stew is still too thick, thin it down by gradually adding water or beef broth until the desired consistency is achieved.

- **3- to 4-quart slow cooker**

2 tbsp	all-purpose flour	30 mL
1/2 tsp	paprika	2 mL
1/2 tsp	dried thyme	2 mL
1/8 tsp	salt	0.5 mL
1/8 tsp	freshly ground black pepper	0.5 mL
1 lb	boneless stewing beef, cut into 1-inch (2.5 cm) cubes	500 g
1 tbsp	vegetable oil (approx.)	15 mL
1 cup	beef broth	250 mL
1	can (7 1/2 oz/213 mL) tomato sauce	1
1	carrot, chopped	1
1	stalk celery, chopped	1
1	clove garlic, minced	1
1/2 cup	diced peeled potatoes	125 mL
1/2 cup	frozen peas, thawed	125 mL

1. In a heavy plastic bag, combine flour, paprika, thyme, salt and pepper. In batches, add beef to bag and toss to coat with flour mixture. Discard excess flour mixture.

2. In a nonstick skillet, heat oil over medium-high heat. Cook beef in batches, adding more oil as needed, for 5 minutes or until browned all over. Using a slotted spoon, transfer to slow cooker stoneware.

3. Add broth to skillet and bring to a boil, scraping up any brown bits from pan. Transfer to stoneware. Stir in tomato sauce, carrot, celery, garlic and potatoes.

4. Cover and cook on Low for 8 to 10 hours or on High for 4 to 5 hours, until bubbling and vegetables are tender.

5. Stir in peas. Cook for 15 to 20 minutes or until heated through.

Multi-Bean Vegetarian Chili for Two

Makes 2 to 3 servings

It's hard to find a recipe for chili that doesn't make a huge pot. My mom and dad like this recipe because it uses a can of mixed beans, so you get a nice variety without a huge quantity. Can you spot the secret ingredient? No, the chocolate syrup is not a mistake. It really does add an interesting element to the sauce for this chili.

Tip

Cajun seasoning is a combination of chiles, pepper, garlic, onions and herbs, and is found in the spice section of the supermarket. It has a little heat, so use as much or as little as your palate can handle. If you can't find it, substitute ¾ tsp (3 mL) ground cumin, ½ tsp (2 mL) each ground thyme and paprika and a pinch of cayenne pepper and ground allspice.

- **3- to 4-quart slow cooker**

1	can (19 oz/540 mL) mixed beans, drained and rinsed	1
1	can (14 oz/398 mL) diced tomatoes, with juice	1
1	can (4½ oz/127 mL) diced mild green chiles	1
1	small zucchini, diced	1
½ cup	frozen corn kernels, thawed	125 mL
½ cup	beer or chicken broth	125 mL
1 tbsp	chocolate syrup	15 mL
1 tbsp	chili powder	15 mL
1 tsp	Cajun seasoning	5 mL
	Sour cream (optional)	
	Shredded Cheddar cheese (optional)	

1. In slow cooker stoneware, stir together beans, tomatoes with juice, green chiles, zucchini, corn, beer, chocolate syrup, chili powder and Cajun seasoning.

2. Cover and cook on Low for 6 to 8 hours or on High for 3 to 4 hours, until bubbling.

3. Ladle into bowls, top each with a dollop of sour cream (if using) and sprinkle with cheese (if using).

Make Ahead

This dish can be assembled up to 12 hours in advance. Prepare through step 1, cover and refrigerate overnight. The next day, place stoneware in slow cooker and proceed with step 2.

Zucchini Ratatouille

Makes 2 to 3 servings

I make this on a regular basis in the summer when I'm harvesting zucchini from my vegetable garden. If I have any leftovers, I like to heat up a bowl for lunch and serve it over rotini. It also makes a great side for grilled chicken or sausage.

Tips

Because eggplant skin can be tough, you may want to peel the eggplant before cubing and cooking it. Alternatively, you can peel it in stripes, leaving some of the skin intact.

Italian seasoning can be purchased premixed in the spice aisle of the grocery store. You can also mix your own from crumbled dried herbs. Combine 2 tsp (10 mL) each basil, marjoram and oregano and 1 tsp (5 mL) dried sage. Store in an airtight container away from heat, moisture and sunlight for up to 1 year.

- **3- to 4-quart slow cooker**

1	can (7½ oz/213 mL) pizza sauce or tomato sauce	1
1½ cups	cubed peeled baby eggplant (see tip, at left)	375 mL
½ cup	coarsely chopped zucchini or yellow summer squash	125 mL
½ cup	coarsely chopped tomato	125 mL
⅓ cup	coarsely chopped red bell pepper	75 mL
¼ cup	finely chopped onion	60 mL
1	clove garlic, minced	1
2 tsp	granulated sugar	10 mL
½ tsp	dried Italian seasoning	2 mL
¼ tsp	salt	1 mL
⅛ tsp	freshly ground black pepper	0.5 mL
1 tbsp	snipped fresh basil	15 mL
3 tbsp	freshly grated Parmesan cheese	45 mL

1. In slow cooker stoneware, combine pizza sauce, eggplant, zucchini, tomato, red pepper, onion, garlic, sugar, Italian seasoning, salt and pepper.

2. Cover and cook on Low for 4½ to 5 hours or on High for 2 to 2½ hours, until bubbling and vegetables are tender.

3. Just before serving, stir in basil. Ladle into bowls and sprinkle with cheese.

Smokin' Mac and Cheese

This updated version of a comfort-food classic gets its exquisite flavor from a touch of smoked cheese. If you have finicky eaters, replace the smoked Gouda with an equal amount of Cheddar. It will still be delicious, just not as poetic. Round it out with a tossed green salad and whole wheat dinner rolls.

Tip

When preparing pasta for the slow cooker, undercook it in boiling salted water first, to remove some of the starch. It will continue to cook in the slow cooker, and the consistency will be perfect rather than overdone.

- **3- to 4-quart slow cooker, stoneware greased**

2 cups	elbow macaroni	500 mL
1	egg, lightly beaten	1
1	can (12 oz/370 mL) evaporated milk	1
¼ cup	milk	60 mL
¼ tsp	salt	1 mL
¼ tsp	freshly ground black pepper	1 mL
¼ tsp	dry mustard	1 mL
⅛ tsp	smoked paprika (optional)	0.5 mL
1 cup	shredded smoked Gouda cheese	250 mL
1	small tomato, chopped	1

1. In a pot of boiling salted water, cook macaroni for 5 minutes. Drain and transfer to prepared slow cooker stoneware.

2. In a bowl, combine egg, evaporated milk, milk, salt, pepper, mustard and paprika (if using). Pour over macaroni. Stir in cheese and tomato.

3. Cover and cook on Low for 5 to 6 hours or until set.

> Gouda, Holland's most famous exported cheese, has a yellow interior dotted with a few holes. The smoked variety is made by placing the rounds over smoldering hickory chips, which gives the rind a brown color without affecting the color of the creamy yellow interior.

Creamy Pesto Chicken and Asparagus

**Makes
2 servings**

This simple chicken and pesto pasta dish can be quickly assembled and put in the slow cooker before you hit the golf course or curling rink. It will be ready for the quick finishing touches when you return.

Tip

Look for fettuccini or linguine pasta packaged like nests — they make it easy to cook only what you need for 2 servings.

- **3- to 4-quart slow cooker**

4	boneless skinless chicken thighs, cut into 1-inch (2.5 cm) cubes	4
	Freshly ground black pepper	
½ cup	chicken broth	125 mL
2 tbsp	basil pesto or sun-dried tomato pesto	30 mL
4 oz	asparagus, chopped	125 g
¼ cup	heavy or whipping (35%) cream	60 mL
2 tbsp	freshly grated Parmesan cheese	30 mL
	Salt	
	Hot cooked fettuccini or rotini pasta	
	Additional freshly grated Parmesan cheese (optional)	

1. Arrange chicken in slow cooker stoneware and sprinkle with ¼ tsp (1 mL) pepper.

2. In a glass measuring cup, combine broth and pesto. Pour over chicken.

3. Cover and cook on Low for 5 to 6 hours or until juices run clear when chicken is pierced.

4. Stir in asparagus, cream and cheese. Cover and cook on High for 15 minutes or until liquid is slightly thickened and asparagus is tender. Season to taste with salt and pepper.

5. Serve over fettuccine, sprinkled with additional cheese, if desired.

No-Hurry Mango Chicken Curry

Makes
2 servings

Not all slow cooker meals look pretty as they cook, but this one is an exception. Simple chicken curry mixed with sweet mangos and red peppers is assembled quickly but simmered slowly. It will satisfy all your curry cravings. Serve over hot basmati or jasmine rice.

Tip

To store gingerroot, peel it and place it in a jar with a tight-fitting lid. Add enough sherry to cover. The sherry will saturate and preserve the ginger. Refrigerate for up to 1 month. Use the infused wine to flavor other chicken dishes.

- **3- to 4-quart slow cooker**

1 tsp	vegetable oil	5 mL
4	boneless skinless chicken thighs	4
½	red bell pepper, chopped	½
1 cup	frozen mango chunks, thawed and drained	250 mL
½ cup	chopped onion	125 mL
1 tbsp	raisins	15 mL
1	clove garlic, minced	1
½ cup	unsweetened applesauce	125 mL
2 tsp	hot or mild curry paste	10 mL
½ tsp	finely grated gingerroot (or ¼ tsp/1 mL ground ginger)	2 mL
¼ tsp	salt	1 mL
⅛ tsp	freshly grated black pepper	0.5 mL
⅓ cup	plain yogurt	75 mL
1 tsp	chopped fresh cilantro or parsley	5 mL

1. In a nonstick skillet, heat oil over medium-high heat. Cook chicken for 2 to 3 minutes per side or until browned all over. Transfer to slow cooker stoneware.

2. Stir in red pepper, mango, onion and raisins.

3. In a bowl, combine garlic, applesauce, curry paste, ginger, salt and pepper. Pour into stoneware.

4. Cover and cook on Low for 6 to 8 hours or on High for 3 to 4 hours, until juices run clear when chicken is pierced with a fork. Just before serving, stir in yogurt and sprinkle with cilantro.

Make Ahead

The ingredients in steps 2 and 3 can be assembled in the stoneware up to 2 days in advance. Cover and refrigerate. When ready to cook, brown the chicken as directed in step 1. Place stoneware in slow cooker, add chicken and proceed with step 4.

Italian Chicken Braciola

These stuffed chicken thighs are so easy to prepare and so tasty served over pasta. Complete the meal with crusty bread for soaking up the sauce and mixed greens tossed with a light vinaigrette.

Tip

Authentic Italian Parmesan cheese (Parmigiano-Reggiano) is expensive, but its flavor is certainly worth the price. Well-wrapped in the refrigerator, a block keeps for months, and it goes a long way when you freshly grate it as you need it.

• **3- to 4-quart slow cooker**

4	slices bacon, diced	4
1	clove garlic, minced	1
½ cup	finely chopped onion	125 mL
1	egg, lightly beaten	1
¼ cup	fine dry bread crumbs	60 mL
¼ cup	freshly grated Parmesan cheese	60 mL
1 tbsp	chopped fresh rosemary (or 1 tsp/5 mL dried)	15 mL
6	boneless skinless chicken thighs	6
1 tbsp	olive oil	15 mL
1 tbsp	butter	15 mL
1	can (19 oz/ 540 mL) diced tomatoes with Italian seasonings, with juice	1
3 tbsp	tomato paste	45 mL

1. In a skillet, cook bacon over medium-high heat, stirring frequently, until crisp. Add garlic and onion; sauté for 2 to 3 minutes or until softened. Remove from heat and stir in egg, bread crumbs, cheese and rosemary.

2. Unfold chicken thighs and place smooth side down on a work surface. Spoon about 2 tbsp (30 mL) of the bacon mixture over each thigh, fold over to enclose filling and secure with a toothpick.

3. In the same skillet, heat oil and butter over medium-high heat. Cook thighs for 2 to 3 minutes per side or until browned all over. Transfer to slow cooker stoneware.

4. In a bowl, combine tomatoes with juice and tomato paste. Pour over chicken.

5. Cover and cook on Low for 5 to 6 hours or on High for 2½ to 3 hours, until juices run clear when chicken is pierced with a fork.

Spicy Lemon Coconut Chicken

Makes 2 to 3 servings

This Thai-influenced chicken treat has lots of exotic flavors, but is so simple to create. The crunch of the green beans and red peppers contrasts nicely with the moist meat.

Tips

One of the perks of cooking bone-in chicken is that the meat retains its tenderness.

Squeezing fresh lemon juice over the chicken enhances the Thai flavors — it really does make a difference to the finished dish.

- **3- to 4-quart slow cooker**

1 tbsp	all-purpose flour	15 mL
½ tsp	ground coriander	2 mL
¼ tsp	ground cumin	1 mL
¼ tsp	salt	1 mL
⅛ tsp	ground allspice	0.5 mL
Pinch	freshly ground black pepper	Pinch
2	chicken leg quarters (about 1½ lbs/750 g)	2
1 tbsp	olive oil	15 mL
¼ cup	chicken broth	60 mL
2 tsp	Thai red curry paste	10 mL
1	small red bell pepper, cut into strips	1
4 oz	green beans, stem ends removed, cut into 1-inch (2.5 cm) lengths	125 g
¼ cup	unsweetened coconut milk	60 mL
	Hot cooked jasmine rice, basmati rice or stir-fried noodles	
½	lemon, cut into wedges	½

1. In a bowl, combine flour, coriander, cumin, salt, allspice and pepper. Coat chicken with flour mixture and set aside.

2. In a nonstick skillet, heat oil over medium-high heat. Cook chicken for 6 to 8 minutes per side or until browned all over. Transfer to slow cooker stoneware.

3. In a bowl, combine broth and curry paste. Pour around chicken in stoneware. Sprinkle with red pepper.

4. Cover and cook on Low for 6 to 8 hours or on High for 3 to 3½ hours, until juices run clear when chicken is pierced with a fork.

5. Stir in green beans and coconut milk. Cover and cook on High for 25 to 30 minutes or until beans are tender.

6. Mound rice on a platter. Spoon chicken, vegetables and sauce on top and squeeze juice from lemon wedges over chicken.

Mu Shu for Two

**Makes
2 servings**

This is one of my son's favorite dinners. Since it only serves two, I originally made it on an evening when just he and I were home, and Jack loved it — any meal wrapped in a tortilla is fine by him. I served it with some lightly blanched asparagus spears, drizzled with an Asian dressing.

Tip

There is no need to peel gingerroot before grating it. Simply scrub it and use a standard box grater with fine holes. You can wrap any unused gingerroot in plastic wrap and freeze it for up to 6 months, then grate the frozen gingerroot as you need it.

- **3- to 4-quart slow cooker**

4	boneless skinless chicken thighs	4
¼ tsp	salt	1 mL
⅛ tsp	freshly ground black pepper	0.5 mL
1	clove garlic, minced	1
1 tsp	minced gingerroot (or ¼ tsp/1 mL ground ginger)	5 mL
¼ cup	soy sauce	60 mL
2 tsp	sesame oil	10 mL
4	10-inch (25 cm) whole wheat flour tortillas	4
¼ cup	hoisin sauce	60 mL
1 cup	broccoli slaw mix	250 mL
¼	red bell pepper, thinly sliced	¼

1. Arrange chicken in slow cooker stoneware. Sprinkle with salt and pepper.

2. In a small bowl, combine garlic, ginger, soy sauce, sesame oil and ¼ cup (60 mL) water. Pour over chicken.

3. Cover and cook on Low for 6 to 7 hours or on High for 3 to 3½ hours, until juices run clear when chicken is pierced with a fork. Using a slotted spoon, transfer chicken to a cutting board. Using two forks, shred meat. Return meat to sauce in stoneware.

4. Preheat oven to 350°F (180°C). Stack tortillas and wrap them in foil. Warm in oven for 10 minutes.

5. Spread 1 tbsp (15 mL) hoisin sauce over each tortilla, then top with one-quarter of the chicken mixture, ¼ cup (60 mL) of the broccoli slaw and red pepper. Fold or roll up tortillas.

> Hoisin sauce is a thick, soy-based sauce that is regularly used in Chinese dishes and stir-fries. The typical ingredients are soybean paste, garlic, vinegar and various seasonings, such as chile peppers. The flavor is sweet, salty and spicy.

Petite Pot Roast

Even two people can enjoy a pot roast without days of leftovers. A cross rib or chuck pot roast has a nice compact size that lends itself to a two-person meal. Surrounded by hearty, home-style vegetables, this roast is delicious and satisfying.

Tip

Slow cooking tenderizes less expensive cuts of meat. Pot roasts benefit from long cooking on Low. If you need to cook this faster, a minimum of 4 hours of simmering on High will produce fork-tender meat.

- **3- to 4-quart slow cooker**

1 tbsp	all-purpose flour	15 mL
¼ tsp	salt	1 mL
⅛ tsp	freshly ground black pepper	0.5 mL
1	boneless beef cross rib or chuck roast (1 to 1½ lbs/500 to 750 g)	1
1 tbsp	vegetable oil	15 mL
4	baby new potatoes, cut in half	4
2	carrots, cut into 1-inch (2.5 cm) pieces	2
1	small parsnip, cut into 1-inch (2.5 cm) pieces	1
1	small onion, cut into wedges	1
1	clove garlic, minced	1
1	bay leaf	1
1 tbsp	tomato paste	15 mL
1 tsp	soy sauce	5 mL
½ tsp	fresh thyme	2 mL
½ cup	fresh or frozen peas, thawed if frozen	125 mL

1. In a bowl, combine flour, salt and pepper. Pat beef dry with paper towels and coat all over with flour mixture.

2. In a large skillet, heat oil over medium-high heat. Cook beef, turning with two wooden spoons, for 7 to 10 minutes or until browned all over. Transfer to slow cooker stoneware.

3. Add potatoes, carrots, parsnip, onion, garlic, bay leaf, tomato paste, soy sauce and thyme to stoneware.

4. Cover and cook on Low for 8 to 10 hours or on High for 4 to 5 hours, until beef is fork-tender. Transfer beef to a warmed platter, cover with foil and let stand for 15 minutes.

5. Meanwhile, stir peas into vegetable mixture in stoneware. Cover and cook on High for 10 to 15 minutes or until heated through. Discard bay leaf.

6. Cut beef across the grain into 6 slices. Using a slotted spoon, arrange vegetables around beef. Spoon cooking liquid over top.

Make Ahead

The ingredients in step 3 can be assembled in the stoneware up to 2 days in advance. Cover and refrigerate. When ready to cook, coat and brown the beef as directed in steps 1 and 2. Place stoneware in slow cooker, add beef and proceed with step 4.

Cranberry Chipotle Pot Roast

Makes 2 to 3 servings

When you're making a pot roast for a small household, either buy a large roast and cut it in half (freeze what you don't need) or look for smaller cuts of beef. The butcher will often cut one for you, if you ask. This recipe was a real hit with my parents' condo neighbors — it got a four-fork rating! Mashed potatoes are a must on the side.

Tip

If the sauce is not thick enough for your liking, here is a quick way to thicken it. Transfer the cooking liquid to a small saucepan and bring it to a boil over medium-high heat. In a small bowl, combine 1 tbsp (15 mL) all-purpose flour and 1 tbsp (15 mL) softened butter; whisk into sauce and cook, stirring, until thickened. Spoon over meat when serving.

- **3- to 4-quart slow cooker**

1	boneless beef cross rib, chuck or rump roast (1½ to 2 lbs/750 g to 1 kg)	1
1	clove garlic, minced	1
½ tsp	dried thyme	2 mL
	Salt and freshly ground black pepper	
2 tsp	vegetable oil	10 mL
1	small onion, cut into thin wedges	1
¾ cup	whole berry cranberry sauce	175 mL
½ to 1 tsp	finely chopped chipotle pepper in adobo sauce	2 to 5 mL

1. Sprinkle beef with garlic, thyme and ⅛ tsp (0.5 mL) each salt and pepper.

2. In a large skillet, heat oil over medium-high heat. Cook beef, turning with two wooden spoons, for 7 to 10 minutes or until browned all over. Transfer to slow cooker stoneware. Arrange onion around beef.

3. In a bowl, combine cranberry sauce and chipotle pepper. Pour over beef.

4. Cover and cook on Low for 8 to 10 hours or on High for 4 to 5 hours, until beef is fork-tender. Using a slotted spoon, transfer beef and onion to a warmed platter, cover with foil and let stand for 10 minutes.

5. Skim off any fat from cooking liquid. Season to taste with salt and pepper. Pour into a gravy boat. Slice roast across the grain and serve with gravy on the side.

Steak and Mushroom Pub Pie

**Makes
2 servings**

On a family trip to
Wales, my son ordered
a pie similar to this in a
quaint pub. Jack loved
it so much, he polished
off the whole thing.
I've recreated it for the
slow cooker, with great
results. Adding a little
butter to the sauce
gives an extra richness
to the filling.

Tips

Serve with boiled
new potatoes, just as
they would in Wales.

If you prefer a
browner crust, you
can bake the topping
in the oven. Top
the cooked stew
as directed, then
transfer stoneware to
a 400°F (200°C) oven
and bake for 30 to
35 minutes or until
topping is golden
brown.

Beer has wonderful
tenderizing
properties, so it's a
great addition to a
dish that includes less
tender cuts of meat,
such as stewing
beef. Although dark
beers, such as stout
and porter, have a
strong flavor, they will
not overpower the
cooked dish. You can
substitute lighter or
non-alcoholic beer,
but the flavor might
not be quite as good.

- **3- to 4-quart slow cooker**

Filling

2 tbsp	all-purpose flour	30 mL
½ tsp	dried thyme	2 mL
¼ tsp	salt	1 mL
⅛ tsp	freshly ground black pepper	0.5 mL
1 lb	stewing beef, cut into ½-inch (1 cm) cubes	500 g
2 tsp	vegetable oil	10 mL
1	bottle (12 oz/341 mL) dark beer, such as Guinness	1
1 cup	quartered button mushrooms	250 mL
¾ cup	chopped onion	175 mL
1 tsp	Worcestershire sauce	5 mL
1 tbsp	butter	15 mL

Topping

1 cup	prepared biscuit mix	250 mL
⅓ cup	milk	75 mL
2 tbsp	shredded Cheddar cheese	30 mL
¼ tsp	dried thyme	1 mL

1. *Filling:* In a bowl, combine flour, thyme, salt and pepper. Add beef and toss to coat with flour mixture.

2. In a large nonstick skillet, heat oil over medium-high heat. Cook beef until browned all over. Using a slotted spoon, transfer to slow cooker stoneware.

3. Add beer to skillet and cook, scraping up any brown bits from pan. Transfer to stoneware. Stir in mushrooms, onion, Worcestershire sauce and butter.

4. Cover and cook on Low for 8 to 10 hours or on High for 4 to 5 hours, until beef is fork-tender.

5. *Topping:* In a bowl, stir together biscuit mix, milk, cheese and thyme until a lumpy dough forms. (Do not overmix.) Drop spoonfuls of dough over stew.

6. Cover and cook on High for 20 to 25 minutes or until a tester inserted in center of topping comes out clean.

Pineapple Ginger Pork

Makes 2 servings

My family has always loved this easy weeknight meal, served over lots of steamed rice. The smell is heavenly, especially when you've been out of the house all day.

Tips

You could also use a pork shoulder chop, cut into pieces, for this dish.

I used a lunch-pack size can of pineapple, which is perfect for this two-person dish. If you have difficulty finding that size, measure out ⅔ cup (150 mL) pineapple and ¼ cup (60 mL) pineapple juice from a regular can, then save the remainder to make a small fruit salad for dessert.

- **3- to 4-quart slow cooker**

12 oz	pork tenderloin, cut into 1-inch (2.5 cm) cubes	375 g
2 tsp	cornstarch, divided	10 mL
2 tbsp	soy sauce, divided	30 mL
1 tsp	sesame oil	5 mL
1	small onion, thinly sliced	1
1	clove garlic, minced	1
1 tbsp	packed brown sugar	15 mL
1 tsp	minced gingerroot (or ¼ tsp/1 mL ground ginger)	5 mL
1	can (5 oz/142 mL) pineapple tidbits, drained, reserving juice	1
¼ cup	chicken broth or water	60 mL
2 tbsp	ketchup	30 mL
1 tbsp	rice vinegar	15 mL
1 tbsp	hoisin sauce	15 mL
½	red bell pepper, thinly sliced	½
½	green bell pepper, thinly sliced	½

1. In a bowl, toss together pork, half the cornstarch, half the soy sauce and sesame oil. Let stand for 30 minutes. Transfer to slow cooker stoneware.

2. In a bowl, combine onion, garlic, brown sugar, ginger, the remaining cornstarch, the remaining soy sauce, pineapple juice, broth, ketchup, vinegar and hoisin sauce. Pour over pork.

3. Cover and cook on Low for 6 to 8 hours or until pork is tender.

4. Add pineapple, red pepper and green pepper to stoneware. Cover and cook on High for 15 minutes or until peppers are tender-crisp and pineapple is warmed through.

Peachy Pork Chops

**Makes
2 servings**

A pleasing combination of peach jam, soy sauce, rice vinegar and fresh ginger gives these chops an exotic Asian flavor. Serve with brown rice and a green vegetable, such as broccoli, for a dinner that welcomes you home at the end of the day.

Tip

You can use pork shoulder (blade) butt chops in this recipe, but you will need to increase the cooking time to 6 to 8 hours on Low or 3 to 4 hours on High. Since these chops tend to release more juices when cooked longer, the sauce will be a little thinner. To thicken it at the end of cooking, combine 2 tsp (10 mL) cornstarch and 1 tbsp (15 mL) cold water; stir into cooking liquid in stoneware (after you've removed the chops). Cover and cook on High for 15 to 20 minutes or until thickened into sauce.

- **3- to 4-quart slow cooker**

2	bone-in pork loin rib chops (about $3/4$ inch/2 cm thick), trimmed	2
2 tsp	vegetable oil	10 mL
$1/2$	small onion, sliced	$1/2$
$1/2$ tsp	grated gingerroot	2 mL
$1/2$ tsp	dry mustard	2 mL
$1/4$ tsp	salt	1 mL
$1/8$ tsp	freshly ground black pepper	0.5 mL
$1/4$ cup	peach jam	60 mL
1 tbsp	soy sauce	15 mL
1 tbsp	rice vinegar	15 mL
$1/2$ cup	long-grain brown rice	125 mL

1. In a nonstick skillet, heat oil over medium-high heat. Cook pork chops for about 5 minutes per side or until browned all over. Transfer to slow cooker stoneware. Arrange onion on top. Sprinkle with ginger, mustard, salt and pepper.

2. In a small bowl, combine jam, soy sauce and vinegar. Pour over pork chops.

3. Cover and cook on Low for 4 to 5 hours or on High for 2 to $2\frac{1}{2}$ hours, until fork-tender.

4. Meanwhile, cook rice according to package directions. Mound rice on a serving platter. Arrange pork chops on top and drizzle with cooking liquid.

Barbecue Pork Chili Ribs

There's no need to fire up the grill for these ribs — they simmer away on their own in a spunky barbecue sauce. Serve with a side of potato salad for an authentic taste of summer. Shred any leftover meat to fill grilled panini the next day.

Tip

Here's a foolproof way to chop an onion: Peel the onion and halve it from top to base. Place each half cut side down on a cutting board. Slice horizontally across each half. Holding the slices together, slice vertically.

- **3- to 4-quart slow cooker**

1½ lbs	pork back ribs, trimmed	750 g
1	small onion, finely chopped	1
1	clove garlic, minced	1
2 tbsp	packed brown sugar	30 mL
½ tsp	chili powder	2 mL
¼ tsp	smoked paprika	1 mL
¼ tsp	celery seeds	1 mL
½ cup	ketchup	125 mL
½ tsp	Worcestershire sauce	2 mL
¼ tsp	hot pepper sauce	1 mL

1. Place ribs in slow cooker stoneware. In a small bowl, combine onion, garlic, brown sugar, chili powder, paprika, celery seeds, ketchup, Worcestershire sauce, hot pepper sauce and ½ cup (125 mL) water. Pour over ribs.

2. Cover and cook on Low for 10 to 12 hours or on High for 5 to 6 hours, until ribs are tender. Using a slotted spoon, transfer ribs to a serving platter and keep warm.

3. Skim off any fat from cooking liquid in stoneware. Transfer cooking liquid to a saucepan and bring to a boil. Reduce heat slightly and boil gently for 5 to 7 minutes or until thickened. Serve sauce on the side.

> **Smoked paprika is made by grinding peppers that have undergone a smoking process. You can find it in various heat levels (from mild to hot). Be careful how much you use, because smoky seasonings can easily overpower the flavor of a dish.**

One-Pot Sausage Supper

All this German-style meal needs is some crusty rolls and your favorite mustard. You can use smoked Polish sausage for this recipe, but I like the fresh variety a little better.

Tip

If there is not much liquid in the ingredients, it is a good idea to grease your stoneware with nonstick cooking spray. Otherwise, when the stoneware heats up, the food can stick, making cleanup difficult. If food does stick, soak the stoneware in hot, soapy water to help remove it.

- **3- to 4-quart slow cooker, stoneware greased**

1 tbsp	vegetable oil	15 mL
2	fresh Oktoberfest or bratwurst sausages	2
1½ cups	frozen hash brown potatoes	375 mL
1	small red bell pepper, chopped (about ½ cup/125 mL)	1
½	red-skinned apple, sliced	½
¼ tsp	caraway seeds	1 mL
¼ tsp	salt	1 mL
⅛ tsp	freshly ground black pepper	0.5 mL
⅓ cup	unsweetened apple juice or apple cider	75 mL
2 tsp	cider vinegar	10 mL
1 cup	drained sauerkraut	250 mL
1 tbsp	chopped fresh parsley	15 mL

1. In a nonstick skillet, heat oil over medium-high heat. Cook sausages, turning, for 6 to 8 minutes or until browned all over. (To make them easier to slice, sausages should not be cooked through.) Transfer to a cutting board. Using a sharp knife, slice into 1-inch (2.5 cm) chunks.

2. In prepared slow cooker stoneware, combine hash browns and red pepper. Arrange sausage, then apple, on top. Sprinkle with caraway seeds, salt and pepper.

3. In a measuring cup, combine apple juice and vinegar. Pour over sausage mixture.

4. Cover and cook on Low for 5 to 6 hours or on High for 2½ to 3 hours, until heated through.

5. Spread sauerkraut over sausage mixture. Cover and cook on High for 25 to 30 minutes or until sauerkraut is heated through. Transfer to a serving dish and sprinkle with parsley.

Double-Duty Dinners

Martha's Maple Chipotle Chicken

**Makes
4 servings,
plus leftovers**

Meaty chicken thighs
star in this hearty dish.
Chicken thighs cook so
well in the slow cooker,
imparting lots of flavor
to the dish while staying
moist and juicy. The
sweet maple syrup
balances nicely with
the smokiness of the
chipotle peppers.

Tips

Tomato paste is now
available in tubes in
many supermarkets
and delis. It keeps
for months in the
refrigerator.

Resist the urge
to lift the lid and
taste or smell
whatever is inside
the slow cooker as
it's cooking. Every
peek will increase
the cooking time by
20 minutes.

- **Minimum 5-quart slow cooker**

2	red bell peppers, cut into 1-inch (2.5 cm) pieces	2
2	carrots, coarsely chopped	2
1	onion, cut into thin wedges	1
3 lbs	boneless skinless chicken thighs	1.5 kg
1	can (19 oz/540 mL) chili-style stewed tomatoes, with juice	1
3 tbsp	tomato paste	45 mL
2 to 3 tbsp	finely chopped chipotle peppers in adobo sauce	30 to 45 mL
2 tbsp	pure maple syrup or packed brown sugar	30 mL
1 tsp	salt	5 mL
	Hot buttered egg noodles	

1. Arrange red peppers, carrots and onion in slow cooker stoneware. Place chicken on top.

2. In a bowl, combine tomatoes with juice, tomato paste, chipotle peppers, maple syrup and salt. Pour over chicken and vegetables.

3. Cover and cook on Low for 8 to 9 hours or on High for 4 to 4½ hours, until juices run clear when chicken is pierced.

4. For Day Two, transfer 8 chicken thighs and 1 cup (250 mL) sauce to separate airtight containers. Let cool, then refrigerate for up to 3 days.

5. Serve the remaining chicken and sauce over hot buttered noodles.

Make Ahead

This dish can be assembled up to 12 hours in advance. Prepare through step 2, cover and refrigerate overnight. The next day, place stoneware in slow cooker and proceed with step 3.

Friday Night Chicken Quesadillas

Day Two

**Makes
4 servings**

When convenience counts, this recipe is the perfect solution. Leftover chicken and sauce make it a snap to put together. Serve with a spinach salad and enjoy a lime-flavored beer on the side.

Tip

Quesadillas can also be pan-fried. Set a large skillet (preferably nonstick or well-seasoned cast iron) over medium-low heat. Add enough vegetable oil to barely coat the bottom. Place the quesadilla in the skillet. When the cheese begins to melt (after about 2 minutes), flip the quesadilla over. Cook for 1 to 2 minutes or until the bottom is warm and lightly toasted.

- *Preheat oven to 400°F (200°C)*
- *Rimmed baking sheet*

8	reserved chicken thighs from Day One	8
1 cup	reserved sauce from Day One	250 mL
8	10-inch (25 cm) flour tortillas	8
2	green onions, sliced	2
1	jalapeño pepper, seeded and diced (optional)	1
2 cups	shredded Monterey Jack or mild Cheddar cheese	500 mL
1 cup	frozen corn kernels, thawed	250 mL
	Hot or mild salsa	
	Sour cream	

1. Place chicken on a cutting board. Using two forks, shred meat; transfer to a bowl. Add sauce and toss to coat.

2. Place 4 tortillas on baking sheet. Top each with chicken mixture, green onions, jalapeño (if using), cheese and corn. Cover each with another tortilla.

3. Bake in preheated oven, turning once, for 15 to 20 minutes or until tortillas are golden and cheese is melted. Transfer to a cutting board and cut into wedges. Serve with salsa and sour cream.

Creamy Chicken with Lemon and Leeks

**Makes
4 servings,
plus leftovers**

The subtle, earthy flavor of leeks naturally complements chicken. Serve this easy entertaining dish with mashed potatoes or rice.

Tips

Leeks contain a lot of sand and must be cleaned carefully. Remove most of the green part and halve the white part lengthwise. Rinse thoroughly under cold running water, spreading leaves apart, and drain in a colander, then slice.

The peel of a citrus fruit contains two parts: the zest and the pith. The zest is the shiny, bright-colored outer layer. The volatile oils found in zest make it extremely flavorful. The pith is the white, fibrous membrane directly below the zest that protects the fruit inside. It can impart a bitter taste if it is not removed.

- **Minimum 5-quart slow cooker**

1	lemon	1
1/3 cup	all-purpose flour	75 mL
3/4 tsp	salt, divided	3 mL
1/2 tsp	freshly ground black pepper	2 mL
6	bone-in skinless chicken breasts (about 2 1/2 lbs/1.25 kg)	6
3 tbsp	butter	45 mL
8	cloves garlic, thinly sliced	8
6	leeks, thinly sliced	6
1 1/2 cups	chicken broth	375 mL
2 tbsp	all-purpose flour	30 mL
1 cup	heavy or whipping (35%) cream	250 mL
	Finely chopped fresh parsley	

1. Finely grate 1/2 tsp (2 mL) zest from lemon, transfer to an airtight container and refrigerate for Day Two. Using a sharp knife, remove the remaining peel (including the white pith) and discard. Seed and thinly slice lemon. Set aside.

2. In a shallow dish, combine the 1/3 cup (75 mL) flour, 1/2 tsp (2 mL) of the salt and pepper. Dredge chicken in flour mixture to coat. Discard any excess flour mixture

3. In a large skillet, melt butter over medium heat. Cook chicken in batches, turning, for 3 to 4 minutes or until browned all over. Drain off fat.

4. Arrange garlic and leeks in slow cooker stoneware. Sprinkle with the remaining salt. Place chicken on top. Arrange the reserved lemon slices over chicken. Pour broth over chicken and vegetables.

5. Cover and cook on Low for 6 to 8 hours or on High for 3 to 4 hours, until chicken is no longer pink inside.

6. For Day Two, remove 2 chicken breasts and let cool. Chop, transfer to an airtight container and refrigerate for up to 3 days.

7. Using a slotted spoon, transfer the remaining chicken to individual serving plates. Spoon leeks over chicken. Cover to keep warm.

Tip

Resist the urge to lift the lid of the slow cooker — every peek will increase the cooking time by 20 minutes.

8. Transfer ½ cup (125 mL) of the cooking liquid to a saucepan. (Discard the remaining cooking liquid.) In a bowl, whisk together the 2 tbsp (30 mL) flour and cream until blended. Pour into saucepan and bring to a boil, whisking. Reduce heat and simmer, whisking, for 3 to 4 minutes or until thickened.

9. Spoon sauce over chicken and leeks. Sprinkle with parsley.

Chicken and Portobello Risotto

Day Two

Makes 4 servings

This is pure comfort food. Although it requires a lot of stirring, the delicious result is worth the effort!

Tips

To prepare the chicken broth, pour it into a large saucepan and bring to a boil over high heat. Cover and reduce heat to low to keep it hot.

If desired, you can sprinkle the finished risotto with additional grated Parmesan cheese.

1 tbsp	olive oil	15 mL
1 tbsp	butter	15 mL
2	large portobello mushrooms, chopped	2
1	onion, chopped	1
1½ cups	Arborio rice	375 mL
½ cup	dry white wine	125 mL
5½ cups	hot chicken broth (see tip, at left)	1.375 mL
	Reserved chopped chicken from Day One	
	Reserved grated lemon zest from Day One	
½ cup	freshly grated Parmesan cheese	125 mL
	Freshly ground black pepper	
	Chopped fresh parsley	

1. In a large skillet, heat oil and butter over medium-high heat. Cook mushrooms and onion, stirring occasionally, for about 8 minutes or until onion is tender and translucent. Add rice and cook, stirring, for 2 minutes.

2. Stir wine into mushroom mixture, loosening rice from bottom of pan. Cook, stirring frequently, for about 2 minutes or until wine is absorbed. Add 1 cup (250 mL) of the broth, reduce heat to medium and simmer, stirring frequently, until broth is absorbed. Continue to add broth, ½ cup (125 mL) at a time, and cook, stirring frequently, until each addition is absorbed before adding the next, until rice is tender. This will take 25 to 30 minutes. While cooking, the mixture should be gently bubbling, so adjust heat as necessary to maintain a simmer.

3. Stir in chicken, lemon zest, Parmesan and ¼ tsp (1 mL) pepper; cook, stirring frequently, until heated through but still creamy.

4. Ladle into individual serving bowls and sprinkle with pepper and parsley.

Honey Mustard Chicken

**Makes
6 servings,
plus leftovers**

. . . .

This tangy-sweet favorite is quick to put together. Cooking the whole meal at once makes things less hectic at dinnertime. Serve with white or brown rice.

Tips

Cooking times for poultry may be longer for larger slow cookers and/or where there is a relatively high proportion of dark to white meat. For predominantly white-meat dishes, be sure to avoid overcooking.

Before measuring honey, rub the inside of the measuring cup with a little vegetable oil. After measuring, the honey will pour out easily, without leaving a sticky mess.

• Minimum 5-quart slow cooker

2	large sweet potatoes	2
1	large onion, halved lengthwise and sliced	1
1	large red bell pepper, chopped	1
8	bone-in skinless chicken breasts (about 4½ lbs/2.25 kg)	8
½ tsp	salt	2 mL
¼ tsp	freshly ground black pepper	1 mL
¼ cup	liquid honey	60 mL
¼ cup	Dijon mustard	60 mL
2 tbsp	curry powder	30 mL
2 tbsp	butter, softened	30 mL
2 tbsp	cornstarch	30 mL
2 tbsp	cold water	30 mL

1. Cut each sweet potato in half lengthwise, then in half crosswise. Cut each quarter into three wedges. In slow cooker stoneware, combine sweet potatoes, onion and red pepper. Arrange chicken on top. Sprinkle with salt and pepper.

2. In a bowl, combine honey, mustard, curry powder and butter. Pour over chicken and vegetables.

3. Cover and cook on Low for 5 to 6 hours or on High for 2½ to 3 hours, until chicken is no longer pink inside.

4. For Day Two, transfer 2 chicken breasts, 1 cup (250 mL) of the vegetables and ½ cup (125 mL) of the cooking liquid to separate airtight containers. Let cool, then refrigerate for up to 3 days.

5. Using a slotted spoon, transfer the remaining chicken and vegetables to a serving platter and cover to keep warm.

6. Strain cooking liquid into a saucepan, discarding solids. In a small bowl, combine cornstarch and water. Bring cooking liquid to a boil over medium-high heat. Whisk in cornstarch mixture. Reduce heat and simmer, stirring, for 2 to 3 minutes or until thickened. Spoon over chicken and vegetables.

Asian Chicken Salad

**Makes
4 servings**

This crunchy, wonderfully satisfying salad uses reserved chicken from the Honey Mustard Chicken. Even the dressing is made from the previous day's cooking liquid.

Tip

Chow mein noodles are usually found in the Asian food section of supermarkets, but some clever grocers stock them in the produce section, since they are often added to salads for extra crunch.

Dressing

½ cup	reserved cooking liquid from Day One	125 mL
½ cup	mayonnaise	125 mL

Salad

2	reserved chicken breasts from Day One	2
1 cup	reserved vegetables from Day One	250 mL
3 cups	shredded napa cabbage or iceberg lettuce	750 mL
1½ cups	broccoli slaw mix	375 mL
½ cup	snow peas, trimmed and thinly sliced lengthwise	125 mL
½ cup	crunchy chow mein noodles	125 mL

1. *Dressing:* In a small bowl, whisk together cooking liquid and mayonnaise until smooth. Set aside.

2. *Salad:* Remove chicken from bones, discarding bones. Chop chicken and reserved vegetables.

3. In a large bowl, combine chicken, vegetables, cabbage, broccoli slaw, snow peas and noodles. Add dressing and toss to coat.

> **Broccoli slaw is a type of coleslaw made with shredded broccoli, carrots and red cabbage. Look for it in the produce department of the supermarket. It is delicious tossed with your favorite coleslaw dressing or with added fruit such as apples and dried cranberries.**

Thai Chicken Noodle Bowls

Day One

Makes 4 servings, plus leftovers

Thai food is known for its symphony of flavors — sweet, salty, spicy and sour. With this slow-simmered dish, you can enjoy two Thai-inspired meals in one week.

Tips

Sriracha chili sauce is found in the Asian food section of the supermarket or in Asian or gourmet food stores. It is a smooth paste of ground sun-ripened chiles and garlic. It adds a delicious spiciness to Thai food, but it's not overpowering.

Canned coconut milk is made from grated soaked coconut pulp — it's not the liquid found inside the coconut. It can be found in the Asian food section of the supermarket or in Asian food stores. Be sure you don't buy coconut cream, often used to make tropical drinks such as piña coladas.

• **Minimum 5-quart slow cooker**

3	large red bell peppers, cut into strips	3
2	onions, sliced	2
1 to 2	serrano chile peppers, seeded and finely chopped	1 to 2
8 oz	cremini mushrooms, sliced	250 g
6	cloves garlic, minced	6
2 tsp	minced gingerroot	10 mL
6	boneless skinless chicken breasts	6
1 cup	tomato sauce	250 mL
1/4 cup	fish sauce	60 mL
2 tbsp	granulated sugar	30 mL
2 tbsp	freshly squeezed lime juice	30 mL
2 tbsp	Sriracha chili sauce	30 mL
1 cup	coconut milk	250 mL
1 1/2 cups	bean sprouts	375 mL
2 tbsp	cornstarch	30 mL
2 tbsp	cold water	30 mL
1	package (6 oz/175 g) rice stick noodles	1
1/2 cup	chopped peanuts	125 mL
	Chopped fresh cilantro	

1. Arrange red peppers, onions, serrano chiles to taste and mushrooms in slow cooker stoneware. Sprinkle with garlic and ginger. Place chicken on top.

2. In a glass measuring cup, combine tomato sauce, fish sauce, sugar, lime juice and chili sauce. Pour over chicken and vegetables.

3. Cover and cook on Low for 6 to 7 hours or on High for 3 to 3 1/2 hours, until chicken is no longer pink inside.

4. Stir in coconut milk and bean sprouts. Cover and cook on High for about 30 minutes or until heated through.

5. For Day Two, transfer 2 chicken breasts, 1 cup (250 mL) of the vegetables and 1/4 cup (60 mL) of the cooking liquid to separate airtight containers. Let cool, then refrigerate for up to 2 days.

6. Using a slotted spoon, transfer the remaining chicken breasts to a cutting board. Slice, cover to keep warm and set aside. Transfer vegetables to a bowl and cover to keep warm.

7. In a small bowl, whisk together cornstarch and water. Transfer the remaining cooking liquid to a saucepan and bring to a boil over medium-high heat. Reduce heat to medium. Whisk in cornstarch mixture and cook, stirring, for 3 to 5 minutes or until thickened.

8. Meanwhile, in a large pot of boiling salted water, cook noodles according to package directions until tender but firm (al dente). Drain and return to pot.

9. Add ½ cup (125 mL) of the sauce and the reserved vegetables to the noodles and toss to coat. Transfer to a serving platter. Top with sliced chicken and spoon the remaining sauce over top. Sprinkle with peanuts and cilantro.

Thai Chicken Pizza

`Day Two`

Makes 4 servings

If you are looking for a pizza that has lots of flavor and is a little different from the rest, this will become one of your favorites. The cilantro on top is a must!

- *Preheat oven to 475°F (240°C), with rack positioned at bottom*

¼ cup	reserved cooking liquid from Day One	60 mL
1 tbsp	peanut butter	15 mL
1 tsp	sesame oil	5 mL
Pinch	hot pepper flakes (optional)	Pinch
1	12-inch (30 cm) baked pizza base or flatbread	1
2	reserved chicken breasts from Day One, chopped	2
1 cup	reserved vegetables from Day One	250 mL
½	red onion, thinly sliced	½
3 cups	shredded mozzarella cheese	750 mL
¼ cup	chopped fresh cilantro	60 mL

1. In a saucepan, combine cooking liquid, peanut butter, sesame oil and hot pepper flakes. Cook over medium heat, stirring often, until heated through. Set aside.

2. Spread sauce over pizza base. Top evenly with chicken, reserved vegetables, red onion, then cheese.

3. Place directly on lowest rack in preheated oven and bake for 10 to 12 minutes or until cheese is bubbling and brown. Sprinkle with cilantro.

Turkey Breast with Sweet Cranberry Soy Gravy

Day One

(see tip, at left)

Makes 6 servings, plus leftovers

Don't wait for the holidays to make a turkey roast. This delicious recipe can be made as a weeknight meal without any special-occasion fuss. Serve it with rice or mashed potatoes and a sauté of colorful peppers on the side.

Tip

If you're using a smaller slow cooker, substitute 2 bone-in turkey breasts (each 3 lbs/1.5 kg).

• **Minimum 6-quart oval slow cooker (see tip, at left)**

1	bone-in double turkey breast (6 to 7 lbs/3 to 3.5 kg)	1
1	can (14 oz/398 mL) whole berry cranberry sauce	1
1	envelope (1½ oz/45 g) onion soup mix	1
	Grated zest and juice of 1 orange	
3 tbsp	cornstarch	45 mL
3 tbsp	soy sauce	45 mL
1 tbsp	granulated sugar	15 mL
1½ tsp	cider vinegar	7 mL
	Salt and freshly ground black pepper	

1. Place turkey, meat side up, in slow cooker stoneware.

2. Transfer 2 tbsp (30 mL) of the cranberry sauce to an airtight container and refrigerate for Day Two. In a bowl, combine the remaining cranberry sauce, soup mix, orange zest and orange juice. Pour over turkey.

3. Cover and cook on High for 3½ to 5 hours or until a meat thermometer inserted into the thickest part of the breast registers 165°F (74°C) and juices run clear when turkey is pierced. Transfer turkey to a cutting board and let stand for 15 minutes.

4. Cut turkey off the bone and thinly slice. Chop 1½ cups (375 mL) for Day Two and transfer to an airtight container. Let cool, then refrigerate for up to 3 days. Cover the remaining sliced turkey to keep warm.

5. Transfer cooking liquid to a saucepan. In a small bowl, whisk together cornstarch and soy sauce until smooth. Stir into cooking liquid, along with sugar and vinegar. Season to taste with salt and pepper. Bring to a boil, then reduce heat and simmer, stirring, for 2 to 3 minutes or until slightly thickened. Spoon over sliced turkey.

Crunchy Turkey and Cranberry Pie

Day Two

Makes 6 servings

This quiche-like recipe is a great way to use up leftover turkey and cranberry sauce, and is a family favorite in my home. If you have enough turkey left from the previous night, make two pies and freeze the second one for a third meal. Serve with a spinach salad.

Tips

Quiche is a great way to use up leftovers. In most cases, egg and cream or milk are the main components of the custard layer, which sits in a flaky bottom crust. But instead of using a pie crust, you could also line the sides and bottom of a pie plate with large croissants that have been split in half.

This dish can be served hot or at room temperature.

• *Preheat oven to 400°F (200°C)*

1	9-inch (23 cm) deep-dish pie shell (unbaked)	1
1 tbsp	Dijon mustard	15 mL
2 tbsp	reserved cranberry sauce from Day One	30 mL
1 cup	shredded Swiss cheese	250 mL
1 cup	shredded Cheddar cheese	250 mL
1 tbsp	butter or margarine	15 mL
1	onion, chopped	1
1	stalk celery, chopped	1
¼ cup	slivered almonds	60 mL
1½ cups	chopped reserved turkey from Day One	375 mL
3	eggs	3
¾ cup	evaporated milk	175 mL
¼ tsp	dried sage	1 mL

1. Bake pie shell in preheated oven for 5 to 7 minutes or until crust is light golden. Remove from oven, leaving oven on, and let cool slightly. Using a pastry brush, brush mustard over inside of pie shell. Spread cranberry sauce over mustard.

2. In a bowl, combine Swiss cheese and Cheddar. Sprinkle half the cheese mixture over cranberry sauce. Set aside.

3. In a nonstick skillet, melt butter over medium heat. Sauté onion, celery and almonds for 3 to 5 minutes or until vegetables are softened.

4. In prepared pie shell, evenly layer onion mixture, turkey and the remaining cheese.

5. In a bowl, whisk eggs until blended; whisk in evaporated milk and sage. Slowly pour into pie shell.

6. Bake for 15 minutes. Reduce heat to 375°F (190°C) and bake for 25 to 30 minutes or until set. (Cover edges of crust with foil, if necessary, to prevent excess browning during the last 10 to 15 minutes.) Let stand for 10 minutes before slicing.

Adobo Barbecue Turkey Thighs

Day One

Makes 6 servings, plus leftovers

Turkey thighs become so tender in this low, slow, Southwest simmer with big, bold flavors. Continue the theme by making the enchiladas for your Day Two dinner.

Tips

For an authentic Southwestern flair, serve this over hominy instead of rice. You can find hominy, either dried or in cans, in the Latin food section of many supermarkets. If you purchase it in cans, just drain, rinse and heat it.

You can freeze the cooked turkey thighs for use at a later time. Transfer to an airtight container and freeze for up to 1 month. When ready to use, let thaw in the refrigerator overnight.

Enchilada sauce is a cooked tomato and chile sauce. Look for it in the Mexican food section of the supermarket.

- **Minimum 5-quart slow cooker**

5	skinless turkey thighs (about 5 lbs/2.5 kg)	5
1	large red or green bell pepper, chopped	1
6	cloves garlic, minced	6
1	can (28 oz/796 mL) crushed tomatoes	1
1	can (10 oz/284 mL) enchilada sauce	1
¼ cup	red wine vinegar	60 mL
2 tbsp	finely chopped chipotle peppers in adobo sauce	30 mL
1 tbsp	chili powder	15 mL
2 tsp	crumbled dried oregano	10 mL
1 tsp	ground cumin	5 mL
1 tsp	salt	5 mL
½ tsp	ground cinnamon	2 mL
3 cups	hot cooked rice	750 mL
	Sour cream (optional)	

1. Arrange turkey thighs in slow cooker stoneware and sprinkle with red pepper.

2. In a bowl, combine garlic, tomatoes, enchilada sauce, vinegar, chipotle peppers, chili powder, oregano, cumin, salt and cinnamon. Pour over turkey.

3. Cover and cook on Low for 8 to 10 hours or on High for 4 to 6 hours, until juices run clear when turkey is pierced and meat is very tender and falling off the bones. Using a slotted spoon, transfer turkey to a cutting board. Skim fat from sauce.

4. For Day Two, transfer 2 turkey thighs and 1 cup (250 mL) of the sauce to separate airtight containers. Let cool, then refrigerate for up to 3 days.

5. Cut the remaining turkey thighs from bones, discarding bones, and cut in half. Serve turkey over rice, topped with sour cream (if using). Serve the remaining sauce on the side.

Make Ahead

This dish can be assembled up to 12 hours in advance. Prepare through step 2, cover and refrigerate overnight. The next day, place stoneware in slow cooker and proceed with step 3.

Amazing Turkey Enchiladas

Makes 6 servings

This rolled tortilla casserole comes together easily. It's a fast fix with loads of family appeal!

Tip

Serve these enchiladas with a selection of garnishes, such as sliced radishes or avocado, chopped tomatoes, shredded lettuce and sour cream. Or try them with Mexican Rice (page 208) alongside.

- *Preheat oven to 350°F (180°C)*
- *13- by 9-inch (33 by 23 cm) glass baking dish, greased*

2	reserved turkey thighs from Day One	2
4 oz	light cream cheese	125 g
3	green onions, finely chopped	3
1 cup	reserved sauce from Day One	250 mL
1/2 cup	plain low-fat yogurt	125 mL
6	10-inch (25 cm) flour tortillas	6
1 1/2 cups	salsa verde	375 mL
1 1/2 cups	shredded Cheddar or Monterey Jack cheese	375 mL
2 tbsp	chopped fresh cilantro or parsley	30 mL

1. Place turkey on a cutting board. Using two forks, shred meat. Discard bones.

2. In large microwave-safe bowl, soften cream cheese on Medium (50%) power for 1 minute. Stir well. Stir in green onions, sauce, yogurt and turkey.

3. Spread about 1/2 cup (125 mL) of the cream cheese mixture along the center of each tortilla and roll up. Arrange tortillas in a single layer, seam side down, in prepared baking dish.

4. Spread salsa over tortillas and sprinkle with cheese. Bake in preheated oven for 30 to 35 minutes or until heated through. Sprinkle with cilantro.

Make Ahead

You can assemble this dish up to 24 hours in advance. Prepare through step 3, cover and refrigerate overnight. When ready to cook, proceed with step 4.

Salsa verde is Spanish for "green salsa." Green salsas are almost always milder than red salsas. In salsa verde, tomatillos replace the tomatoes used in red salsa. The tomatillos give a tangy, zesty flavor to green salsa, which also has underlying flavors of hearty roasted green chiles and onions.

Chili-Glazed Meatloaf

**Makes
6 servings,
plus leftovers**

. . . .

I wouldn't like to tinker with your favorite meatloaf recipe, and I have always included a few in my collection, but this recipe works well for two meals. The trick to making a good meatloaf is to use a blend of meats and work with a light touch when you shape the loaf by hand. Serve this with mashed potatoes and a steamed green vegetable, such as broccoli.

Tips

You can also line the stoneware with a layer of cheesecloth that's large enough to extend up the sides and over the rim.

Meatloaf can be frozen for later use. Let cool to room temperature, wrap in foil and place in a sealable plastic bag. Mark the bag with the date and recipe name and freeze for up to 3 months. Let thaw in the refrigerator overnight.

- **Minimum 5-quart slow cooker**

1½ lbs	lean ground beef	750 g
1½ lbs	lean ground pork	750 g
3	eggs, lightly beaten	3
1	large onion, finely chopped	1
2 cups	fresh bread crumbs	500 mL
2 tsp	salt	10 mL
½ tsp	freshly ground black pepper	2 mL

Chili Sauce Glaze

½ cup	ketchup	125 mL
¼ cup	chili sauce	60 mL
2 tbsp	packed brown sugar	30 mL
½ tsp	dry mustard	2 mL

1. Cut three 2-foot (60 cm) lengths of heavy foil and fold each one in half lengthwise. Place one strip lengthwise along bottom of slow cooker stoneware, bringing the ends up the sides and over the rim. Place two strips widthwise across bottom of stoneware, bringing the ends up the sides and over the rim.

2. In a large bowl, using your hands, combine beef, pork, eggs, onion, bread crumbs, salt and pepper. Shape into two 5-inch (12.5 cm) loaves. Place loaves on foil strips in stoneware.

3. *Chile Sauce Glaze:* In a bowl, combine ketchup, chili sauce, brown sugar and mustard. Spread over loaves.

4. Tucking strip ends under lid, cover and cook on Low for 7 to 8 hours or on High for 3½ to 4 hours, until a meat thermometer inserted in center of loaf registers 170°F (77°C). Remove lid and grasp strip ends to carefully lift out loaves. Transfer one loaf to a serving platter.

5. For Day Two, transfer the other loaf to an airtight container. Let cool, then refrigerate for up to 3 days.

Italian Meatloaf Parmesan

Makes 4 to 6 servings

This is a fantastic way to use up leftover meatloaf. It is so easy to prepare, and even the fussiest eaters will enjoy it. Serve over cooked pasta, such as linguine, and add a tossed green salad on the side.

Tip

Authentic Italian Parmesan cheese (Parmigiano-Reggiano) is expensive, but its flavor is certainly worth the price. Well-wrapped in the refrigerator, a block keeps for months, and it goes a long way when you freshly grate it as you need it.

- *Preheat oven to 350°F (180°C)*
- *Rimmed baking sheet, lined with parchment paper*

	Reserved meatloaf from Day One	
2	eggs, lightly beaten	2
¼ cup	milk	60 mL
½ cup	Italian-seasoned fine dry bread crumbs	125 mL
¼ cup	freshly grated Parmesan cheese	60 mL
2 cups	tomato pasta sauce	500 mL
1 cup	shredded mozzarella cheese	250 mL

1. Cut meatloaf into 6 slices. Set aside.

2. In a shallow bowl, combine eggs and milk. In another shallow bowl, combine bread crumbs and Parmesan.

3. Dip each meatloaf slice in egg mixture, then in bread crumb mixture, coating evenly. Transfer to prepared baking sheet.

4. Bake in preheated oven for 20 minutes. Spoon pasta sauce evenly over meatloaf slices and sprinkle with mozzarella. Bake for about 15 minutes or until cheese is melted and sauce is heated through.

Chinese Five-Spice Beef Short Ribs

**Makes
4 servings,
plus leftovers**

Unlike back ribs, which have more bone than meat, short ribs are covered with layers of meat and fat, and require long, moist-heat cooking to release their succulent flavor. When preparing this recipe, first broil the short ribs to render the excess fat. This allows the intriguing Asian flavors to develop as the ribs simmer in the slow cooker.

Tips

Ready-to-use broth in convenient Tetra-Paks is a handy ingredient and doesn't need to be diluted. Avoid using cubes and powders, which tend to be very salty.

Five-spice powder is commonly used in Chinese-style cooking. Its main components are ground fennel seeds, cloves, cinnamon, star anise (which has a wonderful licorice flavor) and Szechuan peppercorns. While you may find it at some supermarkets, I recommend purchasing it from an Asian market — you will pay a little less, and the flavor will be more authentic.

- **Minimum 5-quart slow cooker**
- *Preheat broiler, with rack set 6 inches (15 cm) below heat source*
- *Broiler pan or rimmed baking sheet, lined with foil*

6 lbs	beef short ribs or braising ribs, cut into 3-inch (7.5 cm) sections	3 kg
2	large red onions, sliced	2
2/3 cup	beef broth	150 mL
1/4 cup	soy sauce	60 mL
1/4 cup	rice vinegar	60 mL
2 tbsp	liquid honey	30 mL
1 tbsp	Chinese five-spice powder	15 mL
1 tsp	ground ginger	5 mL
4	cloves garlic, minced	4
2 cups	hot cooked rice	500 mL

1. Place ribs on prepared pan. Broil, turning often, for 10 to 15 minutes or until browned all over. Transfer to a plate lined with paper towels and let drain.

2. Arrange red onions in slow cooker stoneware. Place ribs on top.

3. In a bowl, combine broth, soy sauce, vinegar, honey, five-spice powder, ginger and garlic. Pour over ribs.

4. Cover and cook on Low for 11 to 12 hours or on High for 5½ to 6 hours, until ribs are tender. Using a slotted spoon, remove ribs and onions and set aside. Pour cooking liquid into a glass measuring cup and skim off fat.

5. For Day Two, transfer half the ribs, half the onions and half the cooking liquid to separate airtight containers. Let cool, then refrigerate for up to 3 days.

6. Serve the remaining ribs, onions and cooking liquid over rice.

Shanghai Beef Stuffed Spuds

**Makes
4 servings**

. . . .

Stuffed baked potatoes are a popular meal in my house, especially with my two teenagers. You can make the potatoes ahead of time, then just reheat and fill them with the hot beef topping. They are perfect for those nights when everyone is on a different schedule. Serve these spuds with a tossed green salad and some corn on the cob for a great family-friendly meal!

Tips

To bake potatoes: Bake in a 400°F (200°C) oven for 1 hour or until potatoes give slightly when squeezed.

To microwave potatoes: Arrange potatoes 1 inch (2.5 cm) apart in a circle on a roasting rack or paper towel in the microwave. Microwave on High, turning halfway through, until potatoes are tender when pierced with a skewer. For 1 large baking potato, cook for 4 to 5 minutes; for two, 6 to 8 minutes; for four, 10 to 12 minutes.

- *Preheat oven to 350°F (180°C)*
- *Shallow baking dish*

4	large baking potatoes (each about 10 oz/300 g), scrubbed	4
	Reserved ribs from Day One	
	Reserved onions from Day One	
	Reserved cooking liquid from Day One	
½ cup	buttermilk	125 mL
1 cup	shredded Cheddar cheese	250 mL
2 tbsp	chopped fresh parsley	30 mL
	Salt and freshly ground black pepper	

1. Using a fork, pierce skin of each potato several times. Bake or microwave potatoes (see tips, at left).

2. Meanwhile, remove meat from ribs, discarding bones, and, using two forks, shred to make about 1½ cups (375 mL). In a saucepan, combine beef, onions and cooking liquid. Cook over medium-high heat, stirring often, until heated through.

3. Cut potatoes in half lengthwise. Carefully scoop out flesh and transfer to a bowl, leaving a ¼-inch (0.5 cm) shell around each half. Set shells aside.

4. Beat buttermilk into potato flesh until smooth. Stir in beef mixture, half the cheese and parsley. Season to taste with salt and pepper. Spoon into shells. Top with the remaining cheese.

5. Arrange in baking dish and bake in preheated oven for 15 minutes or until cheese is melted.

Cubano Pork Roast

**Makes
6 servings,
plus leftovers**

This roast features a winning combination of the warm flavors and spices of Cuba: orange, lime, honey, garlic and cumin. Use the leftovers to make South Beach Pork Panini on Day Two.

Tip

After opening canned chipotle chiles, transfer the peppers and their sauce to a glass jar with an airtight lid, close tightly and store in the refrigerator for up to 1 month. For longer storage, transfer peppers and sauce to a freezer bag and gently press out the air, then seal the bag. Manipulate the bag to separate the peppers so that it will be easy to break off a frozen section of pepper and sauce without thawing the whole package. Freeze for up to 6 months.

- **5- to 6-quart slow cooker**

1	boneless pork loin roast (3½ to 4 lbs/1.75 to 2 kg), trimmed	1
2	cloves garlic, minced	2
1	onion, chopped	1
1	chipotle pepper in adobo sauce, finely chopped	1
1 cup	orange marmalade	250 mL
1 tbsp	liquid honey	15 mL
½ tsp	grated lime zest	2 mL
1 tbsp	freshly squeezed lime juice	15 mL
1 tsp	ground cumin	5 mL
½ tsp	crumbled dried oregano	2 mL
½ tsp	salt	2 mL
¼ tsp	freshly ground black pepper	1 mL
½ cup	chicken broth	125 mL

1. Place pork roast in slow cooker stoneware.

2. In a bowl, stir together garlic, onion, chipotle pepper, marmalade, honey, lime zest, lime juice, cumin, oregano, salt and pepper. Spread over pork. Pour broth around pork.

3. Cover and cook on Low for 5 to 5½ hours or on High for 2½ to 3 hours, until pork is fork-tender. Transfer pork to a cutting board.

4. For Day Two, slice off about one-third of the pork and transfer to an airtight container. Let cool, then refrigerate for up to 3 days.

5. Slice the remaining pork and transfer to a serving platter. If desired, strain cooking liquid and drizzle some on top. (Discard the remaining cooking liquid.)

Make Ahead

This dish can be assembled up to 12 hours in advance. Prepare through step 2, cover and refrigerate overnight. The next day, place stoneware in slow cooker and proceed with step 3.

South Beach Pork Panini

Day Two

Makes
6 servings

Tasty toasted pork sandwiches are Miami's favorite snack and are quickly becoming an icon of American pop food culture.

Tip

If using a skillet, you may wish to press the sandwiches as they cook. Place sandwiches, butter side down, in skillet. Cover with foil and top with a dinner plate. (If necessary, weigh down the plate with 2 to 3 full cans of food.)

• *Preheat panini grill (optional)*

1/3 cup	mayonnaise or roasted garlic mayonnaise	75 mL
1/2	chipotle pepper in adobo sauce, finely chopped	1/2
12	slices sourdough bread	12
1/3 cup	prepared mustard	75 mL
	Reserved pork from Day One, cut into 6 slices	
6	slices Swiss cheese	6
8 oz	shaved Black Forest ham	250 g
6	lengthwise dill pickle slices	6
3 tbsp	butter or margarine, softened	45 mL

1. In a small bowl, combine mayonnaise and chipotle pepper. Spread evenly on 6 of the bread slices and spread mustard on the other 6 slices. On each slice spread with mustard, place 1 slice pork, 1 slice cheese, one-sixth of the ham and 1 slice pickle. Cover with the remaining bread slices. Dividing half the butter evenly, lightly spread over one side of each sandwich.

2. In batches, arrange sandwiches, butter side down, on panini grill (or in a large skillet over medium heat). Lightly spread tops of sandwiches with the remaining butter. Cook for about 8 minutes (or for about 4 minutes per side in skillet) or until cheese has slightly melted and bread is toasted. Cut sandwiches in half.

Family Fun Italian Sausage Sliders

Day One

**Makes
6 servings,
plus leftovers**

· ·

With sliders, you get all the fun of a full-size sausage on a bun in an easy-to-hold package. These are perfect for tailgating, picnics or any other occasion when you want to serve food without the fuss of cutlery or plates. A large Caesar salad will round out the meal.

Tips

In the slow cooker, whole-leaf dried herbs, such as basil and oregano, release their flavor slowly throughout the long cooking process, so they are a better choice than ground herbs.

Adding a little balsamic vinegar to tomato pasta sauce adds richness and brings all the flavors together.

- **Minimum 5-quart slow cooker**
- *Rimmed baking sheet*

10	fresh hot or mild Italian sausages (about 2 lbs/1 kg)	10
6	cloves garlic, minced	6
1	can (28 oz/796 mL) fire-roasted diced tomatoes or San Marzano tomatoes, with juice	1
2 cups	tomato pasta sauce	500 mL
1 tbsp	balsamic vinegar	15 mL
2 tsp	crumbled dried basil	10 mL
1 tsp	dried oregano	5 mL
1/2 tsp	salt	2 mL
1/4 tsp	freshly ground black pepper	1 mL
1/4 tsp	hot pepper flakes	1 mL
12	small French-style dinner rolls or hoagie buns, split	12
12	slices provolone cheese, cut in half	12
3/4 cup	bottled roasted red peppers, drained and cut into thin strips	175 mL

1. In a large nonstick skillet, cook sausages over medium-high heat, turning, for 6 to 8 minutes or until browned all over. Transfer to slow cooker stoneware.

2. Stir in garlic, tomatoes with juice, pasta sauce, vinegar, basil, oregano, salt, black pepper and hot pepper flakes.

3. Cover and cook on Low for 6 to 8 hours or on High for 3 to 4 hours, until bubbling.

4. For Day Two, transfer 4 sausages and 4 cups (1 L) of the sauce to separate airtight containers. Let cool, then refrigerate for up to 3 days.

5. Preheat broiler, with rack set 4 to 5 inches (10 to 12 cm) below heat source. Place roll halves, cut side up, on baking sheet. Cut the remaining sausages in half crosswise. Place 1 sausage half on each bottom roll half. Spoon about 1 tbsp (15 mL) sauce over each and top with 1 half-slice of cheese. Place the remaining half-slices of cheese on top roll halves.

Tip

Resist the urge to lift the lid and taste or smell whatever is inside the slow cooker as it's cooking. Every peek will increase the cooking time by 20 minutes.

6. Broil for 2 to 3 minutes or until cheese is bubbling. Top each sausage with roasted red peppers. Cover with top roll halves. Serve the remaining sauce on the side for dipping.

> San Marzano plum tomatoes are grown in the volcanic soil near Salerno, Italy, long known for producing the most flavorful tomatoes. Deep red and sweet, they are packed in tomato juice and have been the traditional choice of generations of Italian cooks. The production and labeling of this product is restricted by law under the European Union Protected Designation of Origin (DOP). Each can carries a seal of authenticity and is individually numbered.

Saucy Sausage Pasta

Day Two

Makes 6 servings

This rich tomato sauce is highly seasoned by the simmering Italian sausage. Add a few vegetables, and you've got a flavorful pasta sauce that's great over any shape of noodle. A nice Chianti wine and some warm Italian bread complete this quick and easy dinner.

Tip

Authentic Italian Parmesan cheese (Parmigiano-Reggiano) is expensive, but its flavor is certainly worth the price. Well-wrapped in the refrigerator, a block keeps for months, and it goes a long way when you freshly grate it as you need it.

1 tbsp	olive oil	15 mL
1	onion, finely chopped	1
1	large carrot, diced	1
1	red bell pepper, finely chopped	1
4	reserved sausages from Day One, cut into 1-inch (2.5 cm) chunks	4
1	can (14 oz/398 mL) tomato sauce	1
4 cups	reserved sauce from Day One	1 L
1 lb	rotini or penne pasta	500 g
	Freshly grated Parmesan cheese	

1. In a large skillet, heat oil over medium-high heat. Sauté onion, carrot and red pepper for 5 to 7 minutes or until tender. Add sausages, tomato sauce and reserved sauce; bring to a boil. Reduce heat and simmer, stirring occasionally, for 10 to 15 minutes or until sauce is heated through.

2. Meanwhile, in a large pot of boiling salted water, cook pasta according to package directions until tender but firm (al dente). Drain. Toss in sauce to coat pasta.

3. Divide evenly among individual serving bowls and sprinkle with Parmesan.

Greek Lamb Roast Dinner

Day One

Makes 4 servings, plus leftovers

Greek cooks usually roast lamb in liquid until it is well-done and mouth-wateringly tender and juicy. If you have difficulty finding fresh lamb roasts, look for frozen roasts in the supermarket and thaw overnight in the refrigerator. An oval slow cooker works best for this recipe, as you need to fit two small lamb roasts in.

Tips

If the lamb roasts are tied, remove string before sprinkling and rubbing with the shallot mixture, then retie each with butcher's twine.

To zest a lemon, use the fine side of a box grater, making sure not to grate the white pith underneath. Or use a zester, then finely chop the zest. Zesters are inexpensive and widely available at specialty kitchenware shops.

● **Minimum 5-quart oval slow cooker**

1	shallot, minced	1
1 tsp	grated lemon zest	5 mL
1 tsp	garlic powder	5 mL
1 tsp	dried oregano	5 mL
1/2 tsp	dried mint	2 mL
1/2 tsp	dried rosemary	2 mL
1/2 tsp	salt	2 mL
1/4 tsp	freshly ground black pepper	1 mL
2	boneless lamb shoulder roasts (each 2 to 2 1/2 lbs/1 to 1.25 kg), trimmed	2
4	carrots, halved lengthwise and cut into 3-inch (7.5 cm) sticks	4
2	white or red potatoes, quartered	2
1	large onion, cut into wedges	1
1/2 cup	chicken broth	125 mL

1. In a small bowl, combine shallot, lemon zest, garlic powder, oregano, mint, rosemary, salt and pepper. Sprinkle evenly over lamb roasts, rubbing into the meat.

2. In slow cooker stoneware, combine carrots, potatoes, onion and broth. Place roasts on top.

3. Cover and cook on Low for 8 to 9 hours or on High for 4 to 5 hours, until lamb is tender and cooked to desired doneness.

4. For Day Two, transfer one roast to a bowl and let cool. Using two forks, shred lamb and transfer to an airtight container. Refrigerate for up to 3 days.

5. Transfer the other roast to a serving platter and carve into slices. Using a slotted spoon, remove vegetables from stoneware and arrange around meat.

6. Strain cooking liquid into a glass measuring cup and skim off fat. Spoon some of the cooking liquid over meat and vegetables. (Discard the remaining cooking liquid.)

Make Ahead

This dish can be assembled up to 12 hours in advance. Prepare through step 2, cover and refrigerate overnight. The next day, place stoneware in slow cooker and proceed with step 3.

Warm Lamb Gyros with Tzatziki

Makes 4 servings

My favorite part of a gyro (a Greek sandwich made with lamb, tomatoes and onions) is the tzatziki. Serve with a chickpea side salad.

Tip

Use pitas without pockets, since you will be wrapping the pitas around the filling.

- *Preheat oven to 275°F (140°C)*
- *Microwave-safe baking dish*

4	pitas	4
1	reserved shredded lamb roast from Day One	1
2 cups	shredded lettuce	500 mL
2	tomatoes, sliced	2
½	red onion, sliced	½
1 cup	tzatziki (store-bought or see recipe, below)	250 mL
½ cup	crumbled feta cheese	125 mL

1. Stack pitas and wrap in foil. Bake in preheated oven for 10 to 15 minutes or until heated through.

2. Place lamb in baking dish. Cover and microwave on High for 2½ to 3½ minutes, stirring halfway through, until heated through.

3. Place 1 pita on each individual serving plate. Top with lettuce, tomatoes, red onion, lamb, tzatziki and cheese. Wrap up on either side.

Makes about 2 cups (500 mL)

Cucumber, lemon and yogurt combine in this refreshing sauce, which goes perfectly with lamb.

Tzatziki

3 cups	low-fat plain yogurt	750 mL
1	cucumber (unpeeled)	1
1 tsp	salt	5 mL
2 tsp	minced garlic	10 mL
2 tsp	freshly squeezed lemon juice or red wine vinegar	10 mL

1. Line a colander with a large coffee filter or a double layer of paper towels and set over a bowl. Place yogurt in colander and let drain in the refrigerator for 4 hours or until reduced to 1½ cups (375 mL).

2. Meanwhile, grate cucumber, sprinkle with salt and let stand for 20 minutes. Transfer to a sieve and drain, pressing with your palm to squeeze out excess moisture.

3. In a bowl, combine yogurt, cucumber, garlic and lemon juice. Use immediately or cover and refrigerate for up to 5 days.

Desserts

Braised Apricots with Vanilla Mascarpone

A ripe apricot is a thing of beauty, sweetly fragrant and delicious. While apricots are delicious as is, they also braise beautifully. To add a little luxury, this dessert is served with a dollop of vanilla-infused mascarpone, but you can substitute sweetened whipped cream.

Tips

You can substitute 1 tsp (5 mL) vanilla extract for the vanilla bean.

When apricots are not in season, you can use one 14-oz (398 mL) can of apricots, drained. You can also substitute 4 fresh or canned peaches for the apricots.

- **3- to 4-quart slow cooker**

1	vanilla bean, split lengthwise	1
¼ cup	packed brown sugar	60 mL
2 tbsp	butter, melted	30 mL
1 tbsp	freshly squeezed lemon juice or brandy	15 mL
8	firm ripe apricots, halved and pitted	8
½ cup	mascarpone cheese	125 mL
1 tbsp	confectioner's (icing) sugar	15 mL
	Raspberries	

1. In slow cooker stoneware, combine vanilla bean, brown sugar, butter and lemon juice. Add apricots, turn to coat with butter mixture and arrange cut side down in a single layer.

2. Cover and cook on Low for 3 to 4 hours or on High for 1½ to 2 hours, until apricots are tender.

3. Using tongs, remove vanilla bean. Using a sharp paring knife, scrape seeds into a small bowl. Discard pod. Stir mascarpone and confectioner's sugar into vanilla seeds.

4. Using a slotted spoon, transfer apricots to individual serving dishes. Serve warm or at room temperature, topped with mascarpone mixture and raspberries and drizzled with cooking liquid.

> **Vanilla beans are found in glass tubes in the baking aisle of the supermarket. They can be tough pods to open, so a sharp paring knife is a must. Steaming the pod first softens it and makes it a little easier to slice open. Lay the pod flat on a cutting board. Insert the tip of the blade at the center and slice toward one end, then repeat to slice to other end. Once the pod is split open, scrape out the tiny seeds with the blade. They are a little sticky and jammy, so you'll need to scrape them from your blade.**

Bumbleberry Cobbler

**Makes
6 servings**

Bags of frozen mixed berries (or "bumbleberries") are readily available in the supermarket, which makes this dessert a year-round favorite. It is delicious on its own, but if you want to treat yourself, you can add a scoop of ice cream, frozen yogurt or whipped cream.

Tip

To zest a lemon, use the fine side of a box grater, making sure not to grate the white pith underneath. Or use a zester, then finely chop the zest. Zesters are inexpensive and widely available at specialty kitchenware shops.

- **3- to 4-quart slow cooker, stoneware greased**

1	package (21 oz/600 g) frozen mixed berries	1
½ cup	granulated sugar	125 mL
2 tbsp	cornstarch	30 mL
2 tsp	grated lemon zest	10 mL

Topping

1½ cups	all-purpose flour	375 mL
½ cup	packed brown sugar	125 mL
2¼ tsp	baking powder	11 mL
¼ tsp	ground nutmeg	1 mL
¾ cup	milk	175 mL
⅓ cup	butter, melted	75 mL

1. In prepared slow cooker stoneware, gently combine berries, sugar, cornstarch and lemon zest.

2. *Topping:* In a bowl, combine flour, brown sugar, baking powder and nutmeg. Stir in milk and butter just until blended into batter. Drop spoonfuls of batter on berry mixture.

3. Cover and cook on Low for 4 to 5 hours or until a tester inserted in the center of a dumpling comes out clean. Uncover and let stand for about 30 minutes before serving.

Peach and Blueberry Cobbler with Spiced Pecan Topping

Makes 4 to 6 servings

Bags of frozen fruit are so convenient to have on hand. Quick desserts like this one are so easy to put together, you can make a family pleaser even on weeknights. I like this served with a dollop of vanilla-bean ice cream.

Tip

There is no need to defrost frozen berries. As the slow cooker heats up, it will thaw and cook the fruit evenly.

- **3- to 4-quart slow cooker, stoneware greased**

⅔ cup	all-purpose flour	150 mL
½ cup	packed brown sugar	125 mL
1½ tsp	ground cinnamon, divided	7 mL
⅛ tsp	salt	0.5 mL
¼ cup	butter, cut into cubes	60 mL
⅔ cup	coarsely chopped pecans	150 mL
3 cups	fresh or frozen blueberries	750 mL
2 cups	frozen peaches (or about 3 fresh, halved, pitted and sliced)	500 mL
½ cup	granulated sugar	125 mL
¼ tsp	ground nutmeg	1 mL

1. In a small bowl, combine flour, brown sugar, ½ tsp (2 mL) of the cinnamon and salt. Using your fingers, work in butter until mixture readily clumps when pressed. Add pecans and mix until crumbly.

2. In a large bowl, combine blueberries, peaches, granulated sugar, nutmeg and the remaining cinnamon. Transfer to prepared slow cooker stoneware and sprinkle with flour mixture.

3. Cover and cook on Low for 6 to 8 hours or on High for 3 to 4 hours, until fruit is tender and juice is bubbling.

Cran-Raspberry Ambrosia with Warm Dumpling Topping

Makes 4 to 6 servings

Raspberries are truly the "fruit of the gods," and while true ambrosia is a cold dessert, I couldn't resist using that name for this warm version. The airy dumplings form a cake-like topping. If you omit the dumplings, you'll have a wonderful fruit sauce to serve over ice cream or frozen yogurt.

Tip

There is no need to defrost frozen berries. As the slow cooker heats up, it will thaw and cook the fruit evenly.

- **3- to 4-quart slow cooker**

3 cups	fresh or frozen raspberries	750 mL
1 cup	fresh or frozen cranberries	250 mL
½ cup	granulated sugar	125 mL
½ cup	cranberry-raspberry cocktail or unsweetened apple juice	125 mL
2 tbsp	cornstarch	30 mL

Dumplings

1 cup	all-purpose flour	250 mL
2 tbsp	granulated sugar	30 mL
1¼ tsp	baking powder	6 mL
¼ tsp	salt	1 mL
3 tbsp	butter, cubed	45 mL
1	egg, lightly beaten	1
½ cup	milk	125 mL
2 tbsp	packed brown sugar	30 mL
	Whipped cream or frozen yogurt	

1. In slow cooker stoneware, combine raspberries, cranberries, sugar, cranberry-raspberry cocktail and cornstarch.

2. Cover and cook on Low for 5 to 6 hours or on High for 2½ to 3 hours, until bubbling.

3. *Dumplings:* In a bowl, combine flour, granulated sugar, baking powder and salt. Using a pastry blender or two knives, cut in butter until mixture resembles coarse crumbs.

4. In a small glass measuring cup, whisk together egg and milk. Pour into flour mixture and stir until a soft dough forms.

5. Drop spoonfuls of dough on raspberry mixture in stoneware. Sprinkle evenly with brown sugar. Cover and cook on High for 30 to 60 minutes or until a tester inserted in the center of a dumpling comes out clean. Serve warm, with dollops of whipped cream.

Double Chocolate Carrot Cake

Makes 8 to 10 servings

Made with cocoa powder and chocolate chips, this cake has an intense chocolate flavor with bright orange highlights. It's as easy to make as a store-bought mix and every bit as moist.

Tips

To line the bottom of the stoneware, set it on parchment paper and trace around the edge. Remove stoneware and cut out paper, then place in the bottom.

Do not be tempted to use the Low setting to bake this cake. It requires high heat to bake properly.

This cake freezes well. Wrap the cooled cake in plastic wrap, then in foil, and freeze for up to 1 month.

- **3- to 4-quart slow cooker, stoneware greased, bottom lined with parchment paper**

2 cups	all-purpose flour	500 mL
¾ cup	unsweetened cocoa powder	175 mL
1 tsp	baking soda	5 mL
½ tsp	baking powder	2 mL
¼ tsp	salt	1 mL
1½ cups	granulated sugar	375 mL
½ cup	butter, softened	125 mL
3	eggs	3
2 tsp	vanilla extract	10 mL
2 cups	shredded carrots	500 mL
½ cup	semisweet chocolate chips	125 mL
	Confectioner's (icing) sugar	

1. In a bowl, combine flour, cocoa powder, baking soda, baking powder and salt.

2. In another bowl, using an electric mixer, cream sugar and butter until light and fluffy. Beat in eggs and vanilla until smooth. Using a rubber spatula, gently fold in flour mixture just until blended. Fold in carrots and chocolate chips. Spoon batter into prepared slow cooker stoneware.

3. Cover and cook on High for 2 to 2½ hours or until a tester inserted in center of cake comes out clean.

4. Transfer stoneware to a wire rack and let cool for 10 minutes. Run a knife around sides to loosen cake. Turn out onto wire rack and let cool. Dust top with confectioner's sugar before slicing.

Mugga Bittersweet Brownie Decadence

Makes 6 to 8 servings

I couldn't resist trying this recipe when I saw something similar in a magazine. I often pick up a package of gourmet brownie mix for a quick treat. Using it as a base for this slow cooker dessert makes these decadent brownies so moist and chocolatey they disappear in no time.

Tip

Store cocoa powder in an airtight container in a cool, dark place for up to 2 years.

- **Minimum 5-quart slow cooker**
- *6 mugs (each about 6 oz/175 mL), lightly greased*

3	eggs, beaten	3
1	package (18 oz/520 g) brownie mix (about 2½ cups/625 mL)	1
1	package (4-serving size) instant chocolate pudding mix	1
½ cup	semisweet chocolate chips	125 mL
¼ cup	butter, melted	60 mL
2 tbsp	packed brown sugar	30 mL
2 tbsp	unsweetened cocoa powder	30 mL
	Vanilla ice cream or whipped cream	

1. Set prepared mugs in slow cooker stoneware.

2. In a large bowl, combine eggs, brownie mix, pudding mix, chocolate chips and butter (the batter will be very thick). Divide batter evenly among mugs.

3. In a small saucepan, whisk together brown sugar, cocoa powder and ¾ cup (175 mL) water; bring to a boil over medium-high heat. Reduce heat and simmer, stirring, for about 1 minute or until sugar is dissolved. Divide evenly over batter in each mug.

4. Cover and cook on High for 2½ to 3 hours or until a tester inserted in the center of a brownie comes out clean. Turn off heat and let mugs stand in covered stoneware for 30 minutes. Top each mug with ice cream, place on a plate and serve warm.

> Cocoa powder delivers such a rich, deep chocolate flavor, it's hard to beat. Cacao beans are processed into a paste, which is then dried and ground into powder. Dutch-process cocoa powder is a little richer and darker than natural unsweetened cocoa powder, because it has been treated with an alkali, which helps neutralize cocoa's natural acidity.

Blueberry Orange Coffee Cake

Makes 6 to 8 servings

You will find it hard to believe that this addictive coffee cake was made in the slow cooker. Share it with good friends, along with steaming lattes.

Tips

To grease stoneware, use a nonstick vegetable spray or use the cake pan grease available in specialty cake decorating shops or bulk food stores.

There is no need to defrost frozen berries. As the slow cooker heats up, it will thaw and cook the fruit evenly.

To zest an orange, use a Microplane-style rasp grater or citrus zester, ensuring that you don't grate the white pith underneath. Microplanes have tiny razor-like edges, which make quick and easy tasks of grating and cleaning. If you use a zester, finely chop the zest before adding it to the recipe. Microplanes and zesters are widely available at specialty kitchenware shops.

- **3- to 4-quart round slow cooker, stoneware greased**

Topping

¼ cup	packed brown sugar	60 mL
¼ cup	chopped walnuts	60 mL
½ tsp	ground cinnamon	2 mL
2 tbsp	butter, softened	30 mL

Cake

1½ cups	all-purpose flour	375 mL
1 tsp	baking powder	5 mL
1 tsp	ground cinnamon	5 mL
½ tsp	ground nutmeg	2 mL
¼ tsp	baking soda	1 mL
¼ tsp	salt	1 mL
1 cup	fresh or frozen blueberries	250 mL
½ cup	granulated sugar	125 mL
½ cup	butter, softened	125 mL
2	eggs	2
½ cup	sour cream or plain yogurt	125 mL
1 tsp	vanilla extract	5 mL
½ tsp	grated orange zest	2 mL
½ cup	chopped walnuts	125 mL

1. *Topping:* In a bowl, using your fingers, combine brown sugar, walnuts, cinnamon and butter until crumbly. Set aside.

2. *Cake:* In a bowl, combine flour, baking powder, cinnamon, nutmeg, baking soda and salt.

3. Place blueberries in another bowl and add 1 tbsp (15 mL) of the flour mixture; gently toss to coat. Set aside.

Tip

The cooled cake can be wrapped in plastic wrap, then in foil, and frozen for up to 1 month.

4. In a large bowl, using an electric mixer, cream sugar and butter until light and fluffy. Add eggs, one at a time, beating well after each addition. Beat in sour cream, vanilla and orange zest until blended. Using a wooden spoon, stir in flour mixture until just until blended. Gently fold in blueberries and walnuts (the batter will be thick).

5. Spoon batter into prepared slow cooker stoneware. Sprinkle with topping.

6. Cover and cook on High for about 2 hours or until a tester inserted in the center comes out clean. (Do not overcook.) Transfer stoneware to a wire rack and let cool for 15 minutes. Run a knife around sides to loosen cake. Using a spatula, gently ease cake out of stoneware and transfer to a serving plate. Let cool completely before cutting into wedges.

> **Manufacturers designed a kitchen rasp after they discovered that chefs were using the woodworking version to grate citrus fruits. I prefer the citrus zester, which is one of my favorite kitchen tools.**

Warm Chocolate Lava Cake

**Makes
8 servings**

· ·

This decadent dessert
is supremely rich and
incredibly delicious. It
originally developed from
a kitchen error: the chef
simply had no more time
to bake the cake, so he
called it a "lava" cake.
Sometimes less time is
a delicious thing!

Tips

Most recipes use
large eggs. If a recipe
doesn't specify a size,
assume you need
large.

Do not be tempted
to use the Low
setting to bake this
cake. It requires
high heat to bake
properly.

• **4-quart slow cooker, stoneware greased**

2 cups	semisweet chocolate chips	500 mL
¾ cup	butter, cut into cubes	175 mL
6	eggs	6
⅔ cup	granulated sugar	150 mL
2 tsp	vanilla extract	10 mL
2 tbsp	all-purpose flour	30 mL
	Coffee or vanilla ice cream	

1. In a large microwave-safe glass bowl or an 8-cup (2 L) glass measuring cup, combine chocolate chips and butter. Microwave on Medium (50%) for 2½ to 3 minutes, stirring every minute, until melted and smooth.

2. Whisk in eggs, sugar and vanilla until smooth. Whisk in flour until blended and smooth. Spread evenly in prepared slow cooker stoneware.

3. Cover and cook on High for 2 to 2½ hours or until edges are set but center is slightly runny. Serve immediately with ice cream.

Elephant Ears with Hot Caramel Sauce

Makes about 6 to 8 servings

My friend Chris described this sauce as "heaven in a pot." I like to use it as a dessert fondue for dipping the simple French cookies known as palmiers. While the sauce is cooking, you can easily bake a batch of these quick cookies.

Tips

Puff pastry package sizes vary between brands, ranging from 14 to 18 oz (397 to 511 g). If your package is slightly larger or smaller, it will still work fine for this recipe.

Refrigerate any leftover sauce in an airtight container for up to 2 weeks. It can be reheated in a mini slow cooker or microwave.

- **1½- to 3-quart slow cooker**
- *Baking sheets, lined with parchment paper*

Caramel Sauce

1½ cups	packed brown sugar	375 mL
1¼ cups	heavy or whipping (35%) cream	300 mL
¼ tsp	ground cinnamon	1 mL
2 tsp	butter	10 mL
1 tsp	vanilla extract	5 mL

Elephant Ears

	Granulated sugar	
1	package (14 oz/397 g) puff pastry, thawed	1

1. *Sauce:* In slow cooker stoneware, combine brown sugar, cream and cinnamon. Cover and cook on Low for 2½ hours, stirring once or twice. Uncover and cook for 30 to 60 minutes or until thickened slightly. Stir in butter and vanilla.

2. *Elephant Ears:* Meanwhile, sprinkle about ¼ cup (60 mL) sugar over work surface. Roll out pastry into a 12- by 10-inch (30 by 25 cm) rectangle. Sprinkle another ¼ cup (60 mL) sugar over pastry. Roll the left short side inward, stopping in the middle of the dough. Roll up the right side so the two rolls meet in the middle. Press the two rolls together gently. Wrap and refrigerate for 30 minutes.

3. Preheat oven to 400°F (200°C). Cut dough crosswise into slices about ½ inch (1 cm) thick. Lightly sprinkle sugar on each side. Pinch and press the sides of the two rolls together to ensure that they don't unroll during baking. Transfer to prepared baking sheets, placing cookies about 2 inches (5 cm) apart. (They swell dramatically during baking, so only bake 12 at a time.)

4. Bake one sheet at a time for 10 to 15 minutes or until sugar is caramelized and pastry is flaky. Transfer to a wire rack and let cool for 10 minutes.

5. Pour warm sauce into a small serving dish and surround with cookies for dipping.

To-Die-For Butterscotch Custard

Makes
6 servings

Butterscotch pudding is traditionally made with butter and a little Scotch whisky. In this über-creamy version (which is a bit of a cheat), I use butterscotch chips to simplify the recipe. The result is so flavorful, even purists won't complain.

Tips

The cooked custard can also be refrigerated for up to 4 hours or overnight and served cold.

For individual servings, spoon the cream mixture into 6 lightly greased heatproof mugs. Omit foil strips and place mugs in stoneware. Add water and cook as directed.

- **Minimum 5-quart slow cooker**
- *6-cup (1.5 L) soufflé dish or heatproof bowl, lightly greased*

3½ cups	heavy or whipping (35%) cream, divided	875 mL
½	vanilla bean, split lengthwise (see box, page 324)	½
1 cup	butterscotch chips	250 mL
5	egg yolks	5
1½ tsp	packed dark brown sugar	7 mL
½ tsp	salt	2 mL
2 tsp	amaretto (optional)	10 mL
	Whipped cream	
	Caramel sauce	

1. In a heavy saucepan, bring cream and vanilla bean to a simmer over medium heat. Simmer for 3 minutes. Remove from heat and, using tongs, remove vanilla bean. Using a sharp knife, scrape seeds into cream mixture, discarding pod. Add butterscotch chips and let stand for 3 minutes. Whisk until smooth.

2. In a large bowl, whisk together egg yolks, brown sugar, salt and 1 tsp (5 mL) water. Gradually add cream mixture, whisking constantly. Whisk in amaretto (if using). Pour into prepared soufflé dish. Cover tightly with foil and secure with an elastic band.

3. Cut a 2-foot (60 cm) length of foil in half lengthwise to make two strips. Fold each strip in half lengthwise. Crisscross strips on bottom of slow cooker stoneware, bringing the ends up the sides and over the rim. Place soufflé dish in stoneware and pour in enough water to come 1 inch (2.5 cm) up sides of dish. (If dish fits snugly in stoneware, add water before inserting it; see page 15.)

4. Tucking strip ends under lid, cover and cook on High for 2 to 3 hours or until custard is set. Remove lid and grasp strip ends to lift out dish.

5. Spoon into individual serving dishes. Top each with a dollop of whipped cream and drizzle with caramel sauce.

Snickerdoodle Cheesecake

**Makes 6 to
8 servings**

This popular dessert
is often served in
restaurants, but this is
my own version. This
method makes a perfect
cheesecake every time,
without any cracks.
Make sure to use a
large, oval slow cooker
that accommodates the
springform pan. Serve
with a dollop of whipped
cream and some fresh
strawberries on the side.

Tips

If you can't find a
small springform
pan, you can use
a straight-sided
baking dish or soufflé
dish that fits in
the stoneware. The
cheesecake won't
come out of the dish
as cleanly, but it will
still taste good.

This cake is best
made 1 day ahead.
You can also freeze it
for up to 2 weeks.

- **Minimum 6-quart oval slow cooker**
- *7- or 8-inch (18 or 20 cm) springform pan*
- *Vegetable steamer or low rack to fit in stoneware*

Crust

¾ cup	chocolate wafer cookie crumbs	175 mL
1 tbsp	granulated sugar	15 mL
2 tbsp	melted butter	30 mL

Cheesecake

1 lb	cream cheese, softened	500 g
2 tbsp	granulated sugar	30 mL
2	eggs	2
½ cup	heavy or whipping (35%) cream	125 mL
½ tsp	vanilla extract	2 mL
2	Snickers candy bars (each 2 oz/59 g), cut into ½-inch (1 cm) pieces, divided	2

Topping

¼ cup	heavy or whipping (35%) cream	60 mL
2 oz	semisweet chocolate, chopped	60 g

1. *Crust:* In a bowl, combine cookie crumbs, sugar and butter. Press evenly over bottom of springform pan. Chill until ready to use.

2. *Cheesecake:* In a large bowl, using an electric mixer or food processor, combine cream cheese and sugar; beat or process until smooth. One at a time, beat in eggs, mixing well after each addition. Beat in cream and vanilla.

3. Spread three-quarters of the candy pieces evenly over crust. Pour cream cheese mixture evenly over top. Wrap entire pan tightly with foil, securing with an elastic band. Place pan on steamer in slow cooker stoneware. (Do not add any water.)

4. Cover and cook on High for 3 to 3½ hours or until edges are set and center is slightly jiggly. Turn off heat, uncover and let cool for at least 1 hour. Remove from stoneware.

5. *Topping:* In a small saucepan, heat cream and chocolate over medium-low heat, stirring, until smooth. Using a spatula, spread over top of cheesecake. Cover and refrigerate for 4 hours, until chilled, or overnight.

6. Gently run a knife around inside edge of pan to loosen cake. Remove side. Garnish cake with the remaining candy pieces.

Thai Coconut Tapioca Pudding

**Makes
6 servings**

For many people, tapioca pudding was a favorite childhood dessert. Infused with Thai-inspired flavors, this version is updated but still resembles that familiar comfort food. Traditionally, it was served chilled, but we all loved it warm, too.

Tips

Make sure you use pearl tapioca, not instant. Pearl tapioca and Thai basil are readily available at Asian supermarkets. Pearl tapioca is also available at health food markets.

When choosing a mango, color is less important than texture — the softer it is, the riper it is. Some varieties of mango wrinkle a little at the stem when perfectly ripe. An unripe mango will ripen if left at room temperature for a day or two. Once it is ripe, store it in the refrigerator until ready to use.

- **3- to 4-quart slow cooker**

4 cups	whole milk	1 L
½ cup	pearl tapioca	125 mL
½ cup	granulated sugar	125 mL
1 tsp	grated gingerroot	5 mL
¼ tsp	grated lime zest	1 mL
Pinch	cayenne pepper	Pinch
1	4-inch (10 cm) cinnamon stick	1
2	eggs, lightly beaten	2
1	can (14 oz/398 mL) unsweetened coconut milk	1
1	large mango	1
1 tbsp	freshly squeezed lime juice	15 mL
	Thai basil sprigs (optional)	

1. In slow cooker stoneware, combine milk, tapioca, sugar, ginger, lime zest, cayenne and cinnamon stick.

2. Cover and cook on Low for 3 to 4 hours or until thickened, milk is absorbed and most of the tapioca is translucent.

3. In a bowl, whisk together eggs and coconut milk. Stir in 2 to 3 tbsp (30 to 45 mL) of the hot milk mixture and beat well. Pour into stoneware.

4. Cover and cook for 30 minutes. Turn off heat and let cool in covered stoneware for 30 minutes. Discard cinnamon stick.

5. Spoon into individual serving dishes, cover with plastic wrap and refrigerate for at least 2 hours, until chilled, or for up to 3 days. (Or, if desired, serve warm.)

6. Peel mango and cut into cubes. In a bowl, combine mango and lime juice. Spoon over each serving and garnish with a basil sprig.

Pumpkin Croissant Pudding with Tipsy Caramel Sauce

**Makes
6 servings**

This bread pudding recipe came to me from my colleague Dana Shortt, who has a fantastic ready-made food shop and catering business. She serves this up to her customers over the holidays, and it is always a hit. I adapted it to the slow cooker, with delicious results.

Tips

For an extra-boozy hit, soak the raisins in a little rum overnight before using.

You can use dried cranberries in place of the raisins.

Make Ahead

This dish can be assembled up to 24 hours in advance. Complete step 1, cover and refrigerate. Complete step 3, transfer sauce to an airtight container and refrigerate. When ready to cook, place stoneware in slow cooker and proceed with step 2. Just before serving, return sauce to a saucepan and warm over medium-low heat, stirring, until bubbling.

- **4- to 5-quart slow cooker, stoneware greased**

2	eggs	2
1	can (14 oz/398 mL) pumpkin purée (not pie filling)	1
1 cup	packed brown sugar	250 mL
1½ tsp	pumpkin pie spice	7 mL
1½ tsp	ground cinnamon	7 mL
2 cups	table (18%) cream	500 mL
1½ tsp	vanilla extract	7 mL
1	bag (12 oz/375 g) mini croissants (about 24), torn into pieces	1
½ cup	golden raisins	125 mL
½ cup	coarsely chopped pecans	125 mL
	Whipped cream (optional)	

Tipsy Caramel Sauce

1¼ cups	packed brown sugar	300 mL
½ cup	unsalted butter	125 mL
½ cup	heavy or whipping (35%) cream	125 mL
¼ cup	amber or light rum	60 mL

1. In a large bowl, whisk together eggs, pumpkin purée, brown sugar, pumpkin pie spice, cinnamon, cream and vanilla. Fold in croissant pieces and raisins. Spoon into prepared slow cooker stoneware. Sprinkle with pecans.

2. Cover and cook on Low for 3 to 3½ hours or on High for 1½ to 2 hours, until custard is set and a tester inserted in the center comes out clean.

3. *Tipsy Caramel Sauce:* Meanwhile, in a heavy saucepan, whisk brown sugar and butter over medium heat until butter is melted. Whisk in cream and cook, stirring, for about 3 minutes or until sugar is dissolved and sauce is smooth. Remove from heat and stir in rum.

4. Spoon pudding into a serving dish and drizzle with sauce. Garnish with whipped cream (if using).

Pineapple Rhubarb Crumble

Makes 6 to 8 servings

Go ahead and dish out double portions of this warm, sweetly tart crumble; otherwise, everyone will want seconds! Don't be alarmed by the pinch of cayenne — it helps bring out the flavor of the fruit. Serve warm, with a scoop of vanilla ice cream.

Tips

If you use frozen rhubarb for this recipe, increase the cornstarch to 2 tbsp (30 mL), as the rhubarb will get quite watery when it is cooked.

To toast pecans, place in a single layer on a rimmed baking sheet and bake in a 350°F (180°C) oven for 5 to 10 minutes or until golden brown and fragrant.

- **3- to 4-quart slow cooker**

4 cups	chopped rhubarb	1 L
3 cups	chopped fresh pineapple	750 mL
3 tbsp	granulated sugar	45 mL
1 tbsp	cornstarch	15 mL
1 cup	all-purpose flour	250 mL
⅔ cup	packed brown sugar	150 mL
1 tsp	finely grated orange zest	5 mL
1 tsp	ground ginger	5 mL
¼ tsp	ground cinnamon	1 mL
¼ tsp	ground nutmeg	1 mL
Pinch	cayenne pepper	Pinch
⅓ cup	butter, cut into cubes	75 mL
½ cup	chopped pecans, toasted	125 mL

1. In slow cooker stoneware, gently toss together rhubarb, pineapple, granulated sugar and cornstarch.

2. In a bowl, whisk together flour, brown sugar, orange zest, ginger, cinnamon, nutmeg and cayenne. Using a pastry blender or two knives, cut in butter until mixture resembles small peas. Sprinkle over rhubarb mixture. Sprinkle evenly with pecans.

3. Cover and cook on Low for 6 to 8 hours or on High for 3 to 4 hours, until fruit is tender and juice is bubbling. Serve warm.

> **Rhubarb may be used as a fruit, but it is botanically a vegetable. Its thick pink, celery-like stalks are the only edible portion of the plant. The leaves contain oxalic acid and can be toxic. In the spring and early summer, you can find field-grown rhubarb (perhaps from your own garden), but throughout the rest of the year rhubarb is hothouse-grown. You can also find bags of flash-frozen rhubarb in the supermarket.**

Chocolate Pâté with Raspberry Sauce

Makes 10 to 12 servings

I have to admit that I'm not a big chocolate lover. What can I say? I prefer caramel. But this flourless chocolate pâté is so good, even I'm a huge fan. The recipe is a good choice when you're entertaining, because it tastes best when it's made a day ahead. You need to serve it at room temperature, so take it out of the fridge at least an hour before serving.

Tips

When whipping cream, be sure it is well chilled — and for best results, chill the bowl and beaters, too.

Do not be tempted to use the Low setting to bake this pâté. It requires high heat to bake properly.

- **Minimum 6-quart slow cooker**
- *7- or 8-inch (18 or 20 cm) springform pan*
- *Vegetable steamer or low rack to fit in stoneware*

Raspberry Sauce

1	bag (21 oz/600 g) frozen raspberries, partially thawed	1
⅓ cup	confectioner's (icing) sugar	75 mL

Chocolate Pâté

2 oz	bittersweet chocolate, coarsely chopped	60 g
2 cups	semisweet chocolate chips	500 mL
1 cup	unsalted butter	250 mL
6	eggs	6
1½ tbsp	granulated sugar	22 mL

Fresh raspberries (optional)

Whipped cream

1. *Raspberry Sauce:* In a blender or food processor, purée raspberries and confectioner's sugar until smooth. If desired, strain through a fine-mesh sieve to remove seeds. Cover and refrigerate for up to 2 days.

2. *Chocolate Pâté:* In a large microwave-safe glass bowl, combine unsweetened chocolate, chocolate chips and butter. Microwave on Medium (50%) for 1½ to 2 minutes, stirring after 1 minute, until melted and smooth when stirred. (Or melt in a double boiler over hot water.) Whisk in eggs, one at a time, then sugar.

3. Wrap outside of springform pan with foil to prevent leaks. Spread chocolate mixture evenly in pan. Cover top of pan with foil and secure with an elastic band. Place pan on steamer in slow cooker stoneware. (Do not add any water.)

4. Cover and cook on High for 3 hours or until edges are slightly firm but center is still soft and moist. Turn off heat, uncover and let stand for about 30 minutes or until pan is cool enough to handle.

5. Remove pan from stoneware and remove foil. Transfer pan to a wire rack and let cool for 1 hour. Cover and refrigerate for 3 to 4 hours, until chilled and set, or for up to 24 hours. (Pâté is best when made 24 hours ahead.)

6. Let sauce and pâté come to room temperature before serving. Gently run a knife around inside edge of springform pan. Unlatch side and remove ring. Slice pâté with a warm knife. Drizzle each slice with sauce and garnish with raspberries, if desired, and whipped cream.

> **Use a good-quality bittersweet chocolate in this recipe. The cocoa content can range anywhere from 35% to 99%, so check out the ingredients list to see what else is included. A high percentage of solids doesn't guarantee quality, but it does mean there are a lot less fillers. Your best test is your mouth. A good-quality bittersweet chocolate will have an almost chalky mouth feel, but it will coat your mouth evenly, without waxiness or grittiness. It should also have an array of undertones, such as coffee, fruit or acidic notes.**

Creamy Caramel Blondies

Makes 4 to 6 servings

My son, Jack, and I are caramel and butterscotch fanatics! Blondies are often described as brownies without chocolate, which I find silly: blondies have their own unique, delicious personality. While brownies depend on chocolate for their flavor, with blondies it's all about the brown sugar. This tasty dessert combines a cake top over a creamy caramel sauce. Be sure to serve with a big scoop of vanilla ice cream.

Tip

It is best to use individually wrapped soft caramels, but you can substitute ½ cup (125 mL) butterscotch chips.

- **4- to 5-quart slow cooker**

1 cup	all-purpose flour	250 mL
1 tsp	baking powder	5 mL
½ tsp	salt	2 mL
1 cup	packed brown sugar, divided	250 mL
¼ cup	butter, softened	60 mL
1 tsp	vanilla extract	5 mL
½ cup	milk	125 mL
½ cup	soft caramels, wrappers removed	125 mL
1 cup	boiling water	250 mL

1. In a bowl, combine flour, baking powder and salt.

2. In another bowl, using an electric mixer, beat half the brown sugar and butter until creamy. Stir in vanilla. Add flour mixture alternately with milk, making three additions of each and beating well after each addition. Stir in caramels. Spread batter evenly in slow cooker stoneware.

3. In a glass measuring cup, combine the remaining brown sugar and boiling water, stirring until sugar is dissolved. Pour evenly over batter.

4. Cover and cook on High for 2½ to 3 hours or until a toothpick inserted in the center comes out clean.

Index

v = variation